Welcome to the Kaleidoscope
of my life.
Best wishes
Brigitte

FROM *Coffee* TO *Champagne* TO *Coconuts*

Memories *by*
BRIGITTE KASSA

CONTENTS

Acknowledgment

I wish to thank Susan Ploplys for editing and transcribing my handwritten memoir. You have been persistent and resourceful in transcribing my manuscript, and sought with your mind to understand my story in depth. But it has been your heart speaking as you have written the words of my life story. I am very grateful to you Susan!

To my closest friends, Lynne and Terry Lock, thank you for encouraging me to tell my story. With great passion, time and work, Terry paved the way toward the publication of my book. Lynne's enthusiastic vision and perseverance has led to an exploration of this book becoming a potential basis for a television series.

With my deepest gratitude, your devoted friend,
Brigitte Kassa

PROLOGUE

My friends and many other acquaintances whom I met in different parts of the world asked me to write about my adventurous and intriguing life. I never was quite ready for it and answered, "Maybe one day."

I feel that now is the time to write my life story.

I open the sliding glass door from the kitchen leaving the screen door closed, go back to my chair and sit down. I am captivated by the beautiful tropical scenery in front of me. Tall coconut trees with their green palm branches shimmering in the sun which gives them a silvery glitter. I am fascinated by the shades of water in the Caribbean Sea, changing from turquoise to dark blue and everything in between. I can even see the contour of small Owen Island with stretches of white sand beach. What a serene tableau. My eyes wander above the scenery where I see the Magnificent Frigate Birds, the local name is Man O' War, cruising high in the sky and waiting for the Red Footed Booby Birds, Sula Sula, to come back from fishing. Then the Frigate Birds rob the catch of the day from the Booby Birds. I look up to the light blue sky and see a row of curly clouds close together drifting away, it reminds me of a flock of sheep. The surroundings are spectacular. I am living my dream. It is on this island, Little Cayman, the only place in the world where I feel I belong. This is where my late husband and I established our home.

I remember when I was ten years old in Germany and told my aunt with strong determination, that one day I will live on a small tropical island with lots of sunshine and palm trees, surrounded by warm water. Now it will be forty years since I discovered my paradise.

I look down on my glass table covered with my childhood photographs. I reminisce and my past comes alive.

Brigitte Kassa
28th May, 2014

CHAPTER 1

War Child

Every child is born into a world that is not of his or her making. And the life into which one is born shapes each and every one of us. The lucky ones are those who figure out what will make him or her happy. And even luckier are those who successfully pursue their dreams.

I was born the 7th of January 1939 in Berlin, Germany. My parents gave me three names, Brigitte, Hilde and Renate. Kruger was my family name. I am glad my parents chose Brigitte for my first name, I really like my name. My mother's name was Frida, born Gartner, and my father's name was Hermann Kruger. They married in 1935 and owned a small drugstore at Nazareth Kirch Street #45 in Berlin, only one block away from the Main Street, Muller Str. It was a good business. My father was soon drafted into the army in 1940. My mother had to take care of her shop by herself, and hired a nanny for me.

1941

My father got two months leave from the army to visit us and this was the last time that we heard from him during the war.

1942-1945

My first memory was living with my Aunt Berta on my grandparents' farm in Zeckerin, located between Berlin and Dresden, maybe three hours by train from Berlin. Aunt Berta's husband Uncle Martin was also drafted into the army. Aunt Berta had brown hair. Her eyes were gray blue, her cheeks had always a rosy shine like a polished apple. Fine lines were crossing her forehead. She made a friendly impression.

My cousin Margitta, Aunt Berta's daughter, was a pretty girl, one year younger than me, with short dark hair, a round open face, dark eyes gleaming with mischievousness. Her brother Hans, who was five years older, was tall and very handsome, with wavy dark hair. Like Margitta, he had dark brown eyes, but his shone with a warm glow.

My Oma, Grandmother, had just turned seventy, deep lines marked her soft kindly face. She had lost her teeth. I could hardly see her lips. She always wore long dark dresses in blue, gray or black, with long underskirts. Opa, Grandfather, looked very old, he must have been in his eighties. He also had no teeth, he was tall and walked with a cane. He was a grumpy old man. My grandparents had a white stucco house with a little flower garden in front. I loved that old house, it was comfortable and cozy, especially in the winter time. When I first entered the house there was a little mud room where I had to take my shoes, boots or wooden clogs off. Then I changed to slippers to keep my feet warm in the house.

My cousin, Margitta, and I would play a lot in that charming old house. Margitta and I were betting who would arrive first at Oma's and Opa's fireplace in the house. We were outside in the farmyard. Hans drew the starting line and then counted to ten. Off we raced, Margitta pulled the first door open from the mud room and slammed it fast, close in front of me. She ran into the room with her dirty shoes, leaving traces of sand behind her. With a big grin she sat on the bench which surrounded the large fireplace and was usually occupied by one or two cats. I shouted at her, "You are cheating!" She was unmoved. Hans came in and he gave the first prize to me!

In the middle of the room was a large wooden table with some sturdy benches and chairs. Oma and Opa had enormous feather beds built into sleeping nooks on either side of the room. Each bed had a flowered curtain for privacy. This was our favorite play ground; here we amused ourselves in harmony. Margitta and I would climb onto our chosen bed, then we changed our clothes or draped towels or blankets around us, pulled the curtains open and made believe we were in the theater and would act our fantasies out. Sometimes we would misbehave, and our entertainment was teasing Opa. We would watch him walking with the cane and mumbling curses. We were hiding when he passed us. Then we would walk in a row behind him making grimaces and mimicking his limping walk. Suddenly he would stop, turn around and try to hit us with the cane. Sometimes he got one of us. This was our fun.

Every Sunday Oma would roast a goose, duck, rabbit or whatever was available for dinner. Aunt Berta and Uncle Martin had built their own house from bricks across the courtyard from my grandparents' house. It was a much larger house. One Saturday I was very excited, Aunt Berta told me my mother was coming today. Aunt Berta sent Joseph, their farmhand, to the train station to get my mother. Early in the afternoon we heard the carriage stopping outside the big wooden gate. Liesel and Lotte, our horses, were whinnying. Joseph came through the side door to open the big gate.

There she was, my beautiful mother, Frida. She had brown sparkling eyes, high cheekbones, a straight nose and lovely lips. Her features were classic and her skin was a warm olive hue. I ran up to her and put my arms around her legs, that was as far as I could reach. I buried my nose in her skirt and inhaled the scent that was hers alone. She picked me up and gave me a kiss. I pulled on my mother's dress and begged her to take me back with her when she left for Berlin.

"No, Gitti, not this time. I have too much to do in the store. Soon it will be Christmas and I have much to stock up and get ready. After Christmas, I promise to get Lieschen, your nanny, back. Tears came to my eyes.

"How long is that Mutti? "Are you coming back before Christmas?" I asked.

"Oh yes, but now come and look what I brought you from the city. A new dress and shoes; Sunday when you and your cousins go to church, you will look so pretty." There was a Protestant church in the middle of the village. "And look here, a new bow for your hair."

"Mommy, I don't like bows in my hair."

"Don't say that, Brigitte. It is very becoming." Now Mommy called me by my name, not Gitti my nickname. That was not a good sign. It meant she was getting upset with me.

So I agreed. "Thank you Mommy." Then my mother gave Margitta a pretty new blouse and Hans a shirt. The weekend went fast. On Sunday Oma roasted a goose in her big heavy iron pot. Aunt Berta baked a couple of plum and apple cakes. There were many fruit trees on the property and the plums and apples were currently in season.

Every weekend Aunt Berta baked bread and fresh fruit cakes. Joseph gathered firewood for the brick house, in the garden and separate from the farm houses. The brick house was used for baking. It also was a smoke house to cure ham, bacon, sausage and other meats. The side walls had a couple of shelves attached. The middle was filled with a long wooden table where Aunt Berta prepared the food. When the temperature was right, Aunt Berta took a long paddle, put the bread or cake on it, and pushed it onto the iron grill into the large fireplace, which looked like a pizza oven.

When Margitta and I saw the smoke rising from the tall chimney, it was time to play closer to the baking house. The aroma drifted out and made us hungry. Hans joined us as we waited impatiently for the first warm delicious bite which Aunt Berta served us. One of our favorites was streusel Kuchen and Mohn Kuchen, (Poppy Seed Cake). The poppy seeds were mixed with sugar. We gobbled the sweets down and asked for more. It was always a special treat.

My grandparents, Uncle Martin and Aunt Berta owned numerous acres of farmland where various crops grow in the fields. When planting or harvest time came, they employed a few people from the village to help. On the farm itself, Oma and Aunt Berta took care of the animals. Milking the cows and goats, feeding the chickens, ducks, pigs, sheep and geese. Joseph cleaned the stables and took care of the horses. Oma and Aunt Berta made their own butter, the rest of the milk they poured into big containers and put them outside of the gate where they were picked up and the milk sold.

My mother arrived after Christmas in Zeckerin as she had promised. I was very happy when she told me that Lieschen, my nanny, had time for a couple of months to take care of me. Soon we left Zeckerin. I felt sad to leave the freedom of the country with my playmates, but I was looking forward to being close to my mother and the city life.

Alas, it did not last too long. Lieschen quit after three months, she had to take care of her own family. One weekend my mother took me to her brother, Uncle Max, and his wife, Elizabeth. To me she was Aunt Didi, even my uncle and mother called her Didika, or Didi. Maybe it was her Hungarian nickname. We took the tram traveling over one hour from the city to arrive near my uncle and aunt in Heiligensee. This was clearly an upper class neighborhood. The tram stopped at our destination and the house, An der Schneise #13, was not far from the station. We walked maybe ten minutes, passing fenced in flowering gardens with large elegant houses. I asked, "Mommy, is that Uncle Max and Aunt Didi's house?"

"No, Gitti. They also live in a big house, but those houses are called Villen. Look, this is Aunt Didi's and Uncle Max's house." Aunt Didi was looking out the window and waved. It was a tall proud looking two-story home. Uncle Max opened the garden door and greeted us warmly. He was tall, slim and with dark wavy hair, brown eyes, full lips and skin which had the same olive glow as my mother. You could see that they were brother and sister.

Aunt Didi came rushing down the steps. She took me into her arms and hugged me tightly. "Finally you are here Spatzchen, (little sparrow), so she called me.

Aunt Didi was born in Hungary. She never had lost her accent or mannerisms. She grew up in an upper class family. Aunt Didi had dark brown hair which was always pinned up in curls. She had a gentle expression in her brown eyes. However, when she was upset and her temperament took over, her eyes spit fire. Her figure was average, only her legs were skinny. They reminded me of chicken legs.

Since my uncle and aunt did not have any children, they treated me as their own. I liked Uncle Max very much. He carried me on his shoulders around the garden and let me touch the rabbits and chickens in his back yard. Aunt Didi set strict rules which I had to learn and obey. "Brigitte, clean your hands before you sit at the dining table, and don't talk with your mouth full, and always say please and thank you."

I was intimidated by her. "Yes, Aunt Didi, I will remember your words."

Her stern voice changed and with a smile she said, "That is a good Spatzchen." I was happy to be her little sparrow again. My mother told me that I would have to stay for a while with my aunt and uncle. Mother came every weekend to see me since she had to tend to her business in Berlin.

I was content, but the peaceful atmosphere did not last long. One weekend when my mother came from her store to visit us, she was very agitated and had a long talk with Aunt Didi and Uncle Max. I began to worry because I heard my name mentioned several times. Finally my mother took me by the hand and with a sad voice said, "Gitti, tomorrow I have to take you back to Zeckerin. It is much safer there and you have your cousins to play with."

"But Mommy, why?"

"I cannot explain it to you, you are too young to understand. I already have sent a telegram to my family in Zeckerin."

"Mommy, will you come out and visit every weekend like here in Heiligensee?"

"Yes, Gitti. I will try my best." Quietly I helped my mother fill my suitcase. At this moment sirens went off.

I ran to my mother, "What is that Mommy?"

"It's an air raid. We are about to be bombed. Go get your little suitcase, quickly!" It was already packed. We all went down to the cellar where the chickens were all roosting in a row. Uncle Max had made a chicken run out of wire that was like a tunnel between the chicken yard and the cellar. Aunt Didi lit some candles that had been placed there in anticipation. Once the cellar was lighted, the chickens stirred and began to move around. Then they began to pick at the stucco walls.

"Aunt Didi, the chickens are eating the walls."

"That is okay, Spatzchen, they need calcium and that will make the eggshells stronger."

After some time, we heard the sirens again. Uncle Max told us to wait to make sure it was clear to go upstairs. My aunt, uncle and mother were nervously talking. My uncle said, "I have to leave very early in the morning since I am a fire fighter. I don't know when I can come back, Berlin needs me now!"

My mother took me in her arms and with a sad voice she said, "Gitti, we have to change our plan. I will go with my brother to the city and check on my store. I will return as soon as possible. Then I will take you to Zeckerin."

They both left very early when it was still dark. During the day, I helped Aunt Didi around the garden. We waited anxiously for my mother and uncle to come back, but nobody returned. In the evening, Aunt Didi and I chased the chickens through the tunnel. Afterwards I was very tired and fell asleep. The next day, the loud sound of the sirens frightened us. Aunt Didi hollered, "Spatzchen, come fast, help me to get the chickens through the tunnel." It was more difficult to get them to go there during daylight.

Still no word from my mother or uncle. We were very worried. Later that night, after midnight, Aunt Didi shook me awake. There was a big bang and the window next to me exploded, spraying glass all over me. Aunt Didi yelled, "Don't move, the glass will cut you. Wait until I can shake it off of you." She was lying on the floor where she fell when the window was blown out. I lay still in shock. I could feel blood trickling down one of my arms. After the all-clear sirens blew, Aunt Didi slowly got up.

"Spatzchen, are you all right?"

"I think so."

Aunt Didi checked me over, only finding minor cuts. Then she got a dust brush and a pail and swept up as much of the glass as she could. "Tomorrow morning we will be able to see better and we can clean it all up." The room was growing colder with the glass out of the window. We put our coats on and tried to sleep. After daybreak, we cleaned the mess up and Aunt Didi covered the open window with some blankets. For years after this, I often had nightmares.

Finally my mother arrived. Overwhelmed, I ran to her and kissed and hugged her at the same time. I poured my heart out with questions. She held me close in her arms, but with a stern voice said, "Not now, Gitti. We have no time to lose. We have to catch the train which takes you to Zeckerin. Hurry, Get your suitcase and say goodbye to Aunt Didi."

We all had tears in our eyes. Mother and I took the tram to the train station. I was always impressed looking up at that enormous beautiful building. To me it looked like a palace.

Outside, the stone walls were ornamented with stone statues resting on slender columns on both sides of the entrance with a clock in the middle. On the curved rooftop sat a grand bronze angel. Tall glass windows surrounded the building, the entire roof was glass covered. Inside, colored marble columns supported the structure. It was the main train station from Germany. Trains went all over to different countries in Europe.

1944

ANHALTER BAHNHOF, BERLIN

We were horrified as we entered the station to see how overcrowded it was, people were pushing, pulling, hollering; it was awful. I was holding tightly to my mother's hand and was close to tears. "Mommy, why are so many people here?"

"Well, they too want to leave Berlin! But now, I don't want to hear one word more from you Brigitte. Be strong and help us to get to the train. I bought the tickets a couple of days ago." I knew my mother was upset, so I tried my best to cling close to her. She got aggressive too and pushed us forward until we reached the train. The train was letting the steam out as we climbed up. We made it, but had to stand. After a couple of stops, my mother was lucky to get a seat, and I could sit on her lap.

Uncle Martin was waiting at the station with Liesel and Lotte, our two horses, and the wagon. It was a happy wiedersehen, a reunion, with the whole family. Two long wooden tables were standing in the middle of the yard. Covered with fresh hardy food from the farm and accompanied by an assortment of roasted meats and, of course, fresh baked cakes. Margitta, Hans and I had a lot of stories to tell to each other. When my mother left, I was sad and hoped that she would come often to visit me. But her visits became sporadic.

Uncle Martin, Aunt Berta's husband, came home from the war in 1944 because he had been wounded in one of his eyes. It looked as if the eye had popped out and was rolling around. It was scary looking. Also in 1944, my mother's house and her shop were hit during a bombing raid. Aunt Berta came running with tears streaming down her face. "Dear Gitti," and then she sobbed so hard that I could not understand a word. She began again, "I am so sorry dear child, I think your mother is dead. She is buried under her building." She slowly told me details about what had happened in the bombing. I was in shock, could not cry, and just held onto Aunt Berta. A numbness came over my body. Aunt Berta added, "And we still have not heard from your father." I was devastated. Now I had no parents. We tried to get news, but it was difficult to get communication from Berlin.

I was hiding and finally crying. I went to the barn, saw my kinderwagen, baby carriage, standing in the corner. I called the cats. One came out of the barn. I picked her up and put her in the carriage, tucking a pretty ruffled blanket around her. "Now you can be my baby and I will watch over you and will not let you go." But the cat hissed at me and scratched me with her claws as she tried to get away. She sprang out of the wagon and ran away. Crying, I ran to Aunt Berta, who wiped the blood off of my arms with one corner of her apron, and used another corner to wipe away my tears.

Margitta saw her mother tending to me and with a jealous voice told me, "This is my mother, you don't have any more parents."

Aunt Berta slapped Margitta on her face and told her, "Don't be so mean, maybe Aunt Frida is alive." Now Margitta began to cry.

For a long time we did not hear anything from Berlin. We knew that Uncle Max was trying to get information and would do anything to help his sister. Since he was a fireman, he was probably at the site of the bombing. After a while, we got the news that they had dug my mother out of the rubble of her house, and she was alive! They sent her to Carlsbad to recuperate. The doctors had to remove her gallbladder and she needed to recover from the surgery. How happy and proud I was. I ran to Margitta and stuck my tongue out at her. "You see, I have my mommy back! And I will go to Berlin and stay with her!"

How little I knew, and I could not understand why my mother was not coming to visit us right away. Instead, Uncle Max and Aunt Didi came to visit and to tell us about my mother. Uncle Max told us that my mother had to stay in Carlsbad for quite a while to heal. He also said that it was very dangerous to travel. The train he and Aunt Didi were on stopped a couple of times. Each time they had to disembark and lie flat on the ground, hoping that the train would not be bombed. I crawled into my Uncle Max's lap and asked about my mommy. "Why didn't she come with you to see me?" Aunt Didi took me into her arms and consoled me. Both of them held me and stroked my hair. "You have to wait a while until your mother is feeling better," Uncle Max told me. "Right now you are much better off here in the country where there are no bombs falling from the sky. We are going back tomorrow. Since there is no food in Berlin, we will fill our backpacks and hope we make it home."

After Uncle Max and Aunt Didi left, I felt rejected and could not understand why no one wanted to take me to Berlin to see my mother. My blue-green eyes, which usually reflected a joy for life, were filled with sadness. I spent more and more time by myself, and found solace in the company of animals. Every day I walked the ducks to the pond where they would spend the day with the ducks from other farms. Sometimes I lingered sitting in the grass and watching all of the little quackers. It was fun to watch the interaction, which often included fights. In the evening, I would return to the pond and walk the ducks home. Margitta and Hans tried to cheer me up and pull me away from my solitude, but I had no interest in playing with them. I observed them from afar and thinking how strong and healthy they were. I myself had more delicate features, my skin was pale and I was more sensitive by nature. Margitta and Hans, like everyone else in my family, had dark hair. Almost all had brown eyes. I had fine blonde hair but not thin. I thought it was odd that I was the only blondie in our family.

One day Uncle Martin went out to the pub in our village. The three of us followed him, each one carrying an empty container, not for beer, but to fill up with the foam from the beer that was discarded. At home we gave this to a pig which Uncle Martin wanted to fatten up. Happily and noisily, the pig gulped the liquid down. Then the pig laid down on a pile of straw and fell asleep snoring.

Soon the time came to prepare for a feast. Margitta and I knew what that meant. First thing in the morning, the butcher came. We heard the loud squeals from the pig and pressed our pillows more firmly around our ears. Then there was a shot, followed by silence. It was awful. People came from the village to help prepare the meat. The butcher divided the meat, most of which would be cooked, boiled or fried. The fire in the big stove was never allowed to die. The pig skin was a delicious snack when it was fried and salted. The rest of the fat got poured into a stone container and was kept cool. The ham and bacon were hung in the smoke house. The pork was carved, divided and stuffed into the sausage casings, which were made from the intestines of the pig. This all took place in the big kitchen which was built adjoining Aunt Berta's and Uncle Martin's house. It served many different purposes, not just cooking. With the iron hand pump, we got fresh well water. In winter, Aunt Berta put a bathtub in the middle of the kitchen stone floor. Then she warmed big containers of water on the fireplace and poured it in the bathtub. This happened every Saturday. Once a week we got scrubbed clean, with lots of fun splashing the water around. Neither house had plumbing. There was an outhouse which was a short walk from both houses.

1945

I could hear Aunt Berta hollering, "Brigitte, where are you?" I did not answer. I was hiding outside the compound, sitting on the edge of the creek and observing the water swirling around and touching the outside of the brick walls of the animals' stables. I was in my own world. Aunt Berta knew that I felt left out, but that I preferred the solitude. Aunt Berta also knew how to get me out of hiding. Now she added, "Your mother is coming!"

I sprang up and ran in the direction of Aunt Berta's voice. Out of breath, I pulled on her dress. "When? When?" I shouted with excitement.

"She will be here soon. You need to wash up and get ready." My eyes lit up and my spirits lifted. Soon we heard the wagon coming and saw Joseph entering through the outside door. Then he opened up the big gate so that he could drive the wagon, pulled by Liesel and Lotte, into the courtyard.

We all stood in a row; the children in front of Oma and Opa, then Aunt Berta and Uncle Martin. Uncle Martin helped my mother down from the carriage. All the suspense was broken; everybody hugged and kissed, laughed and cried. I stood back a little, reluctant and worried. I was afraid that my mother did not really love me anymore. It had been a year since I had seen her. Mother looked at me, pulled me into her arms, kissed me warmly and said, "It has been too long. This time I am taking you home with me." I could not believe the wonderful news and asked again and again if it was true. I kissed my mommy and laughed and cried with the rest of the family.

Aunt Marta, my mother's older sister, and her daughter, Marianne, arrived from Sonnewalde, the neighboring town. It was one hour by bicycle. Many people from the village came to greet my mother and wish her well. It was a big celebration and a great feast. Mommy looked the same, only very skinny. We enjoyed wonderful relaxing days together. One day my mother said, "It is time to go home, Gitti. But you will not recognize Berlin, it is completely destroyed."

1945, MAY 8TH

The war ended. Mother and I arrived in Berlin. I was now six years old. Berlin was in ruin. People searched through the rubble to find their belongings. Here and there was a house intact. "Sit down, Gitti, here on this piece of wall," my mommy told me. Part of the wall was still standing, but the house behind it was completely destroyed. "Are you hungry?"

"Yes Mommy." My mother took out the sandwich that Aunt Berta had prepared for the trip. Frightened, I looked around me. "Oh Mommy, where is your house?"

"Do you remember, Gitti, when I could not come to see you?"

"Yes, Mommy. I was very sad because I missed you so much!"

With a sad voice, my mother explained, "Our house was destroyed too. What you see here, it looks the same as where we once lived. I was trapped under the bricks and rubble. They were able to dig me out. But I was injured and had to get well before I could come to visit you."

I took my mother's hand and pressed it against my cheek with tears rolling down. "I remember Mommy."

"Cheer up, Gitti. Now we are waiting for Uncle Max to come to pick us up. We will have to stay with Uncle Max and Aunt Didi for a while because my new apartment is not ready yet. It will be a small apartment because I want the biggest room converted into a drugstore, like we had before. Actually it is right next door to where we had our drugstore. This house did not get hit. The other two houses are destroyed." Max knew approximately when we would arrive and where to pick us up. He had his day off, but it was very difficult to find transportation. He asked his colleagues at the fire station if anyone had a vehicle that he could borrow for three hours. He was lucky to find one, because almost everyone rode a bicycle or walked everywhere.

When a vehicle slowly drove down the street towards us, I sprang up and hopped from one leg to the other in excitement, waving furiously. "Mommy, it is Uncle Max. Come, come Mommy!" I loved my Uncle Max very much. His brown eyes had a warm shine like my mother's. After a heartwarming reunion, Uncle Max drove us out of the devastation to his house. After one hour of driving, the scenery changed. We saw woodlands on both sides of the streets.

"Oh, Uncle Max, how wonderful all of the trees are still alive!" My uncle smiled.

"Do you remember where you are, little Brigitte?" My uncle always called me by my name.

"I think we will be close to your house Uncle Max?" Houses with fences and gardens began to appear in the landscape.

"Now we are in Heiligensee and this is our street, an der Schneise," announced my uncle. Soon the houses began to get bigger. This was clearly an upper class neighborhood. I pointed to a much larger house of beautiful construction.

"Is this you're your house, Uncle Max?"

"No Brigitte, this belonged to the family Goldstein." Across the street was another beautiful villa where once the Morgenstern family lived.

"But Uncle Max, why are the gardens full of weeds and the houses abandoned?"

Uncle Max considered my questions and replied, "Well, they left. And then, never came back." A few moments later, Uncle Max exclaimed, "Look at the number on the house Brigitte! Here comes Number 13." Aunt Didi was looking out the window and waved. Uncle Max used his key to open the garden door and Aunt Didi came rushing down the steps. She took me into her arms and hugged me tightly.

"Finally you are here Spatzchen!" I told my aunt that I was very happy to be back, that she and my uncle had survived the war and that their beautiful house was not damaged. "Yes, Spatzchen, we were lucky. Heiligensee was relatively unaffected by the destruction of war." The streets were navigable, but often had big craters from the air attacks.

My mother called to all of us. "Come and look what we brought from Zeckerin!" She opened a big backpack, it was filled with food, potatoes, bread and butter; all of the goods from my family in Zeckerin. Since Uncle Max still had chickens and rabbits in the yard, Aunt Didi cooked a wonderful Hungarian meal, chicken paprika. Afterwards we all were exhausted and went to bed. I had a bed in my aunt's and uncle's bedroom. Mommy slept in the living room on a pullout sofa. I slept very deeply, so happy and relieved to be with my own family.

Early the next morning, my mother and uncle left for the city. Uncle Max told Aunt Didi that he had to be on call at the fire station for the next week. "So, if you don't mind, my sister could sleep in my bed."

"Of course, that would be fine!" Aunt Didi replied. My mother came to me and gave me a kiss. She told me, "I will see you tonight. I have to go to the city to see how the work is progressing for my store."

"It's okay, Mommy, as long as you come back."

Aunt Didi called after my mother, "See if you can purchase some rice or vegetables." Then Aunt Didi called me by my name. "Oh, this must be serious," I thought.

"Come Brigitte and help me with the work in the garden!" She showed me how to make piles of dirt into little mounds. Then she cut the tops from the potatoes with the eyes and put them in the dirt. "And now, Spatzchen, fill all of the water cans. Tell me when you are ready. You can carry the small one." Aunt Didi said Spatzchen, which meant she was content with my work.

It was fun to help. I watered some green leaves, which were sprouting up and asked Aunt Didi, "What are these?"

"Those are spinach, onions and scallions. And the plants in the back with the big leaves are tobacco. That is for your Uncle Max. You can water them every day, this will help them grow."

One day I observed the rabbit family and how admirably they behaved, especially the sweet little babies. I picked one baby rabbit up and told him he would soon be as big as the others. Then I took my small water can and poured water over the baby rabbit to make him grow faster. I ran to Aunt Didi and told her the good news. "Aunt Didi, the small rabbit will grow faster, I watered him just like your plants."

"What did you do?"

I repeated proudly again, "I poured water over the little rabbit to make him grow faster." Aunt Didi was shocked. She ran to where the little rabbit was sitting, drenched.

"Fast, Brigitte, bring me a dry cloth." I ran and got a cloth for Aunt Didi, and she immediately began to dry off the rabbit and scolded me, "Water is only for the plants. Don't you know that?"

"No Aunt Didi, in Zeckerin they had lots of animals, but Margitta and I never helped with anything. We just played."

After a couple of weeks, my mother told me that her apartment was almost ready and that she might not be with me every night. She would be able to sleep in the apartment. To commute each way was very tiring for her. After a long day on her feet, she wanted nothing more than to go to bed. My mother told me that I had to stay with my aunt and uncle and go to school there. "I am very sorry, Gitti, but I cannot take care of you. I open my drugstore at 8:00 in the morning and close at 7:00 in the evening. Please, you have to understand, Gitti."

I was close to tears. "I understand Mommy."

"I will come every Friday and stay until Sunday evening, "my mother promised. That sounded better, but once again I felt alone.

Uncle Max was a professional mason. He had built their house, and became a firefighter later on. The downstairs was rented out to a fabric store. On the second floor was where Uncle Max and Aunt Didi lived. They had a view of the road. The other half of the house was rented to a family with two boys. One day Aunt Didi and Uncle Max asked me to come down into the cellar with them. "We want to show you something." The chicken roost was gone, so was the tunnel. Now the chickens would be staying outside all day and night. I looked with curiosity. Uncle Max took a sledgehammer and banged it against the wall where the chickens once roosted. The cement blocks gave in and Uncle Max took down the fake wall. My eyes widened when I saw all that was behind the wall. It was a treasure. There were Rosenthal porcelain dishes, silver cutlery, money, shoes, and clothing, some that belonged to my mother. I was fascinated.

"It was a horrible time in Berlin." My aunt recalled, "First the Russians came and took everything away that they could lay their hands on. They molested the women. They had never seen flush toilets. Thinking it was drinking water, they filled their bellies from them. I am so relieved, Spatzchen, that you were with your grandparents."

Months were passing. Aunt Didi's garden was flourishing. The spinach was ripe to pick. Mommy came one Friday evening and brought potatoes and chicory, which she got from the black market. Aunt Didi and Mommy brewed the chicory and savored the coffee flavor on Sunday morning. Sometimes Uncle Max would contribute some special treats and surprised them with a little sugar and powdered milk for their coffee. Uncle Max too had the joy of harvesting his tobacco plants and laid the tobacco leaves on the cement walkway to dry. Later on, he would use them to stuff his pipe or would roll them into cigars with great satisfaction. I liked the smell of Uncle Max's pipe.

There was more food available now, mostly from the Americans. I'd never had dry cereal before and did not like it. Aunt Didi spooned it in my mouth but I would not swallow it. I pushed the cereal from one side to the other in my mouth until

Aunt Didi got upset with me. She raised her hand in front of my face and with a threatening voice, she said, "Brigitte, you WILL swallow the cereal right now!" After a couple of times going through that ordeal, I let my imagination wander to Zeckerin and made believe I was eating a fresh prepared sausage.

One day Uncle Max told us that some of the trains were in operation again. "In two days the three of us will go to Zeckerin and get provisions." With joy I jumped up, my dream became reality.

"Oh Uncle Max and Aunt Didi. I am so happy. Now we can eat real food, meats, bread, butter, pies and fruits!" The train station was now in the Russian sector. Berlin was divided into four sections; Germany was defeated by England, France, the United States and Russia.

We lived in the French sector. We took the tram crossing the American sector, then arrived at the train station in the Russian sector. The train was filled to capacity. We had to stand the whole way to Zeckerin. There was a joyful greeting from the family. It was wonderful to see Margitta and Hans again. We had a lot to talk about. I told them about Berlin and how chaotic it was; how hard it was to get food. We heard Uncle Max's voice in the distance, "You three get ready. We are all going mushroom hunting in the woods." Uncle Max had obtained some woodlands from Oma and Opa. It was a lot of fun and we filled a backpack full of mushrooms to take back to Berlin. Aunt Berta and Oma gave us loaves of bread, bacon and ham, as much as we could carry home.

Next day Uncle Martin took us to the train station. Again, lots of people were waiting. They too had backpacks and suitcases filled with food. Uncle Max said, "I want to be the first on the train and get these mushrooms up into the luggage compartment so they won't get crushed. You two stay right behind me." The train arrived, people got agitated and started pushing. Everybody wanted to be first. I held tightly to my Aunt's hand. We saw Uncle Max holding the mushrooms high over his head. We made it, and Aunt Didi even got a seat. At every station, more people got onto the train. We were pressed like sardines in a can. Home again, now Aunt Didi was in her element. She had enough surplus of food to cook with. First thing she made was a big pot full of mushroom soup with herbs from her garden. When we sat down to eat, I saw dead worms floating on top of the soup. "Aunt Didi, I am hungry, but there are worms in the soup."

With a stern voice, Aunt Didi said, "I know there are worms. They are from the mushrooms, but they won't hurt you. Eat now, it is protein." I just couldn't! Aunt Didi came around the table to me and ordered, "Open your mouth Brigitte!" I got scared and opened my mouth. Aunt Didi quickly pushed a spoonful of soup in. I swallowed it. Then she put another spoonful in my mouth and I gagged it down. "Now eat it yourself. You are too skinny and you will eat what is served at the table." I tried to take a spoonful.

With tears in my eyes, I said, "Aunt Didi, I am getting sick." She saw it was true and jumped up to take me quickly to the bathroom. On this evening, Uncle Max and I got a lecture from Aunt Didi. First it was me who got a lecture, "Brigitte, you will be living with us for a while and since we don't have children, we will raise you as our own child. I will teach you manners and etiquette. Sit straight at the table, no elbows on the table, no talking unless your uncle or I ask you something. And when you address us, you say, 'please and thank you.'" I was very intimidated and afraid to say anything.

Next was Uncle Max's turn. "Max, I am not going to Zeckerin anymore. Your family has no manners, and Brigitte speaks the farmers' language. This last visit, your mother's behavior was unacceptable. She was showing me the garden and in the middle of our conversation, I thought I heard water running nearby. I looked down and noticed a puddle between Oma's clogs which was getting larger. With disbelief and shock I looked at Oma, but she kept on talking as if nothing was happening. I turned around and left."

Uncle Max and I broke out into laughter. "You two are laughing! I cannot understand you. I will never visit there again.

Aunt Didi grew up in an upper class family in Hungary, something that defined her and kept her from becoming close to my Uncle Max's family. In Zeckerin they refer to Aunt Didi as "the high dame" because she puts on airs. Her own family disinherited her because she married beneath her class.

From this day on, a different wind blew in the Gartner house. Aunt Didi was strict. I had respect for her and fear at the same time.

1945 – 1951

I was six years and eight months old when the first day of school began in September. Aunt Didi gave me a Schultute, a large cardboard cone filled with sweets in order to make the very first day in school a little less traumatic. I carried it tucked inside my arm. Shyly, I took Aunt Didi's hand and thanked her. "Now Spatzchen, pay attention. This is the way to the school which you must take every day." I felt lighter and the day was brighter, I was Aunt Didi's little sparrow again.

"Please Aunt Didi, do I have to go?"

"Of course, you don't want to be left behind. You have a lot to learn." We passed a wooded area, then a street with nice houses on each side. But closer to the school some houses were bombed out. I was holding tightly to my Aunt's hand; reluctant, scared and excited, I followed her. Then I saw all of the other children with their own Schultute and a photographer taking photos of each one of us. We were 30 pupils, girls and boys mixed. It wasn't long before I learned my way to school quickly and enjoyed the half hour walk. My aunt looked over my school work daily and made sure I did my homework. Whenever Aunt Didi became frustrated with me, I would get a slap on my cheeks.

Winter came, I dreaded this time of year. I was not able to stay warm. Uncle Max gave some rabbit fur to a shoe maker and had warm fur-lined boots made for me. Mommy had found somebody in the city who made a coat for me from the rabbit fur. Aunt Didi put thick woolen stockings on my legs. But nothing worked. As much as I wanted to play with the other children, I never lasted more than ten minutes outside, I stood frozen in the snow and cried. Aunt Didi would come to get me and take me home to the warm living room. Then she would hold my frozen feet against the yellow tiles of the stove; but that hurt even more. Somehow, I made it through each winter.

When the first flowers, lilies of the valley and forget-me-nots, would peek out in spring, in Uncle's and Aunt's garden, I would bend down and joyfully inhale their fragrance. Every morning Aunt Didi brushed my blonde hair, it was long and fine. She would braid and style it with elaborate hair bows. I had to stand very still while she brushed. Once while having my hair brushed, I heard my aunt talking, but it sounded far away. I glanced towards the kitchen window and saw our neighbor's roof spinning around and then everything went black.

"Spatzchen, wake up!" I regained consciousness when I felt a movement under me and heard Aunt Didi's troubled voice. "Are you all right, Spatzchen?" She cradled me in her arms and said, "You got dizzy and fell down. Today you are not going to school. We will find a doctor!" It was quite difficult as there were very few doctors around at this time. We found a general practitioner. He determined that I was anemic and needed to take a spoonful of cod liver oil every day. He also suggested that Aunt Didi allow me to sit down during the morning hair brushing session. I didn't like to take the cod liver oil, but Aunt Didi made sure I did. After a while, I felt stronger and had more energy.

On weekends, my mother came and visited us. I was thrilled when I saw Mommy. She always brought some useful articles with her from her drugstore. First thing she would do when she arrived was to soak in the bathtub, because she did not have one in her apartment. The four of us had a wonderful time together. On Sundays, Aunt Didi would cook her delicious Hungarian dinners, usually we would have rabbit or chicken as a special treat. After dinner, Uncle Max would roll the dry tobacco into a cigar or put it in his pipe. Then I would climb onto his lap, sniff his pipe and tease him. A year went by and times were getting better. Aunt Didi purchased a piano, she informed us that in Hungary it was tradition for the upper class to play an instrument or to be interested in different arts. "And you and I, Brigitte, will take lessons!"

"Please Aunt Didi, I don't like to play the piano! I would like to practice ballet."

"Oh no Brigitte, that is out of the question! Not in my house, you won't dance around and ruin the furniture!" I was very disappointed. Aunt Didi hired a piano teacher to come to the house twice a week. But Aunt Didi was too temperamental and had no patience to learn to play correctly. Now she was more determined that I would play. After I finished my homework, I had to practice the piano. I would have rather played with my friends outside. So I asked my friends to come by during practice time and call me from downstairs to come and play. It was very rare that this worked out, Aunt Didi wouldn't let me go. I thought of another trick. I knew my Aunt liked flowers. So after school, I made a long detour from my usual path home and picked flowers out of other people's gardens. I gave them to Aunt Didi who was pleased and said, "Spatzchen, today you practice only one hour. Then you may go downstairs and play." I was satisfied. I became more and more resourceful in devising ways how not to play the piano. One day on the way home from school, I climbed up on a garden fence and reached down to pick a rose. I pricked my fingers with the thorns, causing them to bleed. I handed Aunt Didi the rose and begged her not to make me play the piano because of my bloody fingers. "But this will be the last time Brigitte. I will not allow this to happen again. I see through your games." Now I was in house arrest and Aunt Didi watched over me. Eventually I began to enjoy playing the piano and progressed quickly. I began to play some familiar operettas and Aunt Didi accompanied me with a melodic whistle. Aunt Didi had diphtheria as a child and it damaged her vocal cords. Now, even though she was unable to sing, she still loved music.

I did not like the long school hours. I was sitting in the back row of my class in silence, wanting to be outdoors and able to run free. I began to rebel, hanging out with three other girls and two boys. After we got out of school, we would roam the neighborhoods and ring the bells at the garden doors. The people had to come out to see who was there; some had quite a long way from the house to the garden door. By then we would be long gone. Some people lived on the second floor and they would throw open the windows and yell, "Who is it?" The worst thing we did was when each one of us threw one stone through windows of a greenhouse. Luckily no one found out and we did not get into trouble.

One day a girlfriend and I put our roller skates on and had fun on the streets. We had to be careful because the streets were uneven and had a lot of potholes left from the war. When a delivery truck passed slowly by, we sped up and caught the back end which we hung onto. With one on each side, we hitched a ride on roller skates. But as the truck went around a curve, we both fell into a pothole and were very skinned up. Blood was streaming from my knees. I did not feel pain. I was afraid of what Aunt Didi would say. We both went limping to our homes. I opened the water faucet in the garden and tried to clean myself up. But the bleeding would not stop. I heard Aunt Didi calling that dinner was ready. I did not make a sound. After a while, Uncle Max came looking for me. He found me by the faucet hunched over and bloody. He was horrified. "Brigitte, child, what happened?" He took me gently in his arms. I told my uncle that I had gone too fast on the roller skates and had fallen in a pothole. I could not tell my uncle the truth about my dangerous escapade, he would have been too upset and worried.

"Please, Uncle Max, hide the roller skates and tell Aunt Didi that I was running too fast and fell in a pothole." Uncle Max always had a soft spot in his heart for me and he had a difficult time being stern. He put the roller skates away. "Please Uncle Max, explain to Aunt Didi that I couldn't come up for dinner. You can tell her that I was worried about staining the furniture or bleeding on the floor."

Uncle Max tried to smooth the way with Aunt Didi. She came downstairs with first aid and medical supplies. When she saw me, she began to holler. Her eyes were blazing fire. "Brigitte, what have you done? You didn't pay attention to the road!"

She went on and on. I just said that I was sorry. I think I was still in shock, I didn't cry, I felt numb. After Aunt Didi calmed down, she said with concern in her voice, "Spatzchen, I think you should lie down now." I agreed. I was embarrassed and ashamed of my behavior. I made a promise to myself to follow the golden rule and therefore conduct myself accordingly.

Life was passing in harmony. Uncle Max got promoted and drove the big fire engine now. He worked and slept at the station for one week, and had the next week off. At home he enjoyed his garden and did all kinds of repairs around the house.

1947

In July, we had school vacation. I was eight years and six months old. Aunt Didi asked me if I would like to go alone to Zeckerin to visit my family. At the end of my stay, Uncle Max would pick me up. "Oh yes, Aunt Didi, that would be wonderful!" My uncle and aunt took me to the train station. First we boarded the tram. We passed the English sector and could see people were busy rebuilding and cleaning up the rubble from the war, like in our French sector. But what a difference in the Russian sector. There was not much activity cleaning up the destruction, it looked gray and sad. We did not recognize the once masterfully built train station, there was only a skeleton left. We saw the remains of the beautiful marble columns piled up in a corner. My spirit was downcast. The traffic was light, only some of the trains were still in working order. Aunt Didi put a sign around my neck with my name on it and the name of the station where I would get off. It was a three hour train ride. I was relieved when I arrived at my destination and saw Uncle Martin, Margitta and Hans waiting at the station with Liesel and Lotte who were pulling the cart. I was thrilled to be back on the farm. There was more food, the company of my cousins and more freedom to play outside. At this point in time, Zeckerin was occupied by French soldiers.

My family had one helper, his name was Jean Claude. He was very nice to Margitta and me. He told us he had a daughter of his own back in France. When he would receive a package from his family, he would share it with us. A special treat was when he gave us a generous piece of chocolate. When Jean Claude had his break from work, we would all play together. Sometimes he would throw us into the air and then catch us. Most of all, we enjoyed playing airplane. Jean Claude would hold one arm and one leg of either Margitta or me. Then he lifted the lucky girl up and swung her with a whirling motion. We had lots of fun. One day I followed him up to the barn where he was taking a break in the hayloft. I plopped myself right down on top of him and told him I wanted to take a nap with him. Jean Claude told me, "No Brigitte, I want to take my nap alone." And he pushed me off of his legs. I thought this was a new game and crawled back up on him. The game continued and I was giggling a lot. Suddenly I felt a little hill under me as I was sliding up and down. Jean Claude turned red and sternly told me to leave him alone.

Margitta was standing outside the barn and was jealous of the fun she could hear that I was having. Margitta's eyes were gleaming with malice and she hissed at me,

"What did you do with Jean Claude up there? I will tell my mother that you had fun with him in the barn!" She took off to tattle to Aunt Berta. Luckily Aunt Berta paid no attention to her story. But she told us to carry food to Uncle Martin, Hans and the rest of the workers in the fields. After delivering the food, we played in the fields which were planted with poppies. We would break the poppies open and eat the seeds; we felt exceptionally happy, laughing a lot and dancing around until we plopped to the ground and fell asleep.

At the end of my vacation, Uncle Max came and picked me up with my backpack full of food which Aunt Berta and Oma had prepared. In spite of all the food I had eaten over the summer, I lost weight and was very skinny. Aunt Didi was concerned. Eventually she determined that I had a tapeworm. She said, "Brigitte, that comes from improperly prepared food. You eat too much pork in Zeckerin."

"Yes, Aunt Didi, I eat plenty of everything." Finding a doctor was difficult and there was almost no medicine available. The natural remedy was for me to eat salt herring and nothing else for three days. Aunt Didi inspected to see if the head of the tapeworm had come out. I didn't have luck the first time, so I had to go through the process again, but the second time was a success.

Excitement was in the air when Uncle Max announced that we all were invited to celebrate New Year's Eve at the fire station with a dinner and a dance. I loved to go to the firehouse. Uncle Max always let me slide down the pole, but not this evening. We all were dressed for the occasion. Mother came too but she was not alone. I was surprised when she presented to me her new friend. His name was Hermann, like Papa's name. He had gray eyes, bushy eyebrows and dark hair that he wore slicked back. He was almost as tall as Uncle Max. He made a friendly impression, but I didn't feel comfortable. We had a great dinner and after the music began to play, Aunt Didi put me in Uncle Max's bed. But I was not sleepy. I listened to the music and was thinking about the stranger whom my mother had brought with her. After midnight, Aunt Didi and Uncle Max woke me up for the trip home on the tram.

My mother's visits became less frequent. She would not stay overnight any more on Saturday. On Sunday she came with Uncle Hermann, as I called him. Sometimes a long discussion went on about my father's disappearance. I heard my mother explaining that since we had not heard anything from him since 1941, she had made the decision to file the paperwork to have him declared dead. The war had ended in 1945 with him still missing. This year it would be seven years.

Then Mother called me, "Gitti, let's go downstairs and sit in the garden. I would like to explain something to you."

"Very good, Mommy, I am coming."

My mother gave me a photograph and pointed out, "Look Gitti. Here you are two years old. You recognize me, of course, and the man in the uniform was your father. Alas, he did not come back from the war."

"I like the photograph, can I have it please, Mommy?"

"Yes, Gitti, you may keep it. And now Gitti, I will share the good news with you. Soon I am marrying Uncle Hermann. His last name is Gramm. I hope you are happy for me?"

I was flabbergasted. I could not say one word. Mommy took me in her arms and thought I was happy for her, which was far from the truth. When I was alone, I began brooding about Uncle Hermann. I disliked him because he took my mommy completely away from me. Aunt Didi saw that I was irritated, displeased and some days detached from the world again. She felt sorry for me and to cheer me up she said, "Spatzchen, today we are going to the Kino, (cinema), to see a movie."

"Oh that would be great Aunt Didi." We took the tram to the next town. It was a very small cinema and people were standing in a long queue to get in. The movie featured beautiful scenery from an island in the sun with lots of palm trees and coconuts. I was enraptured. I didn't know that such an exotic paradise existed. After the movie, I declared with passion to my aunt that one day I would live on a warm sundrenched island with coconuts. The movie put me in a better spirit. My goal was to pursue my dream.

1949-1950

I was still living with my Uncle and Aunt when one morning I opened my eyes and saw a man in uniform standing in front of my bed. I was not scared. I just looked at him curiously. He had blonde hair, blue eyes and he smiled at me. Slowly I recognized the face from the photograph which my mother had given to me. "You are my father," I whispered. He laughingly pulled me from the bed. He kissed and hugged me. Later we found out that the Red Cross had found him deep in Siberia. The Russians never told my father that the war was over. He survived by building himself an igloo to keep himself warm. And he'd been fortunate to have a girl friend who brought him food and vodka. My father stayed with my uncle and aunt for a while, sleeping on a couch in the living room. I was overjoyed to have a father, and we got along in harmony. Soon he got a job on Saturdays and Sundays as a bartender in a beautiful restaurant on Tegeler Sea. The name was Feen Grotte. It was well known. Buses would bring people from all over Berlin. My father tended the bar and was given a room to live in there.

CHAPTER 2

A War Torn Family

War has an uncanny way of disturbing the fragile lives of people and their families.

1951

My mother and her husband wanted me to come live with them. I was delighted and it was exciting to be asked by my mother, but I had never really liked or trusted Hermann Gramm. I also was reluctant to leave Uncle Max and Aunt Didi, they felt like my true family. Moving also meant leaving the tranquil lovely garden area behind and adjusting to the crowded busy city of Berlin. One Saturday my mother and Uncle Hermann picked me up and took me home with them. Another chapter of my life was about to begin. My mother opened the door to the apartment and showed me around. The rooms were smaller and were attached to the store. It was a one bedroom apartment. I didn't let my mother see my disappointment. With a bright voice I asked, "Mommy, where do I sleep?"

"Right here in the living room on the sofa."

'Well,' I thought to myself, 'everything will work out.' Most important was that finally I was close to my mother.

A sunburst woke me up, spreading the rays through the wooden roll up blinds, warming my nose. At the same instant the church bells began ringing. I sprang up, confused, looking around me. Where was I? Slowly I pulled the blinds up. Now I remembered that Mommy and Uncle Hermann brought me to my mother's apartment. On the way from the tram station to here, we had crossed two parks. In the middle of each park stood a church. The first church we passed was a Catholic church. It was the second one, the Protestant church, which was in full view in front of me now. I could not believe people were passing right by my window. I jumped back, I thought that they could see me. But nobody paid attention to me. Then I realized that the people could not see me through the pattern of the drapes; but I clearly saw them. Slowly I approached my sofa bed, sat down and observed with amusement the scenery. Some people went to the church, children were playing in the park, a few elderly couples were sitting on the park benches. Several people were stopping close by my window and I listened in on their conversations without them being aware of me. Abruptly my fun stopped as my mother entered the room. She greeted me with a kiss and said, "Breakfast is ready, we are eating in the kitchen."

Uncle Hermann kissed me too and with a grin he said, "I prepared the breakfast. I hope you like it." I thanked them both. Later on we took a walk through the parks. It was a nice quiet Sunday.

Early next morning, wonderful smells of baked breads and pastries filled the air. I remembered my mother mentioned that right next door to us was a bakery. We had a delicious breakfast together. Then Uncle Hermann said, "I have to leave now to open the other store in Hermsdorf."

"Oh Mommy, I forgot that you have two stores now."

"Yes Gitti, we bought a second store in Hermsdorf. It's a very upscale section of Berlin. This store is much larger. It has two large windows and is more spacious inside than ours here."

"Today is Monday, Brigitte. I will take you to your new school. Please get ready," my mother said with a firm voice. The school was only a block away. It was a very large school. I had come from a much smaller school. Children here of all ages were searching for their assigned classrooms. It was very noisy and I was extremely intimidated. My mother asked for directions to my classroom. In my class were 30 girls of several ages from my age of twelve on up to fifteen. The war had interrupted the schooling for many children and they had to catch up to their respective grades.

When I got home from school the first day, I was very hungry and went to the kitchen. I saw a cucumber salad, my favorite, on the table. But I didn't dare eat the salad. Maybe Mommy had prepared the salad to have for dinner this evening. With Aunt Didi and Uncle Max, I always had to wait to eat at mealtimes. Finally I mustered enough courage to go into the store to ask my mother if I could have some of the salad. "Of course, Gitti. I made the salad for you." My mother was astonished that I would even ask. Everything was so new to me. I became quite shy and timid. After school I would sit on the sofa and hold my stuffed dog in my arms for hours. My mother tried to get me to go out and walk around, but I was stubborn and would not move. One day my mother called me. "Gitti, I need your help in the store. Would you please come?"

"Yes Mommy, I would love to help you!" I wanted to have a closer relationship with my mother. We both were learning how to be a family and how our household should work.

I was very shy in the school and would not talk often. But all that changed when I met Marianne who was placed next to me. Marianne was two years older than I. She had short dyed blonde hair, sparkling brown eyes and a touch of rouge on her lips. Her personality was outgoing and friendly. I was very fond of her. When the teacher asked a question, I would often whisper the answer to Marianne. She would occasionally grab my arm and put it into the air, telling the teacher that I knew the answer but was too shy to speak out loud. I was so embarrassed and my face turned red.

Marianne helped me to gain self-confidence and we became best friends. Marianne played the accordion. Since there was no room in my mother's apartment for a larger instrument, I asked my mother if she would like me to play the accordion. "That is an excellent idea, Gitti." I was pleased. Marianne and I took lessons from Mr. Kirsch. He would come to Mommy's apartment to instruct us. Marianne was a very good player and I was able to catch on quickly.

1952

Come spring, I told my mother that I would like to have shorter hair and a permanent. I wanted to look more grown up like some of my classmates and especially my friend, Marianne. My body was still "sleeping" and showed no signs of maturing. My friend Marianne was two years older and well-developed. Once, out of the blue, I asked Marianne to show me her breasts. Marianne broke out in laughter. "What a silly idea that is, Brigitte!"

"I am just curious, because I have never seen my mother or Aunt Didi without clothes."

"You have weird thoughts, Brigitte." Then Marianne gave me a kiss and left.

Marianne and I were practicing on the accordion almost every day together in the living room of my mother's apartment. The sounds of our music were drifting into the drugstore. My mother's customers were praising us on how wonderfully we played. My mother was so proud of me.

Next day, my mother fulfilled my wish and took me to the hairdresser who cut my long hair and gave me a permanent. Marianne saw me in the school sitting on my bench with my short hair. She became furious. "What have you done with your beautiful long hair, Brigitte?" Then she took a flower vase filled with water. Just before the teacher walked in, she dumped the cool water over my head. All of our classmates broke out into fits of laughter. I felt humiliated and angry. I would not talk to Marianne anymore. Soon after that, Marianne and the older girls were placed in a separate class from me.

Often on Sunday mornings my Mommy and Uncle Hermann would sleep in. I wondered what was going on behind the closed door. I was waiting until Uncle Hermann came out to make our breakfast. Then I would run into the bedroom to cuddle with my mother. The room smelled of alcohol. But I did not care. I simply wanted to feel the warmth of a loving touch from my mother. Since I never had the privilege of sleeping in one bed with my mother, I took this opportunity to do so. My mother put her arm around me and remarked what a big girl I was now. Then we went to the kitchen where Uncle Hermann had set the table and was ready to serve us breakfast.

Uncle Hermann tried to be nice to me. He would pick me up and sit me on his lap; but I was not interested in his affection. When he asked why I didn't call him "Papa Two", I told him that I already had a Papa. He grinned and called me stubborn. At some point, my mother needed help and Uncle Hermann hired a friend of his; her name was Louise. I called her Aunt Louise. She cleaned and did the laundry. The clothes would be washed in the attic in a bath tub and would then hang to dry. The attic was five stories up. It wasn't easy to walk the steps up with a basket full of laundry. In winter, with the bitter cold, the clothes would be frozen stiff. Each tenant had a special day to do his or her own laundry.

My mother, Uncle Hermann, Aunt Louise and her husband became fast friends and would often go out in the evening dancing. Left alone, I would play records and pretend to be a ballerina, dancing around the rooms. I loved music, especially the gypsy music.

After school I was allowed to play ball for an hour with my new friends, girls and boys. We played ball in the lot where a building had been bombed out. This was right around the corner from my mother's store. Then I had to do my homework. This is when I most missed Aunt Didi, who always had spent hours with me. I did not like having to do school work alone. Often my mother called me to help with the store, I liked that better. I was learning a lot, which was a good experience.

CHAPTER 3

A Thorny Road

Every rose has thorns, just as every life has travails.

It was two years since my father had returned from Siberia. He was a hard worker and had made enough money to buy a drug store in Tegel. He also rented space in Tegeler market. I admired him for his fast achievement and adjustment to the busy city of Berlin. Sometimes my father would come to visit, usually on a Saturday morning when he knew that Uncle Hermann had to be away at work. Father would pound on the wooden blinds calling to me, "Sweetheart, let me in." I knew he was quite high, alcohol was his weakness. But then, vodka had saved his life; he survived Siberia. And I was happy that I had a papa. This time Papa brought a young friend with him. Wilhelm was the son of the proprietor of the Feen Grotte, from whom my father rented the bar. This was a well-known establishment. Wilhelm was in his early twenties, very charming and good looking, with blonde hair and blue eyes like my father. Wilhelm and my father were singing joyful songs and talking to my mother and me. Then they wanted more to drink. But my mother served strong coffee with breakfast. Wilhelm put his arms around me, I began to perspire and pushed him gently away. We all laughed and had fun together. Papa and Wilhelm came often and I looked forward to their visits. My mother would often cry after the visits; she realized what she was missing. My father said more than once that Mommy was his one true love and that he would never marry again. That situation helped my mother and me to become closer.

In the afternoon around four o'clock, the aroma of freshly brewed coffee would fill the air and my mother would call to me to take a break for coffee and kuchen. I was proud that my mother asked me to share in the German tradition with her. One day, Uncle Max came by the store in a big fire truck. People came running up, thinking that there was a fire. Uncle Max just grinned and said he wanted to take me for a ride. He had been in the area to put out a fire and took the opportunity to see his sister and me. It was the highlight of my day. On another day, Uncle Max and Aunt Didi had a big surprise for Mommy and me. They had bought their first car. It was green. What an adventure as not many people had cars in the early 1950s. I sat in the back and felt car sick but did not say a word. Aunt Didi turned and looked at me and saw how pale I was. "Oh Spatzchen, you don't look so good! Come, we will change our seats, you sit in the front." Uncle Max went the fastest way home.

One day when I helped my mother in the store, we met a mother and daughter with whom we engaged in a friendly conversation. My mother and I found them to be very sympathetic. The girl's name was Christel and she lived two blocks away on a side street. She and I became good friends. I was shocked when I visited them. They had only two rooms, a tiny kitchen with a table and four chairs, and another small room which was a bedroom-living room combined. A large table took most of the room with four chairs; then there was a bed and a sofa. Christel slept on the sofa. She was not an attractive girl, but was very intelligent. She helped me with my schoolwork. My mother often gave Christel pastries to take home, and I would occasionally give her small gifts like soap or lotion or send some detergent for her mother to use. We had a good relationship. The family was from Poland. I called Christel's mother "Mamushka", she always wore a babushka on her head. My mother and Uncle Hermann would occasionally take me out for dinner with them on Saturday nights. Also on New Year's Eve, we went to a lovely place where there was music and dancing. Life was very nice at this point, I felt content.

1954

On January 7, I turned fifteen. My relationship with my mother had become more open and comfortable. Since she had Aunt Louise to help her on Saturdays, I had to go to help Uncle Hermann in Hernsdorf. He had a young girl as an apprentice who was not very nice to me. She bossed me around and Uncle Hermann just grinned and said nothing. I didn't like his attitude. In April, my mother became very sick and Uncle Hermann took her to a private clinic in Hernsdorf. Aunt Louise and I took care of my mother's store. Mother had an operation and the doctor told her to stay in bed for ten days. I took every opportunity to visit Mother.

The tenth day came and I received a call from Uncle Hermann to come as quickly as possible to the clinic. My heart was pounding fast as I feared the worst. As I entered the clinic, I saw Aunt Didi and Uncle Hermann crying. Uncle Max was heartbroken and cried out loud for his beloved sister. Uncle Hermann told me what had happened. "Your mother got up after the ten days, but from being in bed for so long, a blood clot had formed. When she stood up, the clot traveled to the lungs. "She was able to ring for a doctor, but there was no doctor available when it happened. As a result of the clot, she died!" I could not think, my body was felt paralyzed.

I bent over my mother, gave her a kiss and held her hand. She looked peaceful. Uncle Hermann pulled me away and said to me, "You have to go to the store right now and look after the apprentice." I looked up to Uncle Hermann in disbelief.

"I should go? This is my mother who died and I want to stay."

"No." He dragged me outside, "Go now." And he shut the door behind me. Everyone was so wrapped up in their grief that they paid me no attention. I went to the store, sat in the corner and wept. The apprentice, Gertrude, had no compassion for me, and told me that I had to work while she went for her lunch.

My mother was buried on May 6th, 1954. She was forty-two years old. When I got back to my mother's store after the burial, the whole street was deserted and quiet; no one understood how such a shocking thing could have happened. She was much too young to die. She was well-loved by her friends and clients. I had enjoyed complete companionship with my mother for three years; and the last year was the best. Christel and her family, Aunt Louise and my mother's clients showed compassion for me. At night when no one was around, I spent hours crying. At school, I was staring off into space and withdrawn. My school teacher respected my privacy and left me alone. After school, I worked in my mother's store. Aunt Louise came every day to work with me and stayed until late afternoon. The evenings were dreadful. Uncle Hermann would come home smelling of alcohol and would talk and cry to my mother's pictures. Then he wanted me to sit on his lap. Weeks passed and he became more aggressive. He demanded kisses for food. I would always turn him down and he always would say, "It is only a joke." I felt very uneasy. One evening I was finishing my nightly chore of washing the floor when Uncle Hermann grabbed me from behind and demanded a kiss from me. I threw the bucket of dirty water and rags at him. I wanted to show him that I was not afraid of him. I despised him and my pain and hatred gave me inner strength. I felt anger that he could be so uncaring and thoughtless; that he would try to exploit me.

That Sunday I took the train to visit Uncle Max and Aunt Didi. It was wonderful to be with them in the beautiful and peaceful setting of their home. Aunt Didi made a marvelous meal and she asked me how I was getting along with Uncle Hermann. I told my Uncle and Aunt that I disliked him intensely and detested his behavior. I wanted desperately for them to invite me to live with them again. But alas, they did not. Even though they were my closest relatives, I was too embarrassed to ask. My disappointment and sadness resulted in my building a hard shell around my heart and soul.

No one came to visit me at the store anymore. No one could stand Hermann Gramm. He was a shrewd businessman, was immoral and had no scruples. One evening he asked me to sleep with him "since he missed my mother so much". I told him, definitely not. He grabbed me and began to wrestle with me. When I fell down, he went on top and began kissing me. I went stone still rather than fighting back. With a cold and calm voice, I said, "You can do whatever you want, but in the morning I will report you to the police."

He came to his senses almost immediately and then said, "It was only a joke."

From that night on, I slept with a knife in my bed. He tried to sneak in more time, but I heard the door squeaking, turned on the light and held the knife in my hand. He stopped cold and told me that he "had forgotten something". Then he left and closed the door. That was the last time he made advances on me. Aunt Louise, Christel and her mother were very supportive of me. It was only two months since my mother's death when Uncle Hermann announced that a lady friend of his from Mannheim was coming to live with us. On one hand, I was relieved that now he would give her all of his attention. But on the other hand, I couldn't believe that this was happening so soon after my mother's death. Aunt Louise told me that his new woman was her sister, Micki. Apparently Uncle Hermann and Micki knew each other and were quite close before he married my mother.

Micki was almost as tall as Uncle Hermann, with short brown hair and piercing, steel blue eyes. At first she was friendly to me. Her sister Louise showed her how to sell the products. I would take over the work in the store after school. Micki became less and less friendly and decided that I should be in the back of the store cleaning the rooms while she took care of the store. I complained to Uncle Hermann, "Why can I not work in my mother's store anymore?"

"You must do what Aunt Micki says and help Aunt Louise with the cleaning." Then he added, "If you don't behave, I will send you to the orphanage."

My heart sank. At night I lay awake in bed searching for a solution, a way out of my situation. That Sunday I informed Uncle Hermann and Aunt Micki that I was going to visit my father. They were not very enthusiastic about it, but couldn't say anything against it. I went early morning with the tram, so I could talk to my father before he began his work. I explained everything to him and asked him, "Papa, why can I not live with you?" Papa was sad and told me, "I already researched the possibility," but an official from the court told me that since I was not married and did not own a home, you have to stay where you are. But don't worry, Sweetheart. I have already begun to build a two story house on my girlfriend's property, and when you turn eighteen you will have a place to stay."

"Oh Papa, that means I have to endure three long years with them." We both felt helpless and sorry for each other. It was hard to watch Aunt Micki sleeping in my mother's bed and wearing her furs. I simply did as I was told and kept to myself. One evening they invited Aunt Louise to come over for dinner and told her, in front of me, not to be friendly with Brigitte and not to take her side. Otherwise she would be out of work. Aunt Louise had tears in her eyes but did not say anything. She had a husband and two daughters to take care of.

The Cinderella years had begun. Before I left for school I had to take care of three ovens, clean the ashes out and put newspaper, wood and charcoal in. One was in the living room where I slept. I didn't mind taking care of that one. It was made of a lovely yellow tile. Another one was in the bedroom, I didn't like to go there, but I had to. In the kitchen was a big oven with two fire holes. I felt very depressed and prayed to God to get me away from these people, and kissed my mother's framed pictures good night. One day Aunt Micki came into the living room with a rag in her hand and a mean look in her eyes. "You forgot to wipe the kisses from your mother's pictures."

I jumped up and grabbed her by the wrist, twisting her arm violently. Aunt Micki was dumbfounded and I myself was astounded what a powerful grip I had. Aunt Micki's face turned red and she hurriedly left the room, saying nothing. I felt good and Aunt Micki kept a little distance from me.

Sometime later, I suffered from incredible pain on my side. I went to Dr. Pfluger, a very nice young man in his thirties. He immediately put me into the hospital. I had to have my appendix taken out. When I was released, Aunt Micki immediately put me to work, this time in the store. She demanded that I place the heavy boxes of detergent on a high shelf. The scar broke open. After stitching me up, Dr. Pfluger went to the store and told Aunt Micki that I could not be lifting things. At this point I was sixteen. Uncle Hermann and Aunt Micki got married. I graduated from school, not at the top of the class, not at the bottom, but in the middle of the class. It was now time for high school. I needed to choose what to study. I didn't know what I wanted to learn. I only knew that I wanted to get out of my current situation.

The teacher decided that I should follow in my mother's footsteps and become a professional shop owner. We were fourteen students in the class. The teacher gave us a huge book to study, to learn the ingredients of many products, like soap, lipstick and creams, etc. The class also focused on how to sell goods and to run a successful business. Some subjects were quite interesting. Occasionally I would get out of class early. I did not go straight home because Aunt Micki would put me right to work. Instead, I would stroll through the park, have a seat on a bench, enjoy nature and dream of faraway places, mostly of tropical islands. Sometimes I stayed too long in my peaceful dream world. Then Aunt Micki would question me as to where I was. "Brigitte, work is waiting for you."

"Yes, Aunt Micki, I know. But today we had an extra hour to learn," I lied.

My first school vacation was in 1953. I went to Kronach Oberfranken with my class. We stayed in an old fortress. It was exciting. In 1954, I went with my friend Christel to the Black Forest. The husband of the family with whom we stayed was a forest ranger. The wilderness was wonderful. The family had rescued a young deer, (Bambi), and we were allowed to play with and feed Bambi. It was an enjoyable vacation.

1955

I was sixteen and a half. This time my vacation was a tour that took me to Italy, Austria, Bavaria and ended up in Kempten in Allgau. Kempten was Uncle Hermann's home town. I invited Christel to join me in Kempten. I told her that we have a place to stay, with Uncle Hermann's brother and family. Christel was delighted and arrived the next day. Uncle Hermann's brother, Adolf, and his wife, Anna, received us with open arms. What a difference between the two brothers. Here the atmosphere was warm and friendly. At home it was harsh and very unpleasant. This couple had a son, Adolfchen. He and his friends took us on a motorcycle ride. Christel and I had great fun with them. I also had two admirers. After each vacation, I felt better for a while and tried to ignore the rough treatment from Aunt Micki and Uncle Hermann. In my heart, I felt that one day they would not be without punishment.

One afternoon, Aunt Micki called me. I was cleaning the kitchen. "Brigitte, a gentleman is here to see you." He was a middle aged man and introduced himself as Rudolf Gonzar. He was a well-known baritone singer and star of the opera. His brother and his wife had been very good friends of my mother and I was fond of them. I realized that they probably had asked Rudolf to check in on me. When Aunt Micki realized who the impressive person was, she made a point of being noticed. She even behaved nicely towards me. Mr. Gonzar invited me to one of his performances. Aunt Micki gave me permission to go.

I dressed up for the occasion, which I enjoyed. The first performance I attended was Rosenkavalier, by Johann Strauss. I was captivated by the beautiful performance. Afterwards, Mr. Gonzar took me to a fancy restaurant. From then on, he would send me postcards and letters, as he traveled the world for his work. It was thrilling that a celebrity would be interested in my company. Whenever he had a performance in Berlin, I was invited. Most of all, I enjoyed the elegant dining afterward. Now I was seventeen and took the liberty to go to visit my father most every Saturday or Sunday, with my girlfriend, Christel. The Feen Grotte was a beautiful restaurant, very large. You could sit by the sea or inside. There were a variety of shows, good music and tasty food. My father always reserved a table for us as these events were very exciting. Aunt Micki and Uncle Hermann were resentful.

I often saw Wilhelm in the Feen Grotte and I thought of the time when I first had met him through my mother, when Father and Wilhelm came visiting us. Wilhelm was a charming young man and he would flirt and dance with me. One time I saw him dancing with a much older girl, she wore a lot of makeup and was cheaply dressed. I asked my father who she was. My father told me her name is Elsie, and she is Wilhelm's girlfriend. Wilhelm's father was very unhappy with this situation as she was definitely lower in class than theirs. My father wanted me to marry Wilhelm, so that he would have a built-in drinking partner. I had no interest in getting married. But it made me sad and jealous to see Wilhelm with another woman. Papa always had a collection of young men around him, many of them good looking and wealthy. But they all had one thing in common, drinking. I wanted nothing to do with them.

Christel and I changed our Saturday night destination to a very upscale establishment called Resi. There was a large orchestra that played Glenn Miller hits, boogie-woogie and other American music. But the best and most unique part of this place was the "Rohr Post". This was the only place that had this, each table had a number on a post and a hydraulic tube. One could write a message on a piece of paper with your table number and the number of the receiver; then put it in the hydraulic tube and send it to a chosen person. It was a lot of fun and often this is how a gentleman would ask a lady to dance. This way a woman could check out the person and then make up her mind.

One Sunday when I visited my father, he said he had something strange to tell me. His acquaintance, Professor Gerhard Holman, asked my father if he had a daughter by the name of Brigitte Kruger. My father said yes and then the professor told him that a man named Hermann Gramm had come to his school class. Mr. Gramm had wanted the professor to prevent Brigitte from graduating from the business class. Mr. Gramm had tried to bribe the professor with money and French champagne. He told the professor that he lived in the French sector and got better prices on the champagne. He needed Brigitte as an apprentice, not a professional employee. This way he felt he could get away with paying her less. When my father ended the story, his face was flushed red and he said, "I thanked your Professor Holman profoundly for the information."

I was relieved and glad that my father found out how treacherous Hermann Gramm was, and how he treated me. "Oh, Papa. I am not surprised. I know they are very malicious people. But now I will fight back in my own quiet way. Without making them suspicious. I promise you, Papa, from now on I will study harder and I will make sure that I graduate. I am not going out on Saturdays or Sundays anymore for four months. Then I will be eighteen and graduation is close to the same time."

"Yes, Sweetheart. I know you can do it and by then my house will be ready. You will have a place to stay."

"Oh, Papa, that would be wonderful. I feel like I have a guardian angel who is giving me strength and showing me a new way of hope."

The next Saturday and Sunday I stayed home and Aunt Micki and Uncle Hermann asked me why I wasn't going out as usual. I answered, "I want to study."

"Oh no, you are so good that you don't need to study," they both replied with false smiles.

I played their game and thanked them for the compliment. "Then I will go and see Christel!" I told Christel what my plan was in case Uncle Hermann or Aunt Micki contacted her. "Christel, please help me to get some of my books out from the apartment. I want to sit on a park bench and study. Later, I will leave the books with you."

"That is fine with me," she replied. We both went back to my place and pretended that I had forgotten something. Every weekend and at night I studied hard. I was thankful that the professor had let my father know.

In the store there was a trap door in the floor that was not easy to see. We walked on it. It opened to the cellar where the coal, wood and heavy materials were kept. I had to keep the wooden stairs below the door clean. One morning Aunt Micki called me up from cleaning the stairs, "Brigitte, there are a couple of gentlemen here to see you." I was dirty from being in the cellar. It was Professor Holman and another man. They told Aunt Micki that I should be working in the store, not the cellar. They were from the Chamber of Commerce and Industry, doing a surprise inspection. They were there to confirm that I was correctly performing my job.

I was pleased that the professor and the other gentleman had come at the right moment. I saw panic in Aunt Micki's eyes and her face was red. Finally I had my enjoyment. Professor Holman asked me a lot of questions and I had to show him that I was a good sales person. Then he asked me to gift wrap some perfume and a porcelain coffee set. Professor Holman told me that I did very well and winked at me. He now understood my life better.

One day a small circus set up nearby in town. A gypsy woman from the circus came to buy soap. When I handed her the soap, she looked me in the eyes and said, "You are suffering." Then she took my hand and read my palm. She told me that I would never be happy in Berlin, but that when I turned thirty, I would go for a long journey over water and my life would change for the better. I gave her the soap and thought to myself that she was right about the suffering. But she did not see that my life would soon change when I moved to my father's house. There I would have a peaceful life.

On March 7, 1957, I graduated from the business course. I was declared the second best student in the program. I was thrilled and thanked the professor Holman.

He said, "You deserve it, you worked very hard." I went home to Uncle Hermann and Aunt Micki. This time I wanted to have my sweet revenge. Before I entered the store, I made an unhappy face. My uncle and aunt greeted me with a malicious grin and said, "We know that you did not graduate. Now you must stay with us as an apprentice."

Calmly and with a cynical smile I said, "On the contrary. Here is my certificate. Tomorrow I am leaving you to live with my father. I also want my mother's jewelry and the big white birch armoire." Uncle Hermann and Aunt Micki were stunned. I felt a huge weight lift off of my heart.

CHAPTER 4

Turbulence and Passion

No life is complete without experiencing the highs and lows of true love and passion.

1957

I was eighteen and moved to Tegel into a house that my father had built on land that belonged to his girlfriend, Irmgard Ritter. It was a nice property with a flower shop in the front yard. I was incredibly relieved to breathe fresh air and to have my freedom. Papa had made the attic into a nice, comfortable room for me. The lovely white birch armoire decorated a whole wall. My papa gave me money and I picked out the rest of the furniture; a pullout sofa-bed that was black with yellow dots, chairs that were modern in a yellow and orange fabric and an attractive table. I was happy with and proud of my room, which I had put together by myself. My papa asked his girlfriend to cook for me, but she refused. At first my feelings were hurt. Later I realized that Irmgard didn't do much of anything for anyone. Soon she adopted my father's lifestyle which revolved around drinking.

I began working at my father's store, which was very nice. It was in the Bruno Strasse. Around the corner was Berliner Strasse, which was a main street. One lady worked already for my father. Papa handled the heavy detergents and cleaning supplies, while the lady and I took care of the cosmetics and the rest of the business. I worked eight to ten hours a day, receiving a good salary, and was happy with the situation.

In the summer I received two weeks of vacation. Christel and I went to the North Sea. Christel had a male friend, Gustav, who came along with us. Christel and I stayed in a private home that had a thatched roof, which was typical in this region.

Gustav stayed in a different home, not far from us. He was fifteen years older than Christel, and was very fond of her. We swam every day. One morning we waded very far out and the water suddenly came with a wave as tall as a house. We ran for our lives. We almost made it to safety, just before the wave caught us and knocked us down. We never went back and did not understand why nobody had warned us of the danger.

One day we decided to go into a nearby town for dinner in a nice restaurant. I was in high demand when the dancing began. Around midnight, I went back to our table but could not find Christel or Gustav. They had vanished, just leaving me there. I asked my last dance partner about the best way to get home. He told me by train. He walked me to the station and left. I went inside to buy a ticket but the counter was closed. I sat down on a bench to wait. By now it was nearly 2:00 a.m. in the morning. It was cold and damp. I sat there shivering, vowing never to speak to Christel again. By dawn, I was totally frozen and cramped up. I went to look for a taxi. Finally I found a cab, the driver was a heavy set man with a swarthy face. When I told him my destination and asked if he would drive me there, he said it would cost a lot of money. I did not have enough and told him that I could pay him the rest once I got home. I explained what had happened and I was in excruciating pain from sitting in the cold all night. He agreed to drive me to my place. After half an hour of driving, he looked sideways at me and then stopped the car. He asked me to lift my skirt, he wanted to see my legs. I said no. He told me to get out if he couldn't see my legs. I was in the middle of nowhere, in unbearable pain, and I felt I had no option. So I lifted my skirt a little bit and he began to sweat.

"Higher, higher," he insisted with a hoarse voice. Then he unzipped his pants and pulled himself out. My stomach turned. He demanded that I touch him. Looking the other way, I gave him my hand and he wrapped it around his penis. He guided my hand up and down, and eventually he ejaculated. Then we drove off without saying a word.

The thatched roof from the house where I was staying came into view. "Stop!" I shouted. I jumped out of the car, and he drove off. Christel came running out and told me how worried she had been. I didn't say a word, but simply walked upstairs to our room. I lay down on my stomach and started to cry. Christel began to panic. "I am so sorry," she said. I was furious and let her know it.

"Christel, you should go straight to confession and tell the priest what you and Gustav have done. Christel was a Catholic. I told her something awful had happened, but it could have been much worse. "I could have lost my virginity, at the very least." Christel blamed Gustav for making her leave.

After that, I never felt fully comfortable with Christel again. We went to the night club, Resi, one last time together. I received a note from table #7 through the hydraulic tube. The young man who sent it was sitting with his friend and described himself. After looking at him, I replied, "Yes, I would like to dance with you."

His name was Dario, a very good looking, charming Italian man. Dario and I became good friends. He was just my type; dark hair, very white teeth and a warm glow in his brown eyes. On Saturdays and Sundays we would go sailing in his friend's fast boat. His friend was also his boss. Dario and his boss sold pharmacy products. I was very much taken by Dario and loved to look at him. However, I did not like or trust his boss, Siegfried.

Siegfried was always with us. He told Dario what was on the agenda each day. It was irritating to me. I felt that Siegfried took control over Dario. I wished that Dario and I had more time alone. Dario would pick me up from my father's house and would take me back. This was the only time we had by ourselves. One Sunday

I invited Dario to come upstairs to have a drink and talk without a third person present. He was very pleased. He gave me hot kisses and his hands were all over me. I was very excited.

We didn't even get undressed, my fiery lover just took my panties off. Then I gasped, "Dario, go slowly, it hurts!" I felt a sharp pain, then it went smoother. Before I could enjoy it, it was finished. We rested a while and then we got undressed. I admired Dario's body and reached out, caressed and kissed him. It gave me pleasure. But when I went further down to the very excited part, Dario drew back and pushed me away.

"Where did you learn that? Maybe a French man!" he said with an accusing tone of voice.

I didn't know what I had done wrong and pointed out, "You knew I was a virgin. I was only following my instincts." Dario apologized, and we had missionary style sex. This was the 1950s, no one talked of sex, much less experimented with it, or explained the act to a child. It was taboo. Anyway, I did not have anyone to ask or to confide in.

One day Dario asked me to go home with him. His mother wanted to meet me. That evening his mother cooked lots of pasta and served us red wine. His beautiful sister joined us, it was a lovely evening. His mother insisted that I spend the night there. I ended up sleeping on a pullout sofa in the great room, the bedrooms were all upstairs. I couldn't sleep because I kept expecting Dario to creep downstairs and make love to me. That didn't happen and I was disappointed.

Next day, Sunday, Dario suggested, "Brigitte, would you like to go to the Feen Grotte for a nice dinner and dancing? At the same time you can visit your father."

I was thrilled to be with Dario alone. "Oh yes, Dario, that is an excellent idea." After we greeted my father, who gave us a good table, Dario ordered a bottle of wine. He looked deep into my eyes then and asked me to marry him. I was stunned by his proposal. I didn't know what to say. In my mind, at eighteen, I was just beginning my life and enjoying my freedom. I discovered how deeply I felt that I did not want to get married.

"Oh Dario. I am honored. But I am too young to settle down. I want to see more of the world. It is too soon. We have known each other for only a little over two months. Maybe later." Dario was disappointed and told me that his mother said that if a girl says maybe, it means no.

Early autumn came and it was time to take Siegfried's boat out of the water. We all went to the boatyard. I watched Siegfried and Dario clean the boat and get it ready to put in storage. Mr. Reinhardt, the owner of the shipyard, came by and started talking to me. He was in his late seventies and was very friendly. He said, "Brigitte, why don't you come inside and have a bite to eat with me while they get the boat taken care of?" That sounded like an excellent idea, especially since I didn't like cold weather. I told Dario to let me know when they were done, he nodded. Mr. Reinhardt fixed a lovely platter of cold cuts and Swiss cheese with butter and salt. It was a feast, all of the foods that I never had. We laughed and ate, and Mr. Reinhardt held and kissed my hands. The meal was a huge treat. Since Irmgard didn't cook for me, I was used to only one hot meal a day, which was delivered from the restaurant to my father's store at lunch time. The rest of the day I had to take care of myself, often going without food.

When it was time to go, I gave Mr. Reinhardt a kiss on the cheek and headed back outside. I was smiling and told Dario what a nice time I had had with Mr. Reinhardt. Dario's face darkened. He seemed to be unhappy with me. We all climbed into Siegfried's car. Then Dario yelled at me, "Why did you go with Mr. Reinhardt into his house?" He went on and on until finally I started laughing.

"You are jealous of a seventy year old gentleman! That is ridiculous!" At that moment, Siegfried interrupted, saying that Mr. Reinhardt was known for liking young girls, giving them money and who knows what else. Then he accused me of giving Mr. Reinhardt what he liked.

"That is outrageous, Siegfried! You disgust me. You are a deceitful man!" I cried out. "Dario, I hope you don't believe this evil man!"

Dario turned red and told Siegfried to stop the car. Then he turned to me and said, "Brigitte, get out! I don't want to see you anymore." I got out and they drove off.

In shock and disbelief, I found myself stranded in the middle of Berlin, with no money. I looked for a phone booth and found one on the next corner with a phone book. I called Mr. Reinhardt collect. Twenty minutes later, he picked me up and drove me home in his Mercedes. On the way home, I told him what had happened and how cruel Siegfried was.

I think Siegfried wanted to break up my relationship with Dario. He liked to be in control. When I finally got to my room, I cried with pain, unable to reconcile how Dario could think that of me. I could not stop crying, it must have been early morning before I finally calmed down. I realized how immature and weak Dario was. He was not a man for me. Maybe it all happened for a reason, I consoled myself. My sadness subsided and I felt more peaceful within. I knew that one day Dario would come back with regret in his heart. But it was too late already, my door was closed.

I tried not to think of Dario and concentrated on the work in my father's store. In the evenings I was spending quiet time in my room. One day a young man named Harry came into the store. He was twenty years old, very slim, blue eyes, blond hair and a smiling expression. He began to come around every day and told me that he lived nearby. He always walked with his collie dog. One day he asked me out to dinner at a local bistro. We had an enjoyable evening.

After that, Harry came by the store one day with his friend, Gerhard, who was older, maybe thirty. They invited me to go to their apartment to have dinner. It was an older building owned by a family who rented out the rooms. The lady of the house cooked nice meals for them. I soon grew to dislike Gerhard. He was bald, had dark piercing eyes and he acted strangely. But I really enjoyed being with Harry for how much fun he was.

One Sunday they invited me out to a very nice restaurant in the city. I put my best dress on and we headed out in the late afternoon. Gerhard stopped the car at a beautiful restaurant surrounded by a lovely garden. In the background began the forest, with tall majestic trees which completed the idyllic setting. I asked Harry, "Are we stopping here for our afternoon coffee and cake?" Both men shook their heads at the same time as they changed into waiters' uniforms. Then they walked briskly towards the restaurant.

Ten minutes later, they returned, jumped into the car and we drove off rapidly. Curiously, I asked them, "What was that all about?" But they would not give me an answer. They just kept grinning at each other. When we got to the city, Harry and Gerhard changed back into their suits and we all went to a very upscale restaurant where we had the best of everything.

Finally I found out what had happened at the first restaurant. They had dressed as waiters and picked up the payments that the guests had left on the tables. The restaurant was so large that Gerhard had taken one side of it and Harry the other and the staff did not know what was going on. The three of us laughed about how well the scheme worked.

Sometime later, I asked Harry if he had a job, to which he replied no. Much later, I figured out that Gerhard was the breadwinner and Harry's companion. When I asked Harry about it, he explained that he had come from a very poor family. Gerhard had offered to take care of him. Then Harry asked me if I would like to be his girlfriend. I told him that I just wanted to remain friends. "Also," I explained, "I do not want to participate in any dishonesty or thievery. And I do not like Gerhard."

Soon after, I had a big surprise. Wilhelm, my father's drinking buddy, came in to the store. He was very sweet. He would bring me flowers and chocolate. And one day, he asked me to out with him. I was thrilled. I had always liked Wilhelm. He was maybe five years older than I. I was eighteen. Wilhelm picked me up in an elegant car. My father was pleased, he really wanted him for a son-in-law, a family drinking companion. Wilhelm's father was also very glad that his son had broken up with Elsie.

I thought that it would be a good occasion to ask my father if he would buy me a car. "Papa, I would like to obtain my driver's license and pay for it. Maybe for my next birthday, you would like to buy me a car? It is a long way to walk from your house to the store, especially in the wintertime. You know that I cannot stand the cold. Also, it is dark in the morning when I leave the house, and dark in the evening when I go home."

Papa smiled. He was in a good mood. "We will see, Sweetheart."

Soon I began to take driving lessons. I was excited. Wilhelm and I would go out a lot. He took me to fine restaurants. We had a lot of fun, laughed over silly things and drank. But neither of us wanted to get married. So as not to disappoint our fathers, we kept that a secret. Most Saturdays and Sundays, I stayed overnight at Wilhelm's small apartment in back of the Feen Grotte. We had sex, but I do not remember much of it, because we always had had too much to drink. I think Wilhelm drank because he couldn't be with Elsie, and I had my own reasons.

When I would spend Sunday nights with him, I would take the tram early Monday morning and go to work in my father's store. To settle my stomach, I would drink a couple of bottles of Coca Cola and by noon I would feel better. One evening, when Wilhelm and I were dancing in the Feen Grotte, Elsie came running in, crying. She grabbed Wilhelm, pulling him with her. He followed her outside. Wilhelm never came back.

I was alone again. One week later there was terrible news. Wilhelm and Elsie had been burned alive in Wilhelm's small apartment. They were both smokers and it was thought that they fell asleep smoking. My father and I were in deep mourning. Papa grieved by drinking more, and I by working more. Papa then fired the lady who helped me and told me that I should take care of the store all by myself. That meant that I was responsible for purchasing, setting up displays, selling and cleaning the store. I was not happy about this. At least Papa unpacked the heavier items.

I told my father that I had earned my driver's license. "Please, Papa, would you buy me a car? I am only eighteen and you give me a lot of responsibility."

My father replied, "I would only do that if you drive me to the market at 5 a.m. daily."

As it was, I barely got enough sleep. So I said, "No, Papa. You ask too much of me."

My father ended up buying a car for Wolfgang, who was the son of his girlfriend Irmgard. I was hurt and sad. All admiration for my father faded away. I felt he blamed me for Wilhelm's death. They were best friends and Papa thought of Wilhelm as his future son-in-law. I had a difficult time with the cold winter in Berlin.

I had to walk from my father's house to the store in temperatures that were often twenty degrees below zero. I remember one day is was so cold in my father's store, that I sat on the stove and burned the backside of my work dress. My father smiled when he saw me melting on top of the stove. He seemed to be impervious to the cold and would walk about outside without a coat or gloves on. Since my father survived the harsh long years in Siberia, he did not mind twenty below!

My father's drinking was getting worse. He would occasionally go on binges that lasted up to three days. He had a new group of drinking friends. The owner of some restaurants would let him sleep there. My father was their best client. The first two days, it was difficult to detect much difference in his behavior. He had always been a friendly, happy drunk, especially when things were going his way. However, the third day when my father ran out of money, he would come to the store and take all of the cash. I was furious. Then he would say, "It will be okay, Sweetie. You are strong and you can make it."

The situation got worse when the owner of the establishment had an argument with my father, who lost his temper. My father took a thick phone book and began to tear it in half. People grew afraid of him and his strength.

After a while, my father found a new restaurant, only a block from his house. He became good friends with that owner. They had Russia in common, although his new friend, Rudolf, did not escape from Siberia in as good health as my father. Rudolf had heart problems, asthma and was sickly. Papa, in spite of his time in Siberia, was in very good health.

My spirits were down. I began to brood, how would I get out of this situation? On top of it all, I did not feel well. Sometimes I was very weak, other times my stomach felt upset. I told my father that he had to watch the store for one day while I went to the doctor. I visited my family Dr. Pfluger. His office was in the neighborhood where my mother had her store. Hermann Gramm and Micki still worked there. I was careful to avoid being seen by them. People were standing in a long line to see the doctor. I was in line for over three hours before he saw and recognized me.

"Hello, little Brigitte! What brings you here? I haven't seen you in a long time. I think it was when I took you to the hospital to have your appendix removed, and then your scar broke open. That has to be over five years ago! You have grown into a very beautiful girl." He shouted so loudly that other clients heard him, including some who knew me and my mother. I turned red with embarrassment. Dr. Pfluger was a very good looking man and I had always had a crush on him.

In privacy, I told him that my stomach was upset and I felt nauseous. He asked me, "When did you have your last period, Brigitte?" I had to think that over.

"Maybe two months ago." He had his nurse check me out and confirm that I was almost two and a half months pregnant. I had tears in my eyes as I told him that I did not have a husband.

He recognized the situation and offered, "It was probably a soldier from the occupation, right?"

I understood that Dr. Pfluger wanted to help me. I went along with the story and said, "Yes, he had to go home." The doctor said that he could not personally help me, but he gave me an address for another doctor. I was filled with gratitude and gave him a kiss on his cheek.

Next day I called for an appointment to see the other doctor. Two days later I took the tram to the other end of the city where his office was. When I arrived at the office, again there was a long line. But this was a line of young girls, like me. The doctor checked me out and agreed to do the procedure, but I needed to bring an adult relative with me.

Oh no. Who could I possibly ask? Who could I tell? I thought of Aunt Didi, but knew that she would be appalled that I was in such a low class situation. Then I thought of my mother's friend whom I called Aunt Marta. I was very fond of her, she looked a little like my mother and had always been warm and friendly to me.

Aunt Marta agreed to go to the doctor with me. After the procedure, she took me back to my father's house in a taxi. I told my father what had happened and that it was Wilhelm's baby. My father must have then told Aunt Didi and Uncle Max, because they arrived and were very friendly and solicitous. They had all liked Wilhelm and had approved of our relationship. This made me feel better. Papa had to tend to the store for a few days while I recuperated. My breasts were swollen and dripping. I put Kleenex in my bra to catch the moisture. No one explained to me what was going on with my body, so I just coped on my own. Aunt Didi visited for several days. I thought it very kind of her to be so caring and to spend so much time with me.

One day Aunt Didi became very serious. She looked me in the eyes and asked me if Hermann Gramm had raped me after my mother's death. This question came out of nowhere and I was shocked and deeply hurt. If Aunt Didi and Uncle Max suspected that might have happened, why did they not invite me to live with them? I told Aunt Didi that I had kept that from happening by sleeping with a knife in my bed. A deep sadness descended on me. How could Aunt Didi acknowledge the danger but not take any steps to protect me? All I had wanted at the time was to escape from Hermann Gramm and live with my aunt and uncle. The disappointment in all of the people in my life accumulated and made me think it was time to leave Berlin.

I went back to my father's store and worked hard and saved the money I made. I did not go out. I kept to myself. I was only friendly to the customers who came to the store. I became a loner and tried to figure out how to get away from my depressing environment. My father continued to drink more and more heavily. Rudolf, the restaurant owner, would then call Irmgard, Father's girlfriend, and ask her to come to pick him up because he wanted to close his establishment. Irmgard was never able to influence Father. Now I began to get the calls in the middle of the night to deal with him. I was the only one who could persuade him to come home; although it was not easy. When I went to get him, his first reaction was one of pride. He loved to show off his beautiful daughter to his drinking buddies. Then my father would ask me to join him and his friends for a drink. I would have one or two with them. Then my father and his friends would sing patriotic German songs. After two vodkas, I would remind him that he had promised to accompany me home. He would begin to swear loudly and vehemently in German and Russian demand, "What do you want from me? You look like a goat! I am not coming with you."

When the owner of the bar said that everyone had to go home, all of the drinking partners took off and I was left with the task of getting my father home safely. I bribed him by saying that there was a bottle of vodka at home waiting for him. Home was only one block away, but it was an excruciatingly long walk with him! He would occasionally fall against me, knocking both of us down to the ground.

One time I fell against a garden fence. My father landed on top of me and we both were sliding down to the ground. It was hard to breathe with his weight on top of me and I was scratched and hurting from hitting the fence. At times he would not get up from the pavement, preferring to fall asleep right there. My patience came to an end.

One day, when he was sober, I told him that I wanted to leave the store and his employment. My father begged me not to leave. "Sweetheart, the store and everything I have will be yours after my death."

"No, Papa. I want to be independent and to work for myself, perhaps in a different kind of job. I do not want to wait until you die and inherit the store. I want to accomplish something on my own."

Father was quiet as he considered all that I had said. It was 1958, I was nineteen. For three months my father managed to come home alone and sober at a decent hour. One day he noticed how very unhappy I was. "Brigitte, I see you work very hard. And you do not go out any more. It must be six months or longer since you have visited the Feen Grotte for some fun."

I thought it was maybe a good idea to go out. My father reserved a nice table upstairs, just for me. From there I had a good view over the whole restaurant. It proved to be a good idea, I felt better and was enjoying myself. Someone waved to me and I recognized the salesman from the well-known perfume firm. When the orchestra began to play, he asked me for a dance. It felt so good to dance again! I didn't want to think of Wilhelm. I just wanted to have a good time. After the dance, the salesman, Mr. Schneider, presented me to another gentleman. As I neared the table, my heart began to pound.

"Brigitte Kruger, this is Werner Bab." When Mr. Bab took my hand, an electric shock went through my body. He was extremely handsome. He had dark wavy hair, hazel-green eyes and a light brown tan. He was also dressed elegantly. He asked me for the next dance. The timbre of his voice touched my soul.

I was suddenly quite nervous. Inside I was quivering and on fire. Outside I tried to act composed. With a calm voice, I answered, "With pleasure. I would like to dance with you." We carried on a lovely conversation while dancing, and at the end of the evening Mr. Bab asked me where I lived. I gave him my address and phone number.

A couple of days later he called me and asked if I would like to dine with him after work. The moment I heard his voice, a shiver went through my body. I told him I was busy that night, but could go out the following evening. After I hung up, the palms of my hands were sweaty. I could not figure out why my reaction to him was so strong. The next day, I took a dress and shoes to the store to change into after work. The store had a long corridor with a bathroom and a kitchen. It apparently had been an apartment that had been converted to a store. Evening came and Werner picked me up. He opened the door of his Mercedes, which impressed me even more. We had dinner in a cozy restaurant. Werner asked me all kinds of questions, wanting to get to know me better. Then he told me that he worked in Wittenbergplatz for Mercedes, as a salesman. He lived in America and he spoke English as well as German. I was very much impressed and fascinated by Werner. We drove by his workplace, it was a large facility with all kinds of models of Mercedes.

Every Saturday and Sunday we had a wonderful time. After a while, we also went out twice during the week. One Sunday Werner showed me where he lived on a side street near a large shopping mall. We went upstairs and Werner introduced me to a middle-aged lady who rented the rooms and was his landlord. Werner was thirty-two years old and I was nineteen. The room was decorated with nice Chippendale furniture. Werner took me into his arms and kissed me passionately. I felt aroused and shivered at the same time.

To my horror, I felt something wet running down the inside of my tights. Werner began to undress me all the while kissing and nibbling down my body. I was shocked and ashamed of my wetness. It was the first time I had ever had it happen. I took off my panties by myself, so that I could wipe the moisture away. I unbuttoned his shirt and took it off. Werner kissed his way down towards my most feminine place. I was afraid to let him go there and said,

"Let me kiss you." I slowly began to kiss and savored inch by inch the scent and warmth of his body. He moaned with pleasure. A sensuous response to Werner rushed through my body. It was like melting together and becoming one. That feeling touched my soul deeply, and I was moved to know that Werner felt the same passion. I asked him to go slowly as I thought that if I became too excited and we reached the peak together, I would become pregnant again. I had no knowledge about sex and what could or could not happen. I was trembling with excitement, but was holding back. I didn't want to show my feelings too much. The problem was that I was very much in love with Werner already.

One day he took me firmly in his arms. Speaking in English instead of German, he said softly, "I love you, Brigitte." As much as I loved him, I was too insecure and proud to admit to him out loud how much. My stubbornness would not let me say to him what he wanted to hear. At a later time, I deeply regretted not truthfully expressing my feelings.

One day Werner told me that he was Jewish, that he had been in Auschwitz. He showed me his scars. I had no idea what he was talking about. After all, nobody was talking about it during those days. Most people maybe did not know about the death camps and the extent of violence that had been forced upon the Jews. Werner told me that after they were released from Auschwitz, he and his mother went to America. When she became an actress and did not take care of Werner, he returned to Berlin. His father had killed himself before the Gestapo could arrest him in Berlin. I could not understand how or why a person would return to a place that represented so much pain, suffering and hatred. I felt tremendous compassion for Werner.

One day Werner suggested that we go to the cemetery and try to find his father's gravesite. I was touched and honored that he wanted me to accompany him. I bought a bouquet of flowers. Werner was pleased and impressed by my gesture. We looked for his father's grave for a couple of hours, but couldn't find it. I wanted to leave the flowers on a grave, any grave, but Werner wanted me to bring them away with us. I felt uncomfortable about keeping the flowers, maybe even a little superstitious.

For the next three months, we enjoyed each other intimately. But I would still not let Werner kiss me all of the way down. I couldn't believe how just the sound of his voice on the phone could have such an effect on my body. I was totally mesmerized by Werner and seemed to have no control where he was concerned. My vulnerability amazed and frightened me.

I told Werner about my father and his drinking, explaining how he was drinking less lately. So I wouldn't leave him and the store. Right away, Werner offered to rent another store for me. I told him I was tired of being a store keeper. I would like to do anything else. "I want to come forward in my life, not stand still, doing the same thing every day. I would like to travel and see the world. This is my goal for the future. But right now I need some help in the store. I am always so tired in the evenings."

The next time we saw each other, Werner introduced me to a friend, Inge. Her husband had been injured in the war and couldn't work, but she could work and agreed to help. The very next day, Inge began to work. She brought her little dachshund with her.

Easter came and Werner invited me out to a very well-known spot, Bad Harzberg. But before we left, he bought me a beautiful outfit with shoes and a coat. On Easter morning, I wished him a happy Easter and he looked at me strangely. When I asked him what was wrong, he explained that he was a Jew. He told me that he believed only in God. "I do too," I replied. "In fact, I have an angel that protects me! What is the difference, Werner? To me it makes no difference as long as we are together!" I mentioned that my Aunt and Uncle never went to church. I told Werner, "After my mother's death, I would simply pray to God on my own, without going to church. So what is the big deal?" After our conversation, Werner and I went out and enjoyed the local natural setting.

After the holiday, when we had returned to work, I was troubled by a feeling of impending doom. It began as a constriction in the throat that would then expand to my whole body. One day when Werner and I were close together and I was kissing his chest, tears began flowing. I was not crying. The tears simply flowed out, without me making a sound. I felt as if something in my life was about to change dramatically for the worse, almost as if I were about to lose something.

Werner asked, "Why the tears?" I told him that I didn't know why. On a Saturday, Werner suggested that we go to visit my father at Feen Grotte and have a nice dinner and dance.

"That is a great idea, Werner." Werner and my father had a casual chat, but my father was too busy to really talk. We had a wonderful time. The following

Wednesday, Werner called and asked if I would like to have dinner with him. "Yes, Werner. I would love to. I am looking forward to seeing you!"

I packed a dress and shoes for going out and took them to work the next day. Just before closing time, my father walked into the store. His face was red and he had an angry look about him. I went into the back room to change. My father followed me. "Where are you going?" he asked. I told him that I was going out with Werner. "You are not going out with Werner, he is a Jew!" he spat out.

I shrugged and said, "So what?"

My father was furious and shouted, "No dirty Jew will set foot in my store again!" I protested that I did not care, that Werner was my boyfriend and I was happy for the first time in my life. My father wanted to know why I didn't tell him about Werner's religion. I pointed out that I didn't think it was of any importance. My father said he had found out about Werner from the same salesman who had introduced me to Werner.

"He saw you last Saturday dancing with Werner." The salesman knew that my father was still a Nazi and told him he should break us up. I went back into the store with my father following me. To my surprise, there was Werner, waiting for me. I walked up to him and kissed him. My father acted as if nothing had happened.

Werner and I drove quietly to the restaurant. Finally, he said, "Brigitte, I heard everything that your father said. I have decided not to see you again. I cannot marry you."

I protested that I didn't want to be married. "I only want to be with you." I told Werner that I was ready to quit my father's store and change to his religion. Werner had tears in his eyes as he told me, "You don't understand. It will never work out. You are too young and I don't want to mess up your life. I have gone through too much in my life. One day, you will understand. I am not coming around anymore." With this, he kissed me and left.

Every day I waited for the phone to ring, but there was no call. I cried myself to sleep every night and finally I admitted that I loved him. I hoped that he was suffering as I was.

My father and I began to argue constantly. He started drinking heavily again and regularly visited the store to empty the cash drawer. I began to work on a plan to get out of Berlin. I watched the want ads, looking for a job that would allow me to escape this unhappy life.

One ad in particular caught my eye. "Bar maid wanted, 500 marks per month, room and board provided." The job was located in Wiesbaden, the business was named the Puszta which made me think of Aunt Didi and her Hungarian heritage. The advertisement sounded too good to be true. Already in my young life, I did not trust anyone. So I wrote to the best detective agency I could find, Schimmelpfeng, in Berlin, which is still in business. I hired them for 30 marks.

On November 11, 1958 I received a two page report in which the agency concluded that the business was on-going and reputable. Hermann Schlichter and two owners were listed as principals. Antecedents on all three principals were provided, as well as financial information on the business, adding more credibility to the report. "The Puszta is a good family restaurant, excellent food and décor, and has Hungarian music and dancing on the weekends." I was very happy with the report and sent the Puszta an application and a picture. Very soon, I received a response stating that I had been accepted.

At age nineteen, two months from my twentieth birthday, I was ready to start over. Maybe now I would be able to forget Werner, or at least get some sleep, make some money and move forward with my life. "Now I will show them all." I did not tell anyone of my specific plans. I was sure that my father would not let me go. I did tell my friend, Inge, that I was going to leave Berlin. But I did not tell her where I was going. I told her that the store would now be hers to run. I paid her for a month of work in advance.

Although I had some money saved from my many years of working, I also took what was in the cash register. I felt justified in leaving my father high and dry. I packed my clothes, childhood photographs and the letter from the detective agency; then left for Wiesbaden.

CHAPTER 5

Dangerous Encounter

Only true survivors have both instinct, and the wisdom to listen to it.

I arrived in Wiesbaden early in the afternoon and took a taxi to the Puszta. It was closed. The hours posted indicated that it would reopen in the evening. I walked around the building, it looked very nice. There was a glass cabinet out front where the musicians were showcased. The building was quite large, filling a full block between two streets. I went across the street to wait and get something to eat, for I was hungry. After a good meal with a glass of beer, I asked the owner about the Puszta. He told me that it had a good name, this information gave me great relief.

As opening time drew near, I left the restaurant and went to stand by the front door. I had not waited long before a car came around the corner and stopped in front of me. I was pleased, as I assumed that these were the owners of the Puszta. One gentleman looked Hungarian, with dark brown eyes, a little mustache, and he was balding with some dark hair still on the sides. The other man had reddish hair, bulging blue eyes and was heavyset. They greeted me and told me that they were not affiliated with the Puszta. The red-haired man then informed me that I should not work there, that the Puszta had a very bad reputation.

I replied, "Oh ya?" He suggested that I should go with him, that he owned a family hotel that was a legitimate business. I laughed out loud at him and told him I knew better. I pointed out that I had no idea what kind of person he was. He looked at me soberly and said, "If you can escape, here is my address." He handed me his card and told me that his wife also worked at his hotel. I accepted the card, thanked him and they left.

Shortly afterwards, an employee of the Puszta came and opened the door. He requested that I stay there and wait. I looked around and was impressed. The walls were decorated with lovely paintings, scenes from Hungary. The large dining room had wooden tables and chairs with Hungarian motifs carved on the backs. After a while, the manager came and walked me to his office. We crossed a long corridor which was dimly lit. The office was small. My application and photograph were on his desk. He compared the image to me and was satisfied. He said, "Fraulein Kruger, you are very beautiful." Then he bent over to fill out my paperwork.

My sixth sense was aroused and I looked past him, over his bent head. As I was observing, the wall behind the manager began to move, and opened a little.

What I saw was alarming. There was a gambling table in a room filled with heavy smoke and lots of half-naked girls. Whoever was on that side of the wall quickly closed the opening. Instantly, I looked down at what the manager was writing. He jerked his head up, probably having heard the noise, and looked at me to see if I had perceived anything. I gave him a blank expression. After having had such bad experiences in dealing with people, I had a very good poker face. He was satisfied that I had seen nothing. He asked me, "Would you like to begin tonight?"

I replied calmly and in a tired voice, "No, tomorrow would be better. I am exhausted from traveling." I asked him if I might see where I was going to stay. He agreed and summoned an older man to help me with my suitcase. The old man was limping and puffing, but we finally made it up three flights of stairs to the top floor. I said nothing, not wanting him to know how shocked I was by what I had seen. He opened the door at the top floor, it was the attic. The room was very cold and there were beds lined up in a row like in an army barracks. There was a small sink for washing up. The old man pointed to a bed on the left. I thanked him, showing no emotion, as I felt my heart sink.

This was not a part of my dream! I thought that I had taken all necessary precautions not to get trapped in an underworld business. I had hired the best detective agency in Berlin and had asked different people for references about the Puszta. I knew now, however, that I was in grave danger and I had to get out as quickly as possible. I could not run down the stairs with my suitcase. It was quite likely that someone from the Puszta would see me and halt my departure. So I laid on my bed, put my money in my bra and kept my clothes on. My shoes were set on the floor right by the bed.

It was freezing cold, even with all of my clothes on. After hours and hours of thinking and waiting, I finally heard the girls come up. I closed my eyes feigning sleep. Several girls came in, loudly drunk and quarreling. One of them pointed, "You see the new one there sleeping? Her name is Brigitte and she will be the new mistress for the boss. I saw her photograph and he was very taken by her looks."

"Which boss? Schechter from Poland, or Grina from Rumania?" a girl cried out.

"Maybe she will be the mistress for both bosses," the first replied sarcastically.

I prayed that no one would try to wake me up or steal my things. The girls continued to squabble among themselves about how much money they had made. After an hour or more, they finally all went to sleep. I waited in silence and stillness in my bed until I could see that the sun was rising. Carefully I sat up, reassuring myself that everyone must be sleeping, and rose ever so slowly.

With no sound and holding my shoes in one hand, my suitcase in the other, I tiptoed to the door. My heart was pounding so loudly, I was surprised that no one could hear it. I opened the door inch by inch, walked out and silently pulled it closed behind me. I glided down the stairs noiselessly. At the bottom there was a large wooden door. I prayed that it was not locked. I was lucky! I slipped out the door and into the street.

"Oh what a relief!" If I had not had the initiative to escape right away, I doubted that there would have been a second opportunity to slip away. "What should I do now?" I recalled the gentleman who had given me his card and I thought, "He was right after all." I found the card, walked a couple of streets until I found a taxi and climbed in, reading to him the address on the card. The driver stopped in front of a middle-class hotel and I climbed out. With suitcase in hand, I went to the front desk and a lovely lady greeted me. It was the owner's wife. She had sleek black hair that looked almost blue, dark eyes and a fair complexion. I told the woman my story, how her husband had warned me away from the Puszta and had given me his business card. She welcomed me and said that I would be safe with them and that they would find some work for me.

Her husband was not up yet, he had worked late. She asked a porter to show me to a room. I was very apprehensive after my ordeal at the Puszta. When the porter opened the door, my tension eased. It was a nice room on the second floor with a large armoire, a couple of chairs, a comfy bed and a lovely view of the street. Later on, I walked downstairs for some breakfast and conversed again with Rebecca, the owner's wife, and thanked her for the comfortable room.

After breakfast, Rebecca told me to come back downstairs around lunch time when her husband would be present. At the appointed time, I walked downstairs. The owner gave me a triumphant smile when he saw me and said, "You see, I was right!" I thanked him and blushed with embarrassment. He told me that I was in good hands here. The owner, Lotzie, was Hungarian. He offered me his fleshy hand and squeezed my small hand. Once again, I did not have a good feeling about the situation, but wanted to think positive. I couldn't understand what the lovely Rebecca saw in Lotzie. He was so unattractive and she was so beautiful. They told me that they had a plan for me. Their two children needed a nanny. I would awaken the children, help them get ready and take them to school in the mornings. Then I would assist in the restaurant for lunch, serving behind the bar until it was time to pick the children up from school. I was pleased with this arrangement and was promised a good salary. The children were lovely, a boy and a girl, ages maybe five or six years. Both had dark curly hair and dark brown eyes that shone warmly. They were each a replica of Rebecca. I enjoyed them thoroughly. I slept better, although I still woke up thinking of Werner.

I put all of my energy into the new job and adjusting to the environment so as to spend less time with the painful thoughts of having lost my true love. Occasionally, I would smile when I thought of how Werner had not wanted to mess up my life. And here I was, living with a Jewish family from Hungary.

I met Lotzie's friend, Jeno. He too was from Hungary and also was Jewish. He lived in Monte Carlo and would often come to visit Lotzie. Jeno was around fifty years old, not tall, he had brown eyes and a fringe of brown hair around the sides of his head, a thin mustache that framed his mouth and a strong nose. He was always smoking a cigar. Jeno made a friendly impression. A couple of days passed by without incident.

On the third day I came back from taking the children to school and had just finished changing my clothes, when Lotzie came running up to me. "Stay in your room until I tell you to come out," he ordered. "Don't ask questions, I will tell you later." Then in a low agitated voice he urged me, "Hurry, get into your room!" He left running back downstairs. Not long after, from the top of the stairs, I heard lots of hollering and yelling, all in Hungarian. Two men were arguing with Lotzie. Then there was a moment of silence. A minute or so later, Lotzie reappeared, accompanied by a very young girl. Words were exchanged. The two men looked the girl over and stopped yelling. Then they left.

I hurried back to my room and seconds later Lotzie called up for me to come downstairs. He explained that the two men were from the Puszta. They had accused Lotzie of stealing me away from them. They wanted Brigitte back. They threatened Lotzie with guns while making their demand. Lotzie had shown them the young girl and informed them, "This is Brigitte, and if you take her, I will tell the police. She is our babysitter and too young to go with you. Since the men had not seen my photograph, they believed Lotzie and left. I thanked him for his cleverness. Then I went upstairs, sat down and, as always, every day, everywhere, I gave thanks to God.

The following weeks were more relaxed. Sometimes in the afternoon, Lotzie and Jeno would take me out to show me Wiesbaden and Baden-Baden. We would go to a very nice café house in the afternoons. For the first time I felt content. One day, Lotzie asked me if I wanted to make more money. "Yes, of course," I answered. "What kind of job is it?"

"It would be working at a bar. You won't have to do much, only smile and carry on conversations with the customers." He replied.

I agreed to give the job a try, to see if I liked it. I wanted to be even busier, for more activity meant less time thinking of Werner. Lotzie and Jeno took me to a hair dresser and bought me a little black dress. I was excited about trying some-thing new. The next evening around 9:00, Lotzie and Jeno picked me up from my room and we drove into a different section of Wiesbaden. Lotzie opened the big door to a building, we crossed the hall. On the left side were some stairs, but we continued on to a door which led to an inner courtyard, which we crossed. Lotzie opened the next door which we passed through and then climbed up some stairs all of the way to the top. We were basically going from one house to another. I thought the journey was very strange.

Lotzie opened the final door and we walked into a nicely remodeled attic. Here was a very busy bar, full of people, smoke and loud piano music. Lotzie positioned me behind the bar and told me to take the orders, but that was all. I was not to pour alcohol or take money. I was to call the order to a barkeeper and, when it was ready, I was to serve it to the customer. It was an easy job. Looking at the clientele, I saw quite a mix of people.

Lotzie introduced me to the important ones, lawyers and government officials. Then he brought me back to the bar to work. The rest of the customers were marines, there were also shady characters and girls who danced with customers.

For me it was interesting to meet all different classes of people. I realized that I had landed again in an underground business. As long as they were respectful and didn't get too close to me, all was well. What was important to me was that I made very good money and was saving it for my next step forward. Now I had three jobs; being a nanny in the morning, helping serve lunch and drinks at noon in the family restaurant and at night observing the darker side of life. I listened to the wacky conversations and made a lot of money in tips. I thought it was fun.

One night, a well-dressed man spent a lot of money and then asked if I would like to work for him. He offered me a beautiful apartment, lots of dresses to wear from fashion designers and he told me I wouldn't need to do anything else. I laughed and asked, "What do YOU want?"

"I want to watch you through the keyhole."

I burst out laughing and then noticed Lotzie approaching quickly. Lotzie told the man to leave and never come back. He said that the man was a pimp. Once again, I was thankful for Lotzie's help and protection.

After closing time, Lotzie invited Jeno, a couple of other girls and myself to go out to an expensive night club. He ordered champagne and caviar to show off. It was the first time I savored such delicious gourmet food. Now I was in fine spirits. I was nineteen, had lucrative work in a safe place and enjoyed perks like this! Now I understood why Lotzie slept until noon every day. Everything went quite well for a while.

One day Lotzie and Jeno took me to a fashionable coffee house where we enjoyed our afternoon together. However, Lotzie was beginning to change. He spoke loudly and invited a girl over to our table and flirted with her. He was repulsive and I felt sad and sorry for Rebecca. The next time they asked me out, I declined. I told Jeno privately that I found it disgusting and didn't want to be exposed to Lotzie's behavior. I was stunned when Jeno told me, "He does it because he wants you! He is trying to make you jealous. It is all for show."

This reminded me how my first impression of him was not good. My intuition was accurate. His expensive showing off was leading up to something. I confided in Jeno that I needed to find a new place very soon. Eventually, Lotzie was going to make advances, and I would prefer to avoid that. Jeno confirmed the worst when he told me that Lotzie could be rough. I asked Jeno if he knew of any other places where I could work.

"No Brigitte, I don't know any other places here. But when I go back to Monte Carlo, I will keep you in mind." He gave me his address and telephone number, telling me to call if I needed help. He also cautioned me not to show Lotzie his card, which I later hid upstairs in my room.

For two nights, nothing happened. On the third night, all was quiet until it was time to be paid. I was supposed to get a percentage based on how much liquor I sold, plus tips. As I was coming to collect, one of the other girls suddenly went crazy. She pointed at me and accused me of stealing all of the money from the register. I was flabbergasted, I never touched money or even came near the register. Lotzie looked at the girl and defended me, "Brigitte would never behave in such a way!" Then he screamed at the girl and accused her of being low class and the type to do something like that herself. He grabbed her purse and shook out the contents. Many big bills tumbled out. He lost his temper, his face turned red and he slapped her hard. She fell against the wall, her head split open, blood everywhere on the wall, on the girl and on the floor. I looked at Jeno and realized that it was high time for me to leave.

Jeno and I drove back to the hotel in silence. I undressed and went to bed with thoughts again about how I needed to leave, and very soon!

Soon after going to bed, I heard a knock on the door and asked, "Who is it?" I suspected the worst.

It was Lotzie. "Let me in, I have something important to tell you." I refused to open the door and Lotzie asked me if I was afraid of him. To which I replied that I was not. After much pleading on Lotzie's part, I finally did open the door. I didn't want him to think that I was afraid of him.

"So what is so important?" I demanded of him. He explained that everything he had done, including the slap to the girl's face, he had done for me. "Aha," I thought, "Here comes the trade-off." I told him to get out of my room or I would wake up his wife and children. He turned red and got riled up. He promised to leave once he had seen my breasts. Just to get him to leave, I agreed. "But no touching!"

I slipped one side of my nightgown down my shoulder. He feasted upon the sight, breathing hard. His normally bulging eyes nearly popped out of his head. "You owe this to me since I saved you from the gangsters sent by the Puszta." He begged for one more look, which I reluctantly gave him.

After his visit, I could not sleep. I knew it would be difficult to get away, because he was always around me. I felt like a caged bird. Tossing and turning, I spent much of the night praying to God for help. He must have heard me.

The next night when Lotzie, Jeno and I arrived in the bar, everything seemed as usual. There were already customers enjoying themselves as the pianist was playing. All of a sudden, there was a loud bang. A shot had been fired! Lotzie pulled me out from behind the bar and Jeno came running over. Lotzie spoke rapidly in Hungarian to Jeno, who then grabbed my hand and pulled me running behind him, out the door and past the pianist, who had been shot dead. Jeno took a different route to get out. We went onto a rooftop and then ran from one rooftop to another. Finally we descended some stairs and landed in a completely unknown section of Wiesbaden. We caught a taxi and went back to the hotel. Jeno told me that he would be leaving the next day and suggested that I also make a plan to get away.

Not even one half hour later, there was a banging on my door. "Go away, Lotzie!" I yelled. But the banging continued.

"Police, Police! Open the door." I ignored it, thinking that it was Lotzie trying to confuse me. Then I realized that it really was the police. They were banging on each and every door. When I opened the door, I was questioned, "When did you get home tonight? What were you doing?" They demanded my passport too.

"I have been sleeping since 9:00," I told them. "I am on vacation here in Wiesbaden." The police believed me and left me alone.

The next day, Jeno left. After taking the children to school, I stayed in my room. The police were all over the place. Apparently they had found out that the bar and hotel belonged to Lotzie. Now he was nowhere to be found. I was relieved that he had disappeared. He had been taken away for interrogation by the police.

These were finally the right circumstances for me to leave. My stay had given me a good nest egg. So I packed my suitcase, counted my money and at 6:00 in the morning, I went downstairs. Rebecca listened as I told her that I wanted to quit my jobs for many reasons. She said she understood and gave me a thankful look. Then she paid me my salary and called a taxi for me. I knew at that moment that Rebecca was aware of Lotzie's behavior. She seemed relieved to see me go.

I asked the driver to take me to a small, quiet hotel. When I checked in, I met a girl who was renting the room next door. Doris was tall, had blonde hair and blue eyes. She asked me if I was in Wiesbaden on vacation. I told her no, that I was looking for a job. As it turned out, Doris was working in a very posh and proper club that catered to American officers. The two of us talked a long time. I learned her story and told her mine. Doris was horrified at what I had been through. She promised to see if there was a job opening at her place of work. She asked me if I spoke English and I had to confess that I only knew a bit of English from school. "But I am a fast learner!" I assured her.

The next morning Doris told me to go to the club in the afternoon and apply for a job. I took out the card Jeno had given me and showed it to Doris. She got all excited. "Monte Carlo? Who doesn't want to go to Monte Carlo! You should call him directly!"

"I do want to get out of Germany and see other countries." I said.

"Call Jeno!" Doris insisted.

I phoned Jeno and he took my call. He sounded pleased to hear from me and invited me to Monte Carlo immediately. "You must come right away and escape from Lotzie," he urged. "Lotzie will find you there and then you will never get away." Doris made the arrangements and took me to the train station where there was a once daily train to Monte Carlo. I made it just in time and was thankful for having met such a nice girl, the nicest person since I left Berlin. The train ride was a wonderful experience, bringing back great memories of traveling by train as a child.

CHAPTER 6

Monte Carlo — A Ray of Hope

1958

It is not about what you run away from; but what it is you are running to.

It was the end of December 1958. On the train leaving Germany, I mused over the strenuous year, especially the last two months with so many awful things happening. I was very lucky to have escaped from the criminal underworld, not once, but twice. I must have a guardian angel. I felt my optimism returning as I looked out the train window, viewing the spectacular scenery going by. It was like a dream. Tall palm trees were reaching out to the clear blue sky. Hedges of bougainvillea with showy colorful branches were filling the space between the trees. In the distance, chains of mountains framed the scenery. On the other side I could see the Mediterranean Sea sparkling in the sun. I hoped to leave my painful memories of Werner behind and that my broken heart would mend. As the train slowed on its way into the station, I felt my excitement grow. There was Jeno with his big cigar! He waved with enthusiasm when he saw me. The warm air was filled with the scent of a bouquet of flowers, and I began to relax.

I explained to Jeno that I could only afford a small hotel room for two to three months. Near the station was the Hotel de la Gare, where Jeno had reserved a room for me. It was simple, clean and cheap. I was satisfied with that. The hotel had a little restaurant where Jeno and I had a nice dinner, we had a lot to talk about. Then Jeno said, "Now, have a good night's sleep. I will see you in the morning!" I slept soundly that night, only waking when Jeno knocked at the door 9:00 the next morning.

Still in my nightgown, I greeted him at the door and asked him to come in. The bathroom had a toilet, a sink and a fixture I did not recognize. "What is that?" I asked, pointing to it.

"That is a bidet. You sit on it and rinse your private parts." He answered amused.

"OK, Jeno. Now I will get dressed. Please, will you wait for me in the restaurant? When I come down, I will call Doris to let her know I have arrived safely."

I phoned Doris from the hotel lobby. She answered immediately and informed me that Lotzie and some other men had come running just as my train was leaving the station. They pushed Doris into a corner and demanded to know where I was. Doris told them that I had just left by train and she had no idea where I was going.

She did not know how Lotzie had figured out where I was, and neither did I. Then I thanked Doris and promised her I would stay in touch, before saying good bye.

Jeno took me out for a stroll around Monte Carlo. We walked up hill on the steep Avenue des Spelugues and came to the Café de Paris. It was breathtaking! Before us stood the casino with elaborate Baroque décor, and on our right was the elegant Hotel de Paris, matching the ornate style of the Casino. A lovely roundabout full of colorful flowers was in front of the casino. I was overwhelmed and had many questions. I wanted to see more, so Jeno promised me that he would take me out every day for more sightseeing.

The next morning we strolled from Café de Paris up to the Boulevard de Moulin, which was lined with fashionable boutiques, antique stores and restaurants. We traveled up a staircase and arrived on another street. Then Jeno took another shortcut and announced with a flare, "Now we are in Beausoleil France!" There had been no border or frontier crossing. I was astonished. We entered a little bistro where we enjoyed a strong coffee. Then we walked back down to a lovely restaurant where we talked together over lunch.

After lunch, we walked more until around 5:00 in the afternoon when we ended up in the Café de Paris again. Several of Jeno's friends joined us there. One of them was Mr. Gorovway. Like Jeno, he was a Hungarian. He had been a banker in Budapest. For a long time now, he lived in the Hotel Metropole in Monte Carlo. Every afternoon, Mr. Gorovway entered the casino to gamble small amounts. This was how he made a living. He called it, "Going to his office". Gamblers played with less money during the daytime hours. In the evenings, that changed. That was when the big time gamblers, who played for millions, arrived.

A young Hungarian lady, Piroshka, came to our table. She was slim, had short dyed blond hair and wore glasses. When Jeno introduced us, she greeted me in German. The three of them spoke at least three languages each, but when sitting together, they chatted in Hungarian. I did not mind, as it reminded me of my child-hood when Aunt Didi spoke in Hungarian and taught me some new words. Then another couple arrived. Ilona, a pretty woman in her forties, had black curly hair and brown sparkling eyes, full lips and a wonderful brown suntan. Bela, her hus-band, was tall and a little corpulent. He had brown hair with streaks of gray, wore glasses and had, like Ilona, a good suntan. Bela was an artist, a painter whose work was being shown in an exhibition in Paris. They resided most of the year in Paris, but had an apartment for the winter months in Monte Carlo. Everyone was friendly to me as they conversed in German.

After a while, the temperamental Hungarians fell back into their own language. Bela was a fast talker, much like an Italian. He would wave his arms about and ges-ture with his hands. Mr. Gorovway spoke softly, and Jeno would make comments, puffing away on his big cigar as he tried to calm Bela down. Piroshka brought her long cigarette holder out and carefully fitted a cigarette into it. She radiated a distinct allure.

I was fascinated by all of this, since I love to observe people. It was like watching an entertaining performance on the stage. Then Mr. Gorovway abruptly stood up and announced that it was time for him to go to his office. He excused himself with a little bow and left. As he crossed the little roundabout in front of the casino, the conversation continued in a much calmer manner.

Later, Jeno and I had dinner in a small restaurant, after which he took me back to my hotel room. He said he would begin his work in a nightclub around 10:00 pm, and sometimes worked until 4:00 am. He assured me he would call around 11:00 the next morning.

The days passed by, and every day we visited a new section of Monte Carlo. We wandered down to the port and looked at the expensive yachts. Jeno pointed out the very impressive yacht, Christina, telling me that it belonged to Aristotle Onassis. Then we took a bus to visit Monaco. We viewed the castle and walked on through the ancient village with cobblestone streets. There were little shops along the narrow ways that displayed tropical fruits, cheeses and wines. We stopped at a bistro and sat down to have a glass of wine at a table outside. On the table was a bowl of boiled eggs. Jeno requested cold cuts and a fresh baked baguette. It was a true feast! After our meal, we walked through the picturesque streets of Monaco.

Jeno said that he planned to show me his place of work that evening. I was curious, "Maybe I could work there too, Jeno? But not quite yet, as I would like to enjoy the country, culture and my time off just a little longer."

Jeno smiled, "Well, Brigitte, let me know when you are ready."

I thanked him for showing me so many delightful places. I genuinely liked Jeno, he was like a friend to me, respectful and kind. Jeno was living in a hotel not far from mine, the Hotel Excelsior. As usual, we finished our day at the Café de Paris around 5:00 where we met with his friends. The conversation was animated as usual. On the walk from the café to my hotel, we passed a nightclub. Jeno pointed it out to me, "It is here where I work."

"Oh, it is so easy to find, we pass by it every day! I will come to visit you!"

Jeno reminded me, "But I begin at 10:00 at night."

"That's alright. I would like to see how it will be for me when I work there."

Jeno offered to speak to his boss about a position for me. That night, I put on my best dress, fixed my hair and walked to the nightclub. Jeno presented me to his boss and wife, Janos and Marika, two Hungarian Jews. They warmly greeted me and showed me around the nightclub. The two conversed with me in German. Unfortunately, this exchange in my mother tongue reminded me of Werner and brought sadness to my heart. I accepted a glass of liquor and concentrated on the present. Janos was older than Jeno, perhaps in his early seventies. Marika was younger, around sixty. Janos was a journalist and still worked for a newspaper. Marika and he had escaped the war and were living in Buenos Aires when they met Jeno. I discovered in the conversation that Jeno was an artist there and had managed a dancing group of beautiful ladies. Before the war, Jeno had a nightclub in Budapest that was well-known and frequented by the elite. This was surprising, as Jeno had never mentioned it to me.

Time passed quickly. Guests came and girls put on a show, singing and dancing. It was quite entertaining. I made my way back to the hotel for the night, but could not find restful sleep. Werner had again invaded my dreams and my heart ached.

The weeks were passing. When Jeno had time off, we made longer trips to Nice, Cannes and Menton by train. By bus we traveled into the mountains to Roquebrune and Eze Village, an old village where cars were not allowed. It was marvelous. We had lunch in a picturesque restaurant that clung to a cliff. At first I was sitting close to the window, looked out and pulled back in fright. I begged Jeno to switch positions for I felt as if I was on the edge of a cliff, it was scary. Jeno smiled and we exchanged places. We enjoyed a savory lunch of braised rabbit with aromatic local herbs.

That night Jeno did not have to work at Casanova, the nightclub was closed one night each week. Jeno told me to wear my pretty black dress and to bring my passport along with me. "We are going to the casino tonight!" Jeno picked me up around 9:00. As always, he was elegantly dressed. We entered the casino where I presented my passport.

It took my breath away! The walls and ceiling were ornamental and painted with gold trim. The brilliance of the crystal chandeliers completed the splendor. The women were wearing long dresses and exquisite jewelry, which sparkled from around their wrists and necks. Jeno and I walked slowly from one roulette table to another. Then we visited the baccarat table, where people were gambling with much larger sums. The men all wore tuxedos and looked very attractive. Jeno then escorted me to the Salon Prive, where only the most elite were invited to enter; celebrities, millionaires and royalty. Then we returned to the roulette table. Jeno gave me ten francs and asked me if I had a lucky number. "Seven," I responded without hesitation. He showed me how to place my bet on the red seven. Then he told me to bet seven eleven. I was lucky. Jeno played too and he also won. After this, we went to the bar and enjoyed a glass of champagne. I thanked Jeno for the delightful experience of seeing the incredible glamour of this casino.

Weeks passed. On the nights when we did not go out, I was haunted by thoughts of Werner. I wished that he was with me so that together we could enjoy the set-ting which was both dazzling and picturesque. One day, Jeno and I were the first to arrive at the Café de Paris. I took the opportunity to ask Jeno to write some words in Hungarian for me. I wanted to be able to greet his friends in their lan-guage. I practiced the pronunciations with Jeno, and when his friends arrived, I surprised them all. Jeno was pleased with my thoughtfulness and everyone was impressed. This gave me the confidence to learn more. After the friends left, we lingered over cappuccino. Jeno pointed out one of the other tables, saying that the group of men were industrialists from Italy. The gentleman in the gray suit is the owner of the Fiat car factory. As I turned around to look, Jeno whispered, "Don't stare at them. Just have a peek." Monte Carlo was a haven for the rich and entitled ones; no one disrupted their privacy here.

As time passed, I became increasingly restless; I needed something to do. My free time allowed me to think and dream too often about Werner. I lost my appetite and my heart was constantly racing. I couldn't sleep and grew weaker. One night I went to the nightclub Casanova, where Jeno worked. He, Janos and Marika were happy to see me. I asked them when I might start to work. Janos asked, "How well can you speak French?"

"Not at all," I admitted.

Janos responded by advising me that it was time for me to learn French. "Come back once you are fluent in French and then we will talk about a job." Jeno stood next to me and told them that I had learned some Hungarian, but no French. They were all amused. Only I did not laugh for I was embarrassed that I had not figured out that I needed to learn French. I hadn't given a thought to the future, I was having too much fun. The next day I asked Jeno to please find books and a dictionary that would help me to learn to speak French.

Along with the French textbooks, he brought some magazines from France which made it more interesting to learn. I thanked him, then he took my hand and kissed it. He asked me if I would like to move into his hotel with him. He pointed out that we were together every day already, and were good companions. I considered his offer. Knowing that I was running out of money, and not knowing how to speak French, I realized I needed a job, but didn't have the fluency I needed to get one. It seemed like the logical solution, and I agreed to move in. Jeno had always been a gentleman with me and had waited so long. It was only fair for me to take the next step in our relationship.

The Hotel Excelsior was very old, few people chose to live in it. It was up for sale and to be demolished in the near future. Jeno's room was more spacious than mine, with a queen sized bed, a telephone, a table and two chairs, a bidet and a sink. There was a balcony that looked down on the street. But where was the bathroom with the toilet? Well, that was down the dimly lit corridor. The hotel had probably been built in the early 1900s, when it was not the norm for bathrooms to be in the suites. Before Jeno left for work, he took me gently in his arms and kissed me. No words were spoken. He knew that I was not in love with him, nor was I sexually attracted to him. Jeno was my friend, and I valued him as my savior. After he left, I eagerly began my study of French.

The owner of Hotel Excelsior was a fine gentleman. He politely showed me around the building. The hotel had a pleasant rooftop terrace where I would go to enjoy the sunshine anytime I wanted. I planned to go there in the mornings while Jeno was still sleeping. Jeno knew that I craved the sun, after having spent my life in cold and dreary Germany. He had a little gas stove that he kept on the balcony which he used sometimes for cooking meals. Our neighbor was from Russia and he did the same. He was a masseur for the wealthy clientele of Hotel de Paris. When he cooked, he used a lot of garlic. I could not understand how his clientele could tolerate the smell of him!

Whenever Jeno got up early and wanted to cook, we would go to the market up the hill in Beausoleil France. It was quite a walk up, but always worth it to get fresh vegetables and meats. Jeno and I made more excursions. We stayed overnight in San Remo Italy and enjoyed the local beach and delicious food. When Jeno took me in his arms, he was gentle. It did not happen very often, which suited me fine. He liked to kiss my whole body, toes and fingers included. I was not embarrassed as I had been with Werner. Maybe this was because Jeno was much older than I. And since I was not in love with him, my body did not respond the same as when I was with Werner. It was a pleasurable experience. Jeno was satisfied with what I gave him. He absolutely adored me.

One day, Jeno told me that he thought I should write to my family and let them know that I was alive and well. "Your Uncle Max, Aunt Didi and your father are likely worried about you!"

"I am sure, Jeno, they don't care. I don't want to write them."

But Jeno insisted. Finally I wrote a short note to my father informing him that I was in Monte Carlo and that I was doing well. To my surprise, I received a note back in one week with some news. First, he was glad to hear from me. Then he wrote that the government was looking for me. Hermann Gramm, my step father, had sold my mother's business and the 20,000 Deutch Marks in proceeds belonged to me. The funds were in my father's bank account, waiting for me to claim them. I sent him a telegram that I would visit him soon. Jeno smiled and said, "You see. Something good has come from writing to your father!"

I was thinking of Werner more than the money. My appetite came back and I was looking forward to returning to Berlin. Jeno accompanied me by train to Nice, where I caught a flight to the Berlin Tegel Airport. I hailed a taxi and told the driver that I wished to stay in a bed and breakfast near Kurfurstendamm, the "Fifth Avenue" of Berlin. He drove me to a building on a side street where I asked if he might wait while I checked it out. The proprietor showed me a spacious room furnished with antique furniture which I approved of immediately. After paying the driver, I registered and settled into the lovely accommodations. I hardly slept that night, for I was full of anticipation and could not decide who to call first, my father or Werner.

After breakfast the next morning, I made my first call, to Werner, at the Mercedes showroom where he used to work. I started to tremble when I heard his voice. He was surprised to hear from me, but very pleased. Werner told me he would come to my hotel after work, at 5:00.

Then I took a taxi to my father's store where I found him working with a new lady. I had hoped that he would continue to employ Inge with her Dachshund, but she was gone. Father seemed happy to see me. "I am glad you came back," my father greeted me with a smile. "I can use your help."

I promptly told him that I was living in Monte Carlo and planned to go back almost immediately. His smile vanished. Then I asked about the money from the sale of the store. My father told me that it was in the bank, but that he had spent 5000 DM of the 20,000, and he could use more. I explained to him that I needed all of it. We proceeded to the bank to withdraw the funds, after which we had lunch together and parted with no hard feelings.

I thought to myself how I returned to Berlin just at the right time, thanks to Jeno. If I had come later, or not at all, there would have been not a penny left from the sale of my mother's store. I went back to downtown Berlin and walked the

Kurfurstendamm, looking in the various shops. I found and purchased a beautiful evening dress, and then headed back to the hotel.

Werner came to my room a little after 5:00 and we fell into each other's arms. He looked the same and smelled of Old Spice. Oh how I yearned for him, my body was filled with desire. Werner too was anxious and he began to undress me with trembling hands. "Wait, Werner. Please let's go slowly. I have not seen you for such a long time. Did you miss me?"

We talked then. Werner told me he had moved. "Do you have a nicer place?" I pursued.

"Yes, I have a nicer place now." Then in a much lower, quieter voice, he reluctantly said, "And I am married."

I froze and pulled back away from him. I felt my face turn red. "And you wanted to make love to me? You would cheat on your wife already?"

"You know I always loved you. I married her because she is also Jewish. She was my lawyer in the Nazi civil settlement." He said.

I stood still, but my head was spinning. I would not let him make love to me. That would open up old wounds and then he would leave me. I had hoped that Werner would ask me to stay and vow that we could find a way to make things work for us. It never occurred to me that he would get married. "I will not give in." I stated resolutely. It was important to me that Werner respect his wife and me.

"I have to leave. I will return tomorrow. But now I need a cold shower," Werner said. I let him out and closed the door firmly behind him. I wept all that night and waited two days for him, but he never called or came back. Finally, I boarded a flight back to Monte Carlo.

Jeno picked me up from the Nice Airport. We went by train then to Monte Carlo. He saw my face and asked with sympathy what was wrong. I told him everything. Jeno was kind and felt compassion for me. Jeno and I stayed for one more week in the Hotel Excelsior; then the hotel was sold. We moved to Hotel de la Poste. Our new hotel was located more in the center of town. The entrance was large with marble floors. Inside to the left was a busy post office. Further to the right was a heavy wrought iron ornamental elevator. After the war, the hotel had been turned into an apartment building. Our third floor room was simple, with the bed in the right corner of the room as you walked in. At first glance, it did not look like a bed. The walls and the bed were covered in the same pleated, flowered material. This had the effect of making the bed look like a sofa. Towards the window was a table with two chairs. The view was of the street going downhill. On the left was a small armoire attached to a small buffet. In the bathroom there was a sink, a bidet and a bathtub. I was thrilled to have a bathtub, and relieved that I no longer would have to go down a dark hall to use the bathroom. Unfortunately there was no suitable place for Jeno to put the gas burner that he used for cooking; the balcony was too small. He put it on a shelf in the bathroom. "I hope you will not be cooking in the bathroom, Jeno?" We decided that we would probably only use it to boil water for coffee in the morning.

Our lives continued on as before. Jeno would go to work at night, and I had too much time on my hands. When he was gone, I studied French, but no one ever spoke to me in French. I learned to read and understand much of it. But I did not have the opportunity or confidence to practice conversing in French. After a while, I lost my interest and drive to learn the language. I spent my time looking at newspapers and magazines, but nothing could take my mind off of Werner. I did not sleep well, and still had no appetite. At our usual get-together at the Café de Paris, I began daydreaming, finding escape in my thoughts. When I closed my eyes, I saw Werner and wondered if I should have just become his mistress. Maybe I had made a mistake in not giving all of myself to him. The longing began to consume my life. I had hoped that moving to Monte Carlo would put Werner back into my past and out of my mind. But that did not happen.

One night after I turned off the light switch just above my bed, I felt something crawling on my hair and face. I sprang up and turned the light on to discover two large cockroaches in my bed! I slapped at them with my shoe and couldn't sleep until Jeno came home. Then we slept until 11:00 am. Cockroaches are nocturnal creatures and only come out when it is dark. We told the manager about it and he said he would take care of it. We left the building walking down the beautiful marble steps rather than taking the elevator. When we returned in the evening, we again chose to take the stairs. We noticed that each step had white powder along the back of it. The same powder was in front of our door and all along the walls. Later, we discovered that the powder was DDT.

I began to retreat from life, unable to eat much or sleep well, I was getting weaker by the day. Worse yet, the cockroaches came back. Whenever I turned off the light, they would come crawling out. It was awful. The owner tried to discourage them by sprinkling DDT around the bed. This was not effective. I left the lights on all night in an effort to keep them from coming out. I would wait until Jeno came home and then sleep only four to five hours. Days later, we found out that the roaches had made a nest behind the material above the bed, and came into the room through a hole that had once been used for a telephone line.

I became very sick. I began to run a fever and sweat profusely. At the Café de Paris, I drank a large ice cold lemonade, and still was sweating. Finally, I asked Jeno to please take me home, after which he went to the pharmacy to get me cold medication. But the illness worsened and I continued to sink into a deep depression. Two days later, Jeno called the doctor, who came and listened to my lungs. He told us that I had an infection and then injected me with penicillin. But I continued to get worse. I became so weak that I could not get up. I could barely speak. Jeno had to lean over to hear me whisper, "Turn me over." I was no longer able to do it for myself. Jeno called the doctor again and this time the doctor said that I belonged in the hospital. With a faint breath, I refused. "No, Jeno!" Finally, the doctor said there was one more thing he could try. He came back and gave me a streptomycin injection. If this didn't work, he warned, nothing would. I prayed God to let me die, I was ready.

I must have fallen asleep because when I woke up, Jeno was sitting in a chair by my bed. "Thank God, you made it! Oh Brigitte, I was very worried. Sometimes it looked as if I almost lost you. I was watching you all night," he told me.

The pain disappeared and I felt energy flow into my body. Suddenly I wanted to live and fight. I thanked God for saving me, and made a promise that I would stop feeling self-pity; I would make a good life for myself. I acknowledged that my love for Werner would never leave me, but I recognized that I needed to put it on a shelf in the back of my heart so that I could move forward.

I gained strength while Jeno searched for and found a new apartment for us. It was ideal, a new one-bedroom condominium on the Avenue Grande Bretagne. The avenue was lined with Orange trees which were in bloom. I inhaled the sweet scent and felt an inner calm emerge through my body that gave me strength and lifted my spirits. I enjoyed shopping for furniture and Jeno liked antiques; so we hunted through antique stores. Jeno had already purchased the paint for the living room. The deep velvet red would go with the table, chairs, armoire and buffet all in an antique country style. He contacted his friend, Tiber, who lived in Nice and asked him if he would like the painting job. Tiber always needed money. He began early the next day.

Later we purchased more furniture for the kitchen. Another addition were two parakeets for me! The blue and white bird was named Kiki, and we called the green and yellow one Coco. We went back to see how Tiber was doing with the painting. Jeno turned the key to the apartment and Tiber burst out hollering, "You locked me in here when you left!"

Jeno replied with a smile, "Of course I did! I knew that you would not finish painting if you could leave to sit in a local bistro and drink red wine."

Tiber continued to yell until Jeno finally told him to stop making such a racket and finish the job. "Once you are done, we will all have dinner and drinks." Tiber's mood changed and he hurried up with his work.

CHAPTER 7

The Gipsy Club

AN EXCITING NEW BEGINNING
1960-1966

After we moved into the apartment, I began to sleep better. My spirits and energy improved. Then I had a wonderful idea! "Jeno, why don't we open up our own nightclub? You had a well-known club in Budapest before the war and have told me about it. Here you work for Janos, you know a lot of wealthy people who like and respect you."

Jeno was against the idea, but every day it took on more form for me. Finally, he said, "I don't need much anymore in my life, but I would do it for you."

Encouraged, I suggested that we do something different. I loved Hungarian music, and Jeno had often described the wonderful and inventive shows featuring talented gypsies, young men who were incredible musicians at his night club. "Jeno, you told me that you picked boys off the streets, dressed them up and gave them jobs in your establishment. Now those boys are grown up and are successful musicians in Paris, Germany and other countries. Some even have recording contracts! Surely they would come to play for us?"

Jeno became more interested in the idea with time. Finally he agreed with the concept. "But it must be very elegant to attract an upper scale clientele," he said. "The Russian aristocracy and wealthy Greeks and Italians all love gypsy music. They will bring in other wealthy clients. The gypsies can play anything, any type of music." Excitement was creeping into his voice.

"First we must look for a good location." Jeno knew of a place in the Avenue des Spelugues that was vacant. It used to be a nightclub that catered to American marines. It had been called the Knickerbocker and was closed a while ago. We went to look at the location, it was perfect! The Avenue des Spelugues had a police station on one side and on the other side was a restaurant, Oscar, and then came Tip-Top, a bar and restaurant where customers could sit outdoors as well as in. Next to it was Knickerbocker. It was short walk to the Hotel de Paris, and the casino was five minutes from the Café de Paris. Jeno became animated with his excitement. "I will contact the owner of the Knickerbocker to see what the rent would be."

Lucien, the owner, talked with Jeno, and together they inspected the building. The entrance was a little run down. Inside on the left was a hat check room and on the right was a telephone booth and the bar. Both sides of the wooden floor held banquettes, (benches), and the ceiling was made of mirrors. It had excellent potential. Jeno told Lucien that we needed to think it over. Then Jeno looked at me and said, "If we are going to do this, first I want to go on a cruise with you. You are not strong enough to work nights yet."

We cruised the Mediterranean; Italy, Greece, Turkey and Israel. I was able to sleep well and gained ten pounds. We had a bit of a surprise when we stopped in Tel Aviv. Who should board the ship but Lotzie! He was as surprised as we were. His face turned very red and he apologized profusely to me about his conduct in Wiesbaden. Apparently, Lotzie and his family had left Germany, and now he was working as a dentist in Tel Aviv. It was very odd that we should run into each other.

Once we returned to Monte Carlo, we counted our money. Lucien wanted a three year lease and we needed enough to cover remodeling, advertising and the funds needed to carry the business expenses for the first few months. We pooled our money and decided that there would be sufficient funds to start our business. We painted the outside silver gray, the columns white and the inside red with white trim. The podium was silver-gray satin draped over with red drapes along the sides. There were approximately twenty-two tables with chairs and banquettes. Some were larger than others, for four to six people; others were smaller, for two people. We ordered red and white tablecloths. The small tables had red and the large tables had white cloths. Then we went to a potter and ordered fifty heavy ashtray candleholders with "Gipsy Club Monte Carlo" written on them. We also requested the potter make some pewter colored pots to be used to serve Jeno's homemade specialties, like goulash.

Then Jeno contacted Loizy Balogh, an old and very well-known gypsy cimbalom player. He was currently working at a Parisian establishment, Monseigneur. He was recognized as a great artist amongst the elite and agreed to come to Monte Carlo. He brought with him a bass player and a pianist. We advertised in the newspaper and found a gypsy violin player who lived in Menton, his name was Stanko. We also advertised for and hired a couple from Switzerland; he was a waiter and she was a bartender. We also hired a hat check girl. She was an attractive young French girl with long legs. Jeno had her wear black pantyhose, shoes with a small heel, a white shirt and tie and a black jacket. It was tres chic attire.

To our surprise, people called and asked where we were located and what the name of the previous establishment had been. After finding out that it used to be Knickerbocker, the callers would promptly hang up! Apparently the Knickerbocker had been the scene of many fights among American Marines. Finally the police had closed it down. This was why the rent was so reasonable. We would have a hard time convincing people to give us a chance.

Now we advertised in the newspaper and local visitor books. The Gipsy Club opened at 10:00 pm with Jeno outside, by the entrance, to greet people and escort them in – in style. Johan, the waiter, would then escort them to a table. Behind the bar was Ruth, Johan's wife. She was about 25 years old to Johan's 28. I sat at the end of the bar making out bills and observing everything. Since I was insecure about my French, I made a point of asking the employees to speak only in French to me. I was the boss lady with responsibilities. Slowly I gained confidence in my French and began to speak to our clients.

Each morning Jeno would go to the Gipsy Club to receive the big block of ice that was delivered. Since this was before widespread refrigeration, he would take the block and put it behind the bar. Later, we would place the bottles of beer and vodka there. In the kitchen, we had a refrigerator that made ice cubes for those who wanted them in their drinks. After the ice came, we would go to the market to buy fresh vegetables and meat. Eventually, we bought a small refrigerator for our apartment, mostly for the meat. We had a variety of advertising strategies. Flyers were printed and distributed all over Monte Carlo. We even placed some ads under windshield wipers ourselves.

One evening a young man entered the club and asked for a job. He played the violin. He was originally from Romania, but now he was living in Nice. Jeno gave him an audition and he was fantastic! Molnar was hired on the spot. Now we had two violinists, one piano player and the star, Loizy Balogh on the cimbalom. When Loizy gave a solo performance, I would put the spotlight on him. He often played popular melodies, such as the music from "Third Man" and "Circus Princess". After his work, the musicians would play in a great variety of styles; the waltz, tango, foxtrot, French, Spanish, Greek, Arabian, Hungarian, Russian and German. The only problem was that there were not many clients at first. We persevered and stayed open every night from 10:00 until dawn. Tiptop, next door, was well-established and people would go there after the casino closed. So after 2:00 am Tiptop would be very busy. Jeno told the musicians to play loudly and he would open the door to let the music drift out to the street. Eventually, people looked in and checked us out. Jeno asked his friends to come to help create the illusion of customers. Ilona and Bela, Piroshka and Mr. Gorovway would all come to enjoy themselves and fill seats. Jeno decided he would write to a lady friend of his from Wiesbaden. He invited Margaret to come to visit us. She was pleased to hear from Jeno and would be delighted to visit us. She was also excited about exploring the illustrious Monte Carlo.

Margaret was as stunning a woman as I remembered. She was an albino; very white skin and hair, which was cut short and given a blue rinse. Her eyes were gray-blue, with a circle of pink around the eye color. Margaret worked as a model in Wiesbaden and being tall and so striking, she attracted people's attention where ever she went; many would turn their heads to look.

In the evening, Margaret would visit the casino. She had some money of her own, and she would try her luck. Later on, she would come to the Gipsy Club and then tell us about the latest event at the casino. Margaret made acquaintance with Piroshka. When both sat at the bar, they caught everyone's eyes.

Soon people from the Hotel Paris came. Also we welcomed guests from Hotel Ermitage and Hotel Metropole. Our musicians were formally dressed in tuxedos and sometimes in their native costumes. I sat behind the bar, made the bills and paid the musicians nightly. Jeno advised it was a good plan to pay the musicians after work, because they would gamble their pay away in the daytime and would need to work again. Most of the musicians lived from day to day, it was in their blood.

One night, Jeno introduced Margaret to one of our clients, a wealthy Italian, Count de Sessa. There was an obvious and immediate attraction between the two. Count de Sessa had a charming apartment overlooking the port in Monte Carlo. He lived alone, apart from his family for many years. He and his wife were Catholic, so divorce was not an option. Margaret, who was born in Czechoslovakia but had lived for a long time Wiesbaden. She spoke in German and English, and she was currently learning French. Count de Sessa adored Margaret and was very proud of her. In appreciation to Jeno, he brought his friends to the Gipsy Club. Slowly, our business began to grow. After six months, the Gipsy Club actually made some money.

Musicians sometimes did not like to stay in one place for very long; so I learned quickly to sense when they were getting restless. It was approximately after three months. They all had an element of wanderlust in their blood. Jeno would contact the nightclub, Monseigneur, in Paris and would ask if we could exchange one or two musicians. This establishment had the same style of entertainment and attracted the elite of Paris. This accommodation to the talented musicians enabled Jeno and me to reliably provide our customers the lively music they loved. To my way of thinking, the gypsy culture had three different categories. The lowest level were the traveling gypsies, who were thieves. The middle level were the musicians and artists who held down jobs. And the top level were the wealthy Romany who had mansions, but still would move between different communities and homes.

My private life was routine. Jeno and I would sleep until around 11 am and Jeno would serve me breakfast in bed. Then Jeno would take care of the ice delivery. After that, we would head out to the market, Jeno puffing on his cigar constantly, as always. One day we took a trip to Italy. During a pleasant lunch at a hotel, Jeno took my hand, kissed it and put a ring on my finger. I was shocked speechless! He didn't wait for an answer, he just declared, "Now we will get married in Beausoleil!"

I had never considered getting married and did not want to. When we arrived home and I had time alone, I burst into tears, silently. I felt trapped. Jeno had rescued me a couple of times. I would not be alive if it had not been for Jeno's help. I felt I owed my hand in marriage to him, and considered it a trade-off for my new life. The Gipsy Club fulfilled me, it gave me purpose and I found life in the passionate music. So we were married on the 17th of February, 1961 in Beausoleil. I became Madame Medgyesi. Inside, I felt a deep sadness; but I told myself to look at the bright side and make the best of things.

Business slowly continued to pick up. We were forced to fire Johan, the waiter, as he was dishonest. But his wife, Ruth, remained with us. His firing turned out to be very lucky for us and the club, because of the excellent replacement for him that we were able to find. Leslie, who was from Indonesia, spoke many languages fluently. He had been a dancer in his previous career. He was tall and slim with dark hair and dark eyes. His first night at the club, Leslie was shown how to welcome the clientele, take them to their tables and take their orders. But when the first guests arrived, he absolutely froze, standing in silence, as Jeno and I watched in horror.

"What is the matter?" we asked him.

"I am scared," he confessed.

I laughed and told him how very much afraid I had been in the beginning, and I couldn't even speak the local language. I offered to go through the motions of the job with him, and Jeno did the same. The first few days we worked with Leslie this way. By the end of the week, he had gained his confidence and was able to proceed on his own. Leslie went on to become the best employee we had. Soon, he also became our close friend.

Now our advertising flyers were printed in English and French. Business took off. Jeno hired Yoska Nemeth, a highly celebrated violinist who had, in 1956, won the Grand Prix d'Academe de Records Francais award. He came with his wife, Isa, who was famous for her beautiful voice.

Jeno was spending a lot of money on me. He gave me an exquisite golden bracelet and a light brown fur stole. I felt that the full length fur made me look older. Jeno probably wanted me to look older because of our thirty year age difference. I also felt older within myself. I longed for passionate love and excitement in a relationship. At twenty-three, I had built a façade of calm and understanding, even mothering with Ruth, the barmaid, and the musicians. But inside, I had the desire and longing for more in my life.

Jeno hired two ladies who were attractive and had lovely manners. They provided companionship to the gentlemen who came to the club unaccompanied by women. After Loizy Balog's performance on his cimbalom, he would play dance music, and our two ladies would be in high demand. Usually, after Casino closing time, we were very busy. Some of our gentlemen clients visited the club after 2:00 to unwind from the tension of the casino, to relax and enjoy themselves and to have leisure conversation with our ladies.

Yoska Nemeth and his lovely wife, Isa, along with Loizy Balog made a huge splash for our establishment in Monte Carlo when the local television station, Tele Monte Carlo, featured their special performance at the Gipsy Club one evening before opening. Finally, the elite of Monte Carlo and those living along the Cote d. Azure, began to visit the Gipsy Club. There was one group of wealthy Italian industrialists who came with their ladies and a group of Monegasque, or locals, as well as government officials, such as the financial minister. All began to regularly frequent the Gipsy Club. Jeno, Leslie and I made it a point to greet each customer in his or her respective language. We also requested our musicians play our guests' favorite music so that every client felt special.

One night after the casino closed, a lady came in with a group of people. She introduced herself as Sonya. Jeno and I recognized her from the casino, she knew everyone and was known by everybody. Jeno paid her a compliment with his recognition of her fame. Later Jeno told me that during the war, Sonya was one of

Mussolini's mistresses. She had inherited seven or eight houses from him in Italy. She was a big player in the Casino, and still owned maybe only half of the houses left her due to her heavy gambling losses. Sonya and her entourage became regulars.

Another evening, a gentleman entered, sat at a table and just observed everything that happened. Jeno and I felt that he had something on his mind, and he did not want to be bothered. Leslie politely offered, "If you desire anything, please let me know." The man barely acknowledged him. Many people came and enjoyed themselves that evening. At one point, the staff from the Onassis yacht came to the club. Right away the musicians began to play the Greek music, the Sirtaki. Leslie made an effort to lead the young Greek group to their table, but he could not, for all of the men began to dance and sing. They put their arms around Leslie's shoulder, and there was Leslie, spontaneously dancing the Sirtaki with our Greek guests. Ah, I could see Leslie was fully in his element, since dancing had once been his profession and always his passion. He enjoyed himself tremendously. Other people joined in and danced, the ambience was marvelous! The quiet observer approached the bar and announced to Jeno that on the following day, the Duke and Duchess of Arenberg would be visiting our establishment. Jeno thanked him and offered him a drink, which the man declined; and then he left.

The next night, I put my best dress on and wore the mink stole. Jeno wore his dark blue suit. He did not have a great many clothes, claiming that he did not need any more than what he had. Excitement filled the air at the Gipsy Club, we were all a little nervous. The musicians were arguing over what music to play for the royal couple. Jeno, Leslie and I were discussing what would be the proper way to welcome the royal couple. Around midnight, Jeno announced that the Duke and Duchess had arrived. The musicians played the Hungarian Dance Number 5 from Johannes Brahms just as they entered. Jeno seated them, and Leslie walked behind the Duke. The Duke ordered champagne as the show continued. Yoska, Loizy and the other musicians played their very best. It was a successful night, after which there were few nights when we closed before 5 am. Sometimes, after closing, we would go directly to the meat and vegetable market. This way we could go home to sleep until NOON.

Amid all of the work and our busy days, sadly, my female bird, Kiki, died. I felt sorry for Coco, who had lost his playmate. Whenever I had the time, I would play and talk with him, inviting him out of his cage so he could fly around the living room.

Jeno hired more musicians, sometimes we had a cello player, a bass player and a balalaika player. Leslie and I communicated well with our regular guests, making a point of remembering names, what they liked or didn't like, and what they enjoyed talking about. We all had a lot of fun together. Privately, between Leslie and myself, we gave some of our regular guests' secret nicknames.

A GLAMOROUS SUCCESS

Business flourished at the Gipsy Club. The Duke and Duchess of Arenberg and their entourage became regulars. The Duchess always wanted me to sit at her table, which was a great honor for me as well as for our establishment. I enjoyed it tremendously. The Duchess was an impressive lady, tall and well proportioned, statuesque. She had a lovely face, radiant brown eyes so full of life; but when she was unhappy, her eyes lost their shine and turned darker. In her dark brown hair, she wore a tiara shimmering with diamonds, like the rest of her jewelry. The Duchess was very eccentric. She liked to explore people's characters. I knew that I was one of her candidates. With excitement, I was ready for the challenge. One day the Duchess came with her group and said, "You have champagne, but no caviar. What kind of an establishment is this? You should offer caviar."

Respectfully I answered, "Of course we have caviar. How many dishes would your Highness like?"

"You have Caviar?"

"Yes your Highness, for our special guests such as you!" I excused myself and immediately left to obtain caviar from the Tiptop restaurant next door. Tiptop had everything from spaghetti to caviar, and was open late, like the Gipsy Club.

Another time the Duchess came in with a young Yugoslavian escort. The duchess requested that I sit next to him. I declined, explaining that I preferred to sit by the Duchess. "Don't you like him?" the Duchess asked.

"I do not know your friend. He is very handsome, but it is not for me to like him."

The Duchess was satisfied with my response and said, "Let's dance together." I was relieved that I had passed the test.

The Duchess loved to dance and would always lead. She especially enjoyed the tango, dipping me with great drama. I had so much fun. One night after a gala, the Duke and Duchess came to the club with their entourage. She was dressed in a full length white ermine coat and wearing a sparkling tiara. Everyone was absolutely stunned by how elegant and majestic the Duchess looked.

That night, we knew we were on the right way upward. Jeno, Leslie and I had our private celebration. The Gipsy Club was accepted now by the elite. We were lucky to be in close proximity to such glamour. Monte Carlo was a very safe, quiet place. Ladies were able to go out and wear their furs and jewels without worry.

One night when the Duke and Duchess entered the Gipsy Club, it seemed that they were in the middle of an argument. She told the Duke to sit on the other side of the room opposite her. I had to think quickly how to act. This was a serious situation. The Duchess was in a foul mood. She requested that I approach the Duke and ask him what he would like to drink. Then the Duke asked me to ask the Duchess what SHE wanted to drink. So it went, on and on. Leslie was hiding behind the bar, Jeno went outside. I was the only messenger between the two royalties. Calmly and efficiently, I was crossing the dance floor to relate each message, as if there was nothing unusual going on. After a while, the Duke excused himself and left, he suffered from asthma and was having an attack. The Duchess stopped me to ask, "Why did the Duke leave?" She knew exactly why, as she had heard him coughing. But she was in a mood now to start an argument with me. I quietly explained that the Duke had excused himself because of an asthma attack, and the Duchess let it go. Jeno sent the Duchess a bottle of champagne to loosen her up, and that worked. After the second bottle, we were dancing again and had an animated conversation. Every year, in summertime, the Duchess would go to her villa in Montevideo in South America for three months. When the slow season came, we would close the Gipsy Club for one day a week. That gave us the opportunity to rest and do chores.

One day, I cleaned the apartment, after which Jeno said, "Ilona and Bela will soon be here. We could all drive in Bela's car up to the mountains to try out our new hobby, target practice." Then he continued, "But, if you would like to practice before we go, I could fasten the target chart on the bathroom door and thicken it with cardboard paper behind, so the shot does not go through the door."

"Good thinking, Jeno," I commended. "I will put Coco in the kitchen and get the rifle." When I returned, the target chart was fastened to the bathroom door with thick protective layers of cardboard paper behind and around the target. But Jeno was not in the room. I loaded the rifle and aimed at the target. BANG! A good shot! Close to the middle, but just above, almost perfect. At the same moment, I heard Jeno hollering frantically from inside the bathroom.

"Brigitte, you almost shot me in the forehead! You Meshugginah!" *which is Yiddish for Crazy.* The shot had passed right through the bathroom door to where Jeno was sitting quietly on the toilet, minding his own business.

"Well, Jeno," I calmly replied, "I did not know you were in there. I guess this was not such a good idea after all!"

I brought Coco back out of the kitchen and talked and played with the bird. Coco hopped on my finger, held it tightly and wiggled. He chirped happily away, and was better off than I, in this respect. Then Bela and Ilona arrived. Bela, who loved Coco very much, leaned over the cage to talk to Coco in his usual form, and inadvertently sprayed as he talked. The poor bird retreated to the back of his cage to avoid another shower as he shook and ruffled his feathers to dry.

Jeno's group of friends was expanding. We still continued to gather at Café de Paris every afternoon around 5:00. Our new social group was filled with eccentric, clever, interesting and intriguing individuals. Jeno knew everyone. One of the men, Sandor, worked for Coco Chanel as a tailor. Jeno spoke a long time with Sandor and, to my surprise, the following week, I was wearing an outfit designed by Coco Chanel. Sandor's wife was a Hungarian Gypsy. She spied on her husband because she suspected he had a girlfriend. It was known that she had put sugar in his gas tank for revenge. One time she hid in the back of his car and when the girlfriend climbed in, the wife threatened her with a knife.

One other man in their group made his living by jumping in front of expensive cars. He would make believe that he had been hurt and asked for the police to be called and become involved. Right away, the owner of the car would ask his driver to pay the man off. Some in the group were well-employed, some just barely got by, and some were con artists. I learned a lot about people and their life styles. There was always storytelling and laughter. Most men from the new group were living in Nice, some in Paris.

One day Jeno pointed out that it had been some time since we had gone on a vacation. Business was slow, so we closed the club for two weeks. We went to Munich Germany, with the intent of getting the King of the Gypsies, Toki Horward, to come work with us for the winter season. He was a well-known violinist. Jeno had no trouble finding Toki. Hungarians always seemed to be able to find each other, even without telephones or writing letters. Toki worked in an establishment near the famous Hofbrauhaus. He greeted us warmly and agreed to come to Monte Carlo for the season. Jeno and I enjoyed our vacation and then returned to Monte Carlo. We signed a new contract with Lucien to continue renting the space for another three years. Everyone was happy with the arrangement.

I could not wait to open the club at 10:00 every night. We had bought a record player and some popular records so that there was music when the musicians took a break. We were very pleased when new guests came to our establishment. Some were living in Monte Carlo. One of them was a Russian, Serge. He would bring along his girlfriend. Lucky that at the time we had a Russian musician who played the balalaika and sang, for now we could have vodka parties. We became fast friends with Serge and his girlfriend, Annette. They made a vivacious couple, Serge was tall with light brown hair streaked with gray. He had blue eyes, a short mustache and a friendly expression. Annette had short thick auburn hair, a sparkle in her brown eyes and wore an orange tone lipstick. Her style of dress was tres chic, she was absolutely charming.

Sometimes in the afternoon, Serge would invite Jeno and me to his beautiful condo in Monte Carlo. Annette would serve us all delicious snacks accompanied with ice cold vodka. When they came to the club, we always had a bucket of ice with Vodka ready for them.

There was also Sasha and his group. Sasha's parents were friends of the Duchess. They owned a high end jewelry store next to the Hotel Ermitage. Then in addition to our new regular guests was Walter. He was a Swiss banker overseeing the bank in Monte Carlo. A small man with light brown thin hair and a round face, he always wore a smile. However, his eyes seemed to be in another world. They sometimes shimmered when he talked. He would roll his eyes around. Occasionally they were cloudy. But always, he was in good spirits, and would invite everybody to have a drink with him. He was a very generous tipper with Leslie and the musicians. However, when his movements were getting a little unsteady, I would tell him, "Walter, it is time to go. Tomorrow you have a busy day!" Walter would wipe his hand over his mouth and say, "You are right Madame Brigitte. It is my bedtime." After that, Walter would leave. We not only had fun with our guests, we were also looking after their well-being so as not to let them overdo. Our guests appreciated this attention very much and we earned their respect.

Before the season began, Jeno hired a barmaid to help Leslie. Her name was Yvette. She was French and living near Nice. A petite and pretty brunette, Yvette was at first a little shy behind the bar, but after a few nights of serving, she was comfortable. One night three men came in and Yvette served them whiskey. They had a prolonged conversation with Yvette and paid her compliments, leaving a large tip for her. Leslie and I exchanged glances, we did not like these three men. They spoke French with an accent and we suspected they were from Corsica. Corsicans had a bad reputation. Some were rough with women, they were pimps or gangsters. We hoped that they would never come back. Unfortunately, the very next night, they did. Again, they only wanted to be served by Yvette. She was excited about how much money they gave her again. I saw danger for her and warned her, advising her not to go anywhere with them, even in the daytime. But after the third time that the men came, Yvette disappeared. We were worried when she didn't come to work, but she was an adult and we all hoped for the best.

Approximately one month passed, the winter season was nearing, when we had to deal with a bad accountant. Just before 10:00, we opened the Gipsy Club and, to our horror, a girl covered in blood came running in. It was Yvette! She begged me to hide her. I told Jeno to call the police from our phone booth and to stay in the phone booth until they arrived. Our phone booth was on the right side as you walked into the club; but the door to it was not easy to detect, as it was the same color as the wall.

I took Yvette into the kitchen, pulled down the ladder to the storage area in the ceiling and helped her up the steps. Then I closed the door to the attic and hurried back to the bar. I kept busy with paperwork while Leslie dusted the bottles and straightened the bar. Within minutes, two of the three Corsicans stamped in, looking for Yvette. Leslie and I remained calm and told them we had not seen her. The Corsicans searched through the entire place, the bathroom, the kitchen and behind the bar. Finally, the police arrived, surprising the Corsicans, and they took them away. Jeno was still in the phone booth. I went to tell him it was okay to come out. "It was very smart, Jeno, that you stayed in the booth so the men never saw you." Ten minutes later, the police returned looking for Yvette. I helped her down from the attic so that she could give her statement to them. The police had been searching for these two men. Although Monte Carlo and Monaco had an extensive network of agents, somehow these two had sneaked in. Poor Yvette had to be transported to the hospital. She was very grateful to Jeno, Leslie and me and admitted that she should have listened to my advice. We heard from the police that Yvette had to remain in the hospital for a couple of weeks. She had apparently fallen in love with one of the Corsicans and he then forced her to walk the streets of Nice for him. She refused to go with his friend. His reaction was to tie her to the back of his car which he then drove up the street. Perhaps the rope broke. Luckily, she was able to escape before the men dragged her to her death. The police said that they would patrol the Gipsy Club more closely if the men got out of prison in Nice.

Not even a month later, the two men came back, just as before, around 10:00. We had just opened the club. Jeno was in the kitchen and could overhear the loud accusations about how Leslie and I had called the police. I denied it calmly, pointing out that Leslie and I had been right in front of them the whole time. My heart was beating fast. I had to tell myself, "Keep your composure. Don't panic." Then I informed the men that the police patrolled regularly and they had just happened to come along. I secretly hoped that soon the undercover agents would call the police for us. Eventually, the two men turned on each other, throwing out wild accusations and blame. The next thing we knew, one of the men sprang over the bar, grabbed a bottle of liquor, hit it on the bar and broke the bottle. With it he cut the other man's face. Blood was spurting everywhere. Leslie and I stood frozen in shock at the scene. The police, thankfully, came running in with handcuffs and arrested the men. They had been alerted about the escape of the men from prison and had been keeping an eye on the Gipsy Club. The two men were then extradited to Corsica. We never hired another girl to work at the Gipsy Club. And we never needed to.

Jacqueline from Nice, Monica from Germany, and Michele and Lucille from Menton were young single ladies who would play small amounts at the casino, and would then bring their dates into the Gipsy Club. Sometimes the ladies would come alone. They were well dressed, gentile and good conversationalists. Jeno would offer them drinks at the bar and we would all have a good time chatting. Often our single customers would join us and the gentlemen were pleased to have a dance partner. I think that Jeno, Leslie and I made a good team. Jeno brought his expertise to the Gipsy Club. Leslie was a great addition to the club with his fluency in several languages and his elegant manners, he was friendly and entertaining. Many of our customers seemed to enjoy my company, perhaps because I could sense how they wanted to be treated. I was respectful and had a dry sense of humor that they liked, and the ability to make clever remarks in an insightful and amusing way. Our clients returned because they felt at ease, they could relax and joke around with us.

One gentleman from England visited us periodically. Horace was always impeccably dressed and spoke the Queen's English, mostly to Leslie, who was pleased whenever Jeno announced, "A Bentley is approaching! It is probably Mr. Horace!" We did not have many guests when Mr. Horace arrived early. He was greeted by our musician who played his favorite melody. With a smile, Mr. Horace would settle down at the bar. He was a handsome man, average height, a squarish face, his brown hair slightly wavy and he wore a friendly expression. Mr. Horace would engage Leslie in interesting conversation.

One evening I was busy writing out bills when, suddenly, Mr. Horace turned to me and, speaking in French, asked if I would like to join him and Leslie in a bottle of Champagne. I accepted with pleasure, "Mr. Horace, Thank you!" Now all three of us were conversing in French. After the second bottle, the conversation took on a very strange twist. Mr. Horace looked at me with a twinkle in his eyes and said, "Madame Brigitte, I do not know why my head is itching. What do you think I should do?"

I was thinking to myself, "Oh now we have another person who likes to play games." I replied with a stern face," I think, Mr. Horace, you should lift your hands, and with your fingers you should scratch your head!"

Mr. Horace chuckled and said, "I tried it, but it doesn't help!"

The conversation grew more and more peculiar. Mr. Horace asked me more questions. So I suggested that he had head lice and they were having a party. He liked that idea and laughed, "Oh yeah?" He sounded amused with the idea.

I became more imaginative and continued, "Maybe you have little lice and they pinch you, some are little girl lice in pink ribbons and the little boys are in blue." He was really getting into this conversation. Who can tell what he was thinking about or what was amusing him. Mr. Horace was one of our most bizarre guests. We had fun and I enjoyed the challenge and the Champagne.

The winter season began. Toki Horvath arrived, and we had a great opening. The Duchess returned from South America, she really liked Toki. She requested that he sit at her table and play for her again and again. She tried to monopolize his attention, but she did not understand the gypsy heart. It did not matter how much money she gave him. When other guests began to arrive, he would go to play for them. This intrigued the Duchess, who undoubtedly saw Toki as a wonderful new toy to play with. Many times she invited Toki to sit with her and her entourage, then she would ask him to play classical music. Toki was very happy to do so. The Champagne was flowing, everyone was enjoying themselves; but Toki never spent the whole evening at the Duchess's table, as she requested.

Business continued to thrive and guests continued to arrive. Sasha came with his entourage. Then an Italian group followed. Next a Greek group entered. The musicians were playing the Sirtaki. Leslie pulled Jacqueline and the other girls onto the dance floor. Everyone joined in and they all had a wonderful time. The musicians were playing from the Greek Sirtaki, the traditional Russian music, like

Kalinka and Troika, to the waltz. The ambiance was marvelous. These were splendid evenings.

A lovely lady from England, Abigail, came into the Club, sometimes with friends and sometimes alone. She was in her early thirties, very attractive with dark hair and radiant violet eyes. Her voice was so stunning that Leslie and I would beg her to sing. She sang arias from Carmen and other operas. Once in a while, performers of the Opera de Monte Carlo would visit the club and would sing for us. We were all entertained by some of our guests. There were also some regular guests from Menton, in particular a young man named Martino, who caught my eye. Martino also had a great voice and would occasionally sing for us. Most of all, he was an extraordinarily good dancer. Jeno gave him permission to dance with me. I was in heaven! Jeno knew I loved to dance, but he never danced with me. One night during a dance, Martino told me that he had dreamt of me at night. I was simply enjoying myself while dancing with Martino, but now I would have to be careful not to further encourage him.

One night, two men arrived and posted themselves on each side of the room, their backs to the walls. We did not question them as we thought they were the secret police. The next day, a tall middle-aged man entered and spoke at length with Leslie. He came three nights in a row, and on the third he told us that he was the chauffeur for the Maharajah of Jetpour. He announced that the Maharajah would join us the following evening. We were all very excited, royalty was coming to visit our club. The next evening, Jeno informed us that a white Rolls Royce was in view, driving slowly from the Hotel de Paris. Leslie instructed everyone on how to greet the Maharajah. When he entered, we each greeted him formally. He smiled warmly at us. The Maharajah was of medium height and a little corpulent around the middle. He had large dark brown eyes, dark hair and full lips; I thought to myself, "Kiss Lips". He walked with a cane. Jeno offered to seat him, but he preferred to remain at the bar and chat with Leslie and me. We were exceedingly honored. Leslie spoke with him fluently in English. Then the Maharajah turned to me and asked me in French if I would care to sit and have Champagne with him. I accepted, saying that it would be an honor. I learned that the two men were his security, they had been sent to make sure the club was a safe establishment for him to visit. We had a light conversation with lots of laughter. After that night, he came almost every evening. Sometimes he drank whisky and I would enjoy Champagne.

The Maharajah wanted to dance with me, but only for a short time because of his injury. He was from Bombay, now Mumbai, and one day a journalist asked to take some photographs at his palace and also on Safari, to see tigers in the wild. So his Highness took the journalist on Safari. As he was taking the photos of the wild tiger, the Maharajah warned him to keep his distance. But the journalist, excited about his opportunity, did not listen to the warnings and came too close. The tiger turned and attacked. The Maharajah threw himself in between the tiger and the journalist and was himself injured. The journalist was saved, but the Maharajah was injured for life. I was very touched with his noble act.

A couple of nights later, the Maharajah asked Jeno if I could accompany him to the Sporting d'Ete. Jeno gave permission. The chauffeur drove us in the white Rolls Royce to the location. What glamour and glitter. We sat at the bar and people would come by to greet the Maharajah. He told me that he would be introducing me to his nephew and the nephew's mother, the Maharani of Baroda. She was an exotic beauty with light brown skin, jet black hair and a sparkle in her dark eyes. Her sari was exquisite, and the glitter of her diamonds gave a finishing touch. Her son was between eighteen and twenty and resembled his mother. He wore a Nehru style jacket with diamond buttons. The Maharajah presented me to his relatives who were very friendly. The son said that he would pay a visit to the Gipsy Club later. The chauffeur drove us back to the club where the Maharajah told his driver that he was free to enjoy himself at the bar.

Back at the Gipsy Club we had more Champagne and danced slowly. Later on, his nephew came to join us at our table. When he left our table to talk with Leslie, Jeno offered the nephew a drink, he accepted. Leslie was happy to have the opportunity to speak with the young prince. Jeno was pleased with the Maharajah's interest in the club and gave permission for me to go out several more nights with him. At the same time, his visits helped increase our business, setting a high standard for the Gipsy Club. I thoroughly enjoyed the excursions. At the Sporting d'Ete, we had a little table and enjoyed gourmet snacks after midnight. Often we were served smoked salmon, pate de foie gras and caviar. What enjoyable times these were! The Maharajah stayed for one month in the Hotel de Paris; and when it was time for him to go, I felt sad. But he promised to return in six months and we both looked forward to the next visit.

The Gipsy Club was in full bloom in the summer. One night, while our musicians were playing a waltz, one older gentleman, to our surprise, began to dance. He moved gracefully, making believe convincingly that he was dancing with a partner in his arm. It was very funny. This was our first meeting with Henry, an Englishman affiliated with Cal Tex Gasoline. For many years he lived in Monte Carlo and enjoyed his life with a little help from vodka. He too became one of our regulars.

Occasionally the summer nights were too hot and we would move the music into the street. The piano was moved outside and the pianist would begin to play, the violinist and guitarist would follow and play in harmony. The police kindly closed the street to accommodate the dancers whenever Onassis and his entourage came. Then the fun would begin. Our musicians played Greek music and Onassis's guests were dancing in the street. As the gaiety increased, our guests and Leslie joined in the fun and danced with them. We respected Mr. Onassis's privacy and did not take any photographs of him. However, some of his guests permitted us to take photos of them.

1963

In the summer of 1963, changes were coming to Monte Carlo. To the horror of the locals, slot machines were brought into Cafe de Paris and other locations. Onassis, who had been the financier since 1953 of La Societe des Bains de mer de Monaco, had a falling out with them. A group of French bankers took over and Onassis withdrew from the finance business. New money had arrived and brought in new clientele. The serenity of the area was replaced by the noise of tour buses, and tourists in shorts with cameras, loud voices and poor manners. The aura of the sleeping beauty of Monte Carlo awakened. Wealthy elite would host private events in their villas. The Gipsy Club was still busy, many of the regulars continued to come. The Duchess never seemed to tire of the club and would often take musicians back to her home after the club closed at 5:00. Toki would never go, as much as she wanted him to. He always told her that he was too tired.

1964

In the summer of 1964, Jeno's friends from Paris came for a visit. We all spent time on the beach together. One morning, I did not feel well. I thought perhaps I had had too much to drink the night before. But after two days, Jeno took me to the doctor. The doctor checked me out and finding nothing wrong, asked me when my last period was. I had to really think because this was something I didn't pay much attention to. I gave him a probable date and he told me that he would order a pregnancy test.

A couple of days later, he called to give us the "good news". I was two months pregnant. Jeno and I looked at each other in shock and disbelief. Jeno suddenly became a beast and accused me of being unfaithful. I pointed out that we spent almost all of our time together. Jeno nervously drew on his cigar and exclaimed, "My previous wife never got pregnant. Therefore, it is not possible that I got you pregnant!"

I replied calmly, "Perhaps your former wife was herself barren and not you, Jeno." That stopped him cold. After a while he also calmed down, but I was hurt by his accusation, and was never able to look at him the same way. He had shown a side of himself that I did not like nor could I trust. Together we decided that we did not want a child. First of all, it was not a love match marriage. Secondly, our occupation, work place and small apartment did not provide an appropriate environment for raising a child. Our problem now was that we lived in a French Catholic community where abortion was not an option.

Jeno confided our situation to his Parisian friends. They were a young couple in their early thirties. His name was Pauli, he was a Hungarian Jew. His partner, Kristel, was from Munich Germany. They immediately responded that they would want the baby, as they could not have one of their own. But I was unwilling, it was not a good option for me. If I were to have the baby, I would want to raise the child myself. Pauli and Kristel were very disappointed, but they promised to find someone to help once they returned to Paris. Jeno and I enjoyed our time with these two friends. They owned a car and it was a treat to take field trips with them to different places. One week after they left, I began to bleed quite a bit. I was hopeful that I was miscarrying. Jeno and I went to see the doctor, who was not sympathetic. He was a small, skinny man and looked unhealthy. We admitted to him that we wanted him to end the pregnancy. The doctor decided that he could give me an injection that would make me lose the baby.

Every day for a week we visited the doctor and he gave me injections. Unfortunately, the treatment was not successful. I began to feel better and the bleeding stopped. When we asked the doctor about the results of his treatment, he smiled and told us, "Now you will have a healthy baby. I have been giving Brigitte vitamin B12 shots." I was outraged and sad.

Within days we received a letter from Pauli with a name and address for someone who could help. We bought a little cage for Coco and took him with us by train to Paris. We took a room in a small hotel and went to the address Pauli had given us. A couple greeted and welcomed us into their apartment. The lady took me into a very small room lined with coats. In the middle was a table covered with white linen. I undressed and laid down on the table. The two strapped down my arms and legs and, without administering any anesthetic, the man began to operate on me. I closed my eyes, did not say a word or even cry out. But silent tears streamed down my cheeks. The pain was excruciating. Sweat poured out of me. I was lying in a pool of wetness. The wife put a cool cloth on my forehead and held my hand.

At one point, I heard them flush the fetus down the toilet. They told me that I had had a boy, exclaiming that never before had anyone remained silent throughout the procedure. When they helped me back to the living room, Jeno was shocked by my appearance. My skin was ghostly pale, my eyes were sunken and had black circles. Later, we heard from Pauli and Kristel, that I had been the last patient. The police arrested the couple and shut down their business.

Jeno brought me back to the hotel by taxi and we stayed there for four days. Jeno would bring me food and the maid would clean around the bed. But I was most appreciative of Coco, who was there to keep me company. On the second day of being bed-ridden, Coco spoke his first words to me, "Cheri, Joli, Bonjour!" After years of talking to him, now he was talking back to me! I was very pleased and asked Jeno to let Coco out before he left to visit his friends. Coco sat on my hand and talked to me. With all of the time I now had to myself while healing, I thought about what I would have done if the baby had been Werner's. Of course, I would have kept the child and loved his baby. Once again, I had too much time to think, and it was Werner who invaded my thoughts.

Jeno and I headed back to Monte Carlo. We were astounded by how much construction was going on. Princess Grace gave Monte Carlo a new look. The beautiful villas were surrounded by upcoming new high rise condominiums. We heard that Onassis and left as had other people from old wealth.

Another season began. Toki Horwarth returned and brought a new cimbalom player with him, because Loizy had another engagement in Paris. Toki had attracted other great musicians and artists from around the world; celebrities like the French pianist Samson Francois and Gregory Cziffra, who played classical music solo in Nice. The whole group from Monte Carlo Opera returned to the club, including a well-known singer, Alan Vanzo from Paris. Sometimes they would sing, always inviting me to sit with them. Jeno made some additions to the music at the club. Elec Bacsek played Jazz for a couple of nights before traveling to New York to make a recording. One time we had a young group of musicians from Spain who imitated the Beatles. This variety helped us draw in the younger crowd, which was now a part of the new Monte Carlo.

SAMSON FRANCOIS

Monte Carlo felt very much more Americanized, some of which was due to the increase in filming for Hollywood movie projects. Many actors, actresses, directors and producers frequented the club. Often we did not recognize them; but we were very excited when James Garner paid us a visit. He was a very handsome and friendly man. He stayed at the bar and invited me to join him in a drink. We enjoyed a lively conversation.

One night, Zsa Zsa Gabor entered the club. The musicians began playing Hungarian melodies. Jeno spoke with her at great length in their mother language. Zsa Zsa returned the next night with her husband, Mr. Hilton. Jeno introduced me to Zsa Zsa and I greeted her in Hungarian. She was very impressed and, joking with Jeno she said, "I like her, I will take her back to Hollywood with me!" Jeno took a photograph of us two that evening.

I enjoyed and valued the opportunity to meet such interesting and famous people. Jeno was well-liked, but one famous writer from Paris preferred to talk with me. I was puzzled when he told me, "Jeno never should have married you; he is much too old. He knew what he was doing and took advantage of you. You were too young to understand."

I was a bit offended and defended Jeno's actions. "You do not know the circumstances."

"Brigitte, you talk to me with a smile, but I detect profound sadness in your eyes," he said gently.

It did make me feel good that such an intellectual person took a personal interest in me. Then he added, "From now on, I will call you Tristesse, sad eyes."

One night after midnight, loud noises from outside the club drew our attention. Jeno, Leslie and I went outdoors to take a look. We saw a convoy of four police motorcycles, then a Rolls Royse, then four more police on motorcycles pass by. We went back inside, so as not to be gawking. Someone told us that it was the Sheik Ibn Saud of Saudi Arabia. He and his entourage and harem had taken over the whole top floor of the Hotel Negresco in Nice. We thought no more of it until later on. As if a gust of wind had blown open the door to the club, several policemen burst in. They positioned themselves around the club. Finally, the son of Ibn Saud appeared. He strode right up to the bar, spoke with Leslie and then noticed me. He invited me to share a bottle of Champagne with him. He was ravishingly handsome and we had an entertaining conversation. Then he told us that he would be returning the following evening.

The next evening, the young Prince entered without his escort of police. We were enjoying the champagne and he was flirting with me, calling me "Beauty". We had a delightful evening, our conversation was stimulating. The third night, the young prince came rushing into the club to tell us that he would like to present us to his father. After this announcement, he swiftly left. Sure enough, the Sheik of Saudi Arabia entered with his son, who made formal introductions. The Sheik was dressed in his royal attire and proceeded directly to the bar where he ordered two cafes. But like the Duchess, he wanted to test us. Leslie asked the Sheik if he wanted an expresso or a cappuccino. The Sheik requested the expresso. So Leslie slipped out to the Tiptop and obtained it for him. The Sheik drank his café and exchanged a few words with Leslie. Not wanting to seem pushy, I retired to my chair.

The Sheik and his son left. But moments later, the handsome Prince came back to inform us that his father liked the Gipsy Club. We had passed the test! The Prince stayed for quite a while, drank Champagne and flirted with me. He was seated in front of the bar and I behind the bar in my usual place. He did not ask me to sit on the bench with him, I felt this was most respectful and again, we had a wonderful evening filled with fun and laughter. Before he left that evening, he gave me a beautiful gold coin, telling me that it was official currency from their kingdom. "I will come back," he promised me. "Tomorrow evening, I will bring more coins so that you can make a beautiful necklace out of them." Then he stood up, leaned over the bar and gave me a kiss. "Goodbye, my Beauty, until tomorrow!"

I felt the blood rush to my head. Leslie noted, "Madame Brigitte, you are blushing." Now I was twenty-five years old and six years had passed since I had left Berlin and Werner. This was the first time I felt attracted to another man and my heart was beating fast.

The following night, I waited with anticipation, but the charming Prince did not return. I was very disappointed. The following day, the newspaper reported what had happened. The Sheik had had a heart attack and the whole family flew him to Switzerland for medical care. I felt great sympathy for the young Prince, but it was good to know why he did not return as promised.

My private life was very much routine. Since the horrible experience in Paris, Jeno and I were no longer intimate. At one point, Jeno had to go to the doctor, but he never explained why. This more distant relationship is how it worked out best for both of us.

Margaret, who now lived with the Count de Sessa, continued to visit us often during the day. Occasionally the two would invite Jeno and me for dinner. We reciprocated by inviting them for drinks at the club. Margaret had begun to have pain in her hands, which was worsening. The doctor said that she had rheumatoid arthritis. As the disease progressed, she become more and more crippled, to the point where she could no longer hold a cup. It was very troubling to see. Luckily she had Gino, the Count, to take care of her. He could afford all of the medical expenses and medications. But doctors only helped for a while. Still, Margaret and Gino would go out once or twice a week. One time, Gino brought a group of Italian friends to the Gipsy Club and right away they loved the music and sang along. Margaret suddenly rose and announced that she wanted to go somewhere else. Gino was shocked, as were their friends. But Gino was a true gentleman. He gave into her wishes and left, with their friends following behind reluctantly.

I could not understand Margaret's actions, so I did not contact her. Maybe she was jealous of me. After several months, she came over to our apartment with a bottle of vodka and asked why I had not called her. I told her how rude she had been to leave so suddenly and she replied, "Well, I wanted to go somewhere else where I could be the center of attention."

I turned to Jeno and right there, in front of Margaret, I said, "You see, I was right, Jeno." Jeno never wanted to confront anyone, he always stayed in the background. Although Margaret and I stayed in contact, I never felt the same way about her.

At home, I played with Coco and taught him more words. During the slow season, we closed the Gipsy Club once a week. One evening, Jeno said, "Let's go to see Piroshka perform a show at a nightclub in Nice!" I didn't know that Piroshka was working. I saw her only in the afternoons at the Café de Paris, after which she would accompany Mr. Gorovway to the casino to play.

Jeno said, "Sometimes when she needs money, she will look for work. She's very good in her act."

I was curious, I couldn't imagine Piroshka in any act. She wore thick glasses. "How can she dance or do whatever she does with those glasses on?" I asked.

"You will see," Jeno said.

Otherwise, she was attractive enough, with her short blond colored hair, with her long cigarette holder between her well-manicured fingers. She was madly in love with Mr. Gorovway and followed him like a faithful little puppy. Mr. Gorovway was only interested in going to the casino and playing with his little terrier, Igor, on the beach every day.

The nightclub was in a well-known hotel in Nice. We saw Piroshka's act and it was truly astonishing. First she came out with glasses and gray hair, walking very slowly. She approached the podium where there was an easel for sketching. The music accompanied her actions as she quickly made a sketch. She drew herself as a nurse, pulled the sketch down and then removed some clothing and looked like the nurse in the sketch. Then she made another sketch and became that character. One after another, she continued through a series of drawings, ending up as a harem girl. The accompanying music was perfect, becoming more and more suggestive as she finally stood before us, topless, at the end of the show. We enthusiastically applauded her performance.

Jeno invited Piroshka to join us at our table. I exclaimed how amazing her performance was and the three of us went on a drinking spree, traveling from one club to another.

One day, I said to Jeno, "We have saved quite a bit of money. I would like to have a larger apartment so that we can invite friends over."

Jeno replied, "Yes, I was thinking we could buy one of the new condos which are popping up all over Monte Carlo, if the coming season is successful."

I became excited now that I would have a new project to look forward to. I promised myself that I would put all of my energy and love into the club. When I had some time alone, I closed my eyes and gave intensive thought to a special guest, who I hoped would visit the Gipsy Club that night. When we left our apartment in the evening, walking to the club, I told Jeno about my intuition and said, "Jeno, I think Mr. Benett or Serge or this person or that will come to the club tonight, and so it was.

Another season began at the Gipsy Club. The great gambler, Sonya, still came regularly to the club. She had already lost much of her fortune and continued to do so, occasionally losing as much as one of her villas in one night's gambling. We treated her just the same, even when she was unable to pay. It was often that we would not give customers their bills at the end of an evening if we knew that a few nights later they would have the money to pay the bill. We found that this sort of courtesy and understanding resulted in a mutually rewarding relationship. One night, one of our regular guests, Walter the banker, came in. His eyes were glittering and he rolled them around more than usual. It looked as if he was high on drugs. He asked me, "What should I do, Madame Brigitte?"

I asked him, "What is bothering you?"

But he just kept asking what he should do. He wouldn't say anything else. "Just tell me what to do!"

Finally, I told him to return to his hotel, sleep it off and, "Tomorrow you will know what to do."

"Yes, Madame Brigitte. You are right. I will know what to do!" This was the last time we saw Walter. The next day there was a big article in the newspaper. Walter had shot himself. Apparently he had misused bank funds and knew that he was going to be caught. Alas, throughout the years, there were several people we came to know who, for one reason or another, took their own lives.

We received news that the Maharajah had left India and would soon be in Monte Carlo. I had been looking forward to his arrival. This time, he arrived and spoke with Jeno, asking him for my hand in marriage. "But I am married!" I exclaimed.

"It does not matter," the Maharajah explained. "So am I."

"But I don't want to be the second wife," I laughingly told him.

"Then you will be my first wife," he assured me. With a serious voice, the Maharajah informed me that he had told his wife about me and she was happy with the arrangement. Jeno looked on dumfounded and then he smiled, excused himself and left. There I was alone again with a tricky situation. This time I did not know what to say or how to react. I felt awkward, "Was he serious?" I asked myself. Maybe he was, because his culture permitted him to have more than one wife.

Finally I decided on a plan. The next day, I said, "Your Highness, your offer is a great honor, but it is also a very big surprise for me and I need time to think about this."

The Maharajah was satisfied with my answer, and he invited me to the Sporting d'Ete, where we saw many celebrities including Elizabeth Taylor and Jack Warner.

One day the Maharajah invited Jeno and me for tea at the Hotel de Paris. We went to the hotel and waited in anticipation of his arrival. But he did not arrive. After half an hour of waiting, we asked the front desk to ring his room. There was no answer. I was offended and, with agitation, I said to Jeno, "Let's go. I am very displeased by the manners of the Maharajah."

When we opened up the Gipsy Club at 10:00, Leslie asked me if something was wrong. "Yes! You'd better believe it!" I related to Leslie what had happened.

He laughed and said, "You should see your eyes right now. They have turned green and are glowing! Have you thought that maybe something happened to the Maharajah?"

"Of course not," I answered with a grim look.

It was after 2:00 am when the Maharajah and his chauffeur entered. I kept my distance, staying behind the bar, sitting in my chair. He rushed immediately over to me and came behind the bar, kneeling in front of me, asking for my forgiveness. He explained that he could not make it for tea because he had been in prison in Italy.

I looked at him in disbelief. "Please, come up off your knees and tell me the story," I directed.

Apparently, the night before, after he left the Gipsy Club, he was invited by Emil Barelli, a well-known orchestra leader, along with the entire ballet company, to go out on a Kris Craft boat. Everybody was drinking in excess. The boat was cruising around and went further and further away from Monte Carlo, ending up in Italy. The driver wanted to show off and did a couple of spins. Some of the girls and the Maharajah himself, ended up in the water. The Italian police fished them out and put all of them in jail. It had taken the police hours to sort out who was who, as none of them had identification. People from Monte Carlo had to come to Italy to identify them. Finally, they were picked up and driven back to Monte Carlo. We all broke out in roaring laughter when the Maharajah finished relating his adventure.

For a long time, this event was the talk of the town. The Maharajah invited me the next day to lunch in a beautiful restaurant up in the mountains. He reassured me how serious he was about marrying me. I thanked him and told him that I had secretly called his lips "Kiss Lips". He gave me a kiss, which I liked, and then he took my hands and covered them with his kisses. The Maharajah told me that he was leaving in two days, and that, as always, he had a wonderful time with me. We exchanged addresses and finished our late lunch. On the way back to Monte Carlo, I felt sad that he was leaving so soon. We were both very quiet and he kissed me warmly before he dropped me off. That night, the Maharajah came by the Gipsy Club, but he did not stay long. I tried to put on a happy face, but felt as if my fun times were all ending. I had the feeling that I would never see him again.

The Gipsy Club experienced another sensational evening when the gorgeous Brigitte Bardot walked in with the handsome Gunter Sachs. They made a charming couple and were casual and friendly as they talked with us and our musicians. After a while, Brigitte requested Chico, our Spanish gypsy guitarist, to play a flamenco dance. Chico's eyes lit up and he began to play, sing and dance. Spontaneously, Brigitte rose and danced to the music with sexy movements. We were all clapping to the rhythm of the music. It was absolutely brilliant!

The Duchess of Arenberg had changed her tactics. She was calmer, and her mood swings were not so erratic and unpredictable as before. Now she invited me to the Sporting d'Ete for dinner and to different restaurants for lunch. Two times, she invited Jeno and myself to her villa, along with other friends. One evening the Duchess asked me why we did not invite her to our place.

"Oh la Duchess, we have only a small apartment and would be embarrassed to have you over!" But the Duchess insisted. We obliged, although we could not understand why she would want to see our simple apartment.

One afternoon, at our request, she came to visit. Jeno served Champagne with some canapes. The Duchess commented, "Your place is very small, but taste-fully decorated."

A couple of nights later, when she came to the club, she invited me to accompany her to Montevideo Uruguay, as her companion. I was thrilled. Now I knew why the Duchess wanted to see our place; we needed to pass her inspection. Oh yes, I wanted to see the world and travel to faraway places, maybe I would find a sunny island, I was thinking to myself. I thanked the Duchess for the great honor of her invitation, and told her that I would speak to Jeno.

At first, Jeno was somewhat receptive to the idea. But after thinking it over at length, he realized that he could not manage the Gipsy Club on his own for three to four months. He reminded me of how very moody the Duchess was. "What if she decides to discard you while you are there? You could end up stranded in South America."

I thought it over and decided that Jeno was right. Together, Jeno and I told the Duchess that I would have to get my passport renewed and that would take months. But we thanked her for thinking of me.

We had one new interesting guest. Leslie and I gave him a nickname, Romeo. He was a very wealthy Italian who was a shareholder in mining precious stones in South America. He was charming, tall and slim with dark hair and a strong Roman nose. The first evening he arrived with his wife, a gorgeous lady. A couple of days later, he entered with a different woman, and we pretended we had never seen him before. So it went, on and on, he never had the same lady accompany him twice. He appreciated our discretion. In the end, he became excited over me and came behind the bar to kiss me. But I acted amused, and gently pushed him away.

Many of our regular guests liked to come behind the bar and have fun with Leslie and me. I realized that I had reached a point in my life where I was feeling self-confident and good about my achievements. Not only was the Gipsy Club well-received and accepted by the elite, but we too were treated with friendliness and respect. Perhaps it was time to get in touch with Aunt Didi and Uncle Max. I sent them a letter, inviting them to come to Monte Carlo. They came to visit and loved the country and surrounding area. Aunt Didi enjoyed speaking in Hungarian to Jeno, but still did not approve of the age difference between Jeno and me.

I never told my aunt and uncle how and where I had met Jeno. They would have been horrified to know about my bad encounter in Wiesbaden. Aunt Didi loved the Hungarian music, but did not like the late hours. She didn't understand that it was not only a nightclub, but that Jeno, Leslie and I made it so much more than a nightclub. After they left, I began again to long for Werner. I wanted to see him and finally resolve that yearning. Now, after I was successful and married, I felt strong enough to keep my emotions under control, and to face Werner. I sent him a card and told him that Jeno and I had a club. Not long after, I received a card in response that he was coming to visit Monte Carlo. I became excited and showed the message to Jeno, who did not say anything. One evening, Werner showed up at the club. I did not expect him so soon.

At first I was stunned and felt as if all of my blood had rushed to my head. Jeno came over and asked me if he was my friend from Berlin. I pulled myself together and introduced Werner to Jeno and Leslie. All three carried on a light conversation. Finally, Werner invited Jeno and me to lunch the following day and asked if we might show him around Monte Carlo. Jeno was gracious and said that he was busy, but that I could show Werner around. Jeno knew that we wanted to be alone. I was sleepless that night. All of my good intentions were melting away. My feelings for Werner were as strong as before. I realized that if Werner would ask me to leave with him, I would go in a moment. Even after all I had been through.

The next day, I went to his hotel and asked the front desk to call Werner. His response was that I should come up to his room. I knocked on the door, he opened it and we fell into each other's arms. We exchanged kisses with great tenderness and passion, and then sat down to talk. Werner said his wife had passed away the previous year. She was only thirty-eight when she died of cancer. "Now I am free and you are married, Brigitte!"

I tried to explain about my marriage to Werner. "I never felt with Jeno what I feel with you, Werner!"

Werner acknowledged, "I know, Brigitte, it has always been the same for me." Four years had passed and we both were feeling the same love for each other. Then Werner continued, "But Jeno is a good man. Monte Carlo is a beautiful and warm place, perfect for you!"

I understood that Werner had no intention of taking me with him. "You know, Werner, that Jeno has the same religious beliefs as you?"

"Yes, I know, Brigitte. Now, how long would you like me to stay?"

"I would like you to stay forever, but I see that it is not what you desire. I don't want to reopen all of my old wounds and then you leave me here! If you really love me, then leave as soon as possible!"

Werner took me in his arms and lamented, "Yes, Brigitte. I understand."

When I saw Jeno later, he commented that I did not look very happy. I didn't respond. That evening, when Werner came to the club, he invited Jeno and me to lunch the following day. Jeno was pleased and invited Werner to an early dinner at our place. Jeno was a great cook and the conversation was light. After dinner, Werner told us that he would be leaving the next day. I felt sad but knew it was better this way. Jeno commented to me that, "Maybe Werner does not love you deeply enough." I thought he might be right. After Werner left, I put all of my energy again into the club. I did the bookkeeping, ordered all of the supplies and everything else that needed to be done. I worked as hard as I could, to forget.

CHAPTER 8

The Gipsy Club II

1965

RED CROSS GALA

Jeno and I made a new friend, Rene. He told us that he was once Secretary to King Faisal of Iraq. When the government was overthrown, they had fled through the desert; he went one way and the King went the other. Rene invited us to his elegant flat and displayed for us the precious jewelry that he had saved for the King. What a story! It was wonderful to have such an interesting new friend. Rene also told us that he often went to Switzerland to visit his daughter who was very ill with a lung disease. She had to remain in a private clinic there. One night he asked Jeno if he could invite me to the Red Cross Gala at the Sporting d'Ete. We attended with another couple, Rene's friends, and we four enjoyed the spectacular event and superb dinner.

DRIVING PRINCESS GRACE'S CAR

Rene, who was a friend of Princess Grace de Monaco, told Jeno one night that he had a big surprise for the two of us. Princess Grace wanted to sell her car, a German model Borgward Isabella. Jeno was excited about the car, but I was less so. I had obtained a license to drive in Berlin, but it had been years ago, and Jeno had no interest in driving. I was going to have to do all of the chauffeuring. The next day, Rene brought the car around and Jeno paid for it on the spot. Once we closed the club in the wee hours of the morning, I had the road all to myself and could practice to my heart's content.

Every morning, Jeno would direct me, and I would practice a little more. Parking in front of our apartment was a true challenge, but I soon mastered the art of driving again. Eventually my confidence grew and I began to drive during the day in traffic. The first time that I drove in daylight hours, the police stopped traffic for me. They recognized the car as belonging to Princess Grace! The second time I drove in the day, the police stopped me and asked me to get new plates. The original diplomat plates were still on the car. After I received the new ones, I was more comfortable driving around and traveled longer and longer distances.

One day, Jeno wanted to visit Nice. I was apprehensive, because the road, Moyenne Corniche, was considered a dangerous road. It was up in the mountains and had many switchbacks. I was afraid to drive on it, and would rather have gone by train. But I drove it that day, and made it back in time to open the Gipsy Club. That night, as Jeno and I were getting ready to go to the club, I told Jeno that I had a feeling that Trevor, the gentleman from England, would be coming to the club that night. Sure enough, after a couple of hours, Mr. Trevor entered the club and told us that he was thinking all day of us and the club. I related that I too had had the feeling that he would come this night. I had begun to look deep inside myself to see if I could predict who would come to the club each evening. Most of the time, I was right. My intuition was improving. Sometimes I could tell the correct birthdays of our guests. It reminded me of when I was a child living with my mother and was left alone. I would think intensely of a particular person to see if I could make events occur or people visit.

1966

NEW YEAR'S EVE

The Gipsy Club was packed, champagne and Vodka were flowing. Music was filling the air, and people were singing and dancing. Jeno took my shoe and drank champagne from it. Serge took my other shoe and drank from it. Then the Russians began to throw their glasses on the floor after toasting. Everyone followed suit, dancing on the crushed and broken glass. It was a fantastic celebration. Needless to say, the next day there was not one glass left in the club. It took us two days to put everything back in order, but it was worth it. Those were all of my friends. Sometimes, I wished that I could be a guest of the Gipsy Club rather than an owner. What fun that would have been!

DARK CLOUDS HANG OVER THE GIPSY CLUB

Monte Carlo continued to change. Busses with tourists wearing colorful shirts and carrying cameras were arriving all of the time. More condominiums were being built. Slowly, the *Elite* disappeared. Some went to new playgrounds, like Portofino. Others preferred to hold private parties in their luxurious villas in Cap d'Ail, Cap Martin and Cap Ferrat. It was hurting the Gipsy Club, and the ambiance was changing. Some of our regulars continued to come, but it was not enough on a daily basis. It was expensive to keep the club open every day and to maintain the high standards our clientele had become accustomed to. The group of Monegasque, *locals*, only came in once a week. Even they changed, becoming more forward and feisty, often demanding that I dance with them. I did not want to dance with just anyone, I preferred to keep my distance and be respected. Most of the men were married and some approached me inappropriately.

One in particular, Emil, was a local finance minister about forty years old and single. He told me that he was madly in love with me. I kept my distance since I knew he was an out-of-control alcoholic. I was polite with him while being careful I was not sending him the wrong signals. That was not enough. My disinterest seemed only to inspire more aggressive behavior from him. The more I stayed away, the more he pressed me to stay near. One night, when Jeno and I went to open up the club, there was Emil, barricading the door with a huge bunch of roses. He was completely drunk, kneeling in front of me on the street at the entrance to the club, and begging me to marry him. Jeno stood behind me and said nothing. I pulled Emil to his feet and shook him, telling him, "You know full well that I am married and have no interest in you. I don't want you to come here to the club anymore!" The other Monegasques appeared out of nowhere and grabbed seats outside at the Tiptop. They did not want to miss this show! I called for them to take their friend home, and off they went with him. A few days later, I heard that someone had checked Emil into a clinic to "dry out". I was relieved that not only would he be indisposed now and unable to bother me at the club, but also that he would be getting some help.

After the New Year's Eve party, the following weeks were quiet. The Maharajah had not returned, although I had received several beautiful hand painted cards from him. Business was so slow, we had to dive into our savings to prop it up. Jeno changed too. He was becoming increasingly paranoid. Leslie and I always enjoyed working together. We had pet names for familiar clients, and would say them to each other, giggling, when they entered the club. Jeno had always been right there when this was happening. But now he was reacting negatively. At closing time, he would grumble to me that I was laughing and talking about him too. I was flabbergasted, "What do you mean, Jeno?" I asked.

"You and Leslie talk and laugh at me," he complained. I became angry with Jeno, unable to understand what he was talking about. When we arrived at home, Jeno climbed into the bed and was instantly asleep. But I was unable to find rest because the situation had me so upset. Worse yet, some of Jeno's acquaintants came from Paris, and they needed money, which Jeno gave to them. They proceeded to the casino where they promptly lost it. Then they asked for more. Jeno was playing the "big man" and gave them more and more money. We could not afford this! Every penny was needed to keep the club open. It was so bad that one day Jeno asked me to get my fur coat. We took it to the pawn shop for some cash. I was furious. It was wrong for him to give money to these people who were well and able to work for their money. Now, I called Jeno a Meshugginah and threatened to leave him if he didn't change this behavior. "If you must help these people, put them to work at the club, cleaning or something!"

Jeno was astonished and then he laughed, "So, you are right, Little Mommy."

From that day on, Jeno called me "Little Mommy". Since he could not say no, he would send the people to me and we would put them to work. One by one, they disappeared. Now Jeno became jealous of my attentions to Coco, my Cockatiel, and then was jealous of Leslie. Jeno knew that Leslie was not interested in women. Leslie was very discreet in his private live. On occasion we would see him walking with another gentleman, but we never discussed his sexual preferences. Still, Jeno was jealous of the friendship that Leslie and I had. The span of years between

Jeno, and Leslie and me made it difficult for Jeno to understand our young, light-hearted fun.

I was getting restless and ready to move on. At twenty-seven years, I was too young to be miserable. I worked hard, which I liked. But I would not accept the ridiculous, jealous accusations. Above all, I had been living without a love life for years. I had a passport, a driver's license and my car. All I needed now was a good plan. Spain sounded like an alternative. I just wanted to disappear as I did from Berlin. It became a waiting game. I was ready to go the next time Jeno grew angry with me. However, to my surprise, business at the Gipsy Club picked up and Jeno changed his attitude, becoming more agreeable again.

We now had new clients; people from England, France, Italy, Germany and America were now coming in. They were mostly business men, who would come to Monte Carlo after completing their business dealings. A very good looking business man from America came in one night. He had gone to a cabaret and enjoyed his meal, but it was upsetting his stomach. So he went for a walk and found the Gipsy Club. He heard the most amazing violin music from outside and came in to enjoy more. He spoke with Leslie all in English and asked him to translate his story to me. He drank whisky and I enjoyed his conversation which was translated through Leslie. He related that he had come directly from Paris, but home was in New Jersey, where he owned a small factory. It was his first time in Monte Carlo and he loved it! This business man returned every night.

Leslie and I nicknamed him "The Ship". He would lean against the bar and move his upper body around like a ship on water with waves rolling about. His name was Basil. At the end of the week, he came in with a couple, and they asked if I might come to sit at the table with them. I was pleased and the champagne was flowing again. His friends were leaving, but Basil was staying on in Monte Carlo. He told me that he had planned to leave the next day, but did not want to go. We exchanged a few more pleasantries and then Basil asked Leslie for a Gipsy Club business card. He left with a smile.

The same week, another gentleman visited the club. Leslie and I had a lively conversation with him. He returned next evening and, without saying a word, he gave Leslie a diamond ring and offered me a golden bracelet set with ten 1945 Mexican dos pesos coins. Before we could say anything, the gentleman ran quickly out of the club. Leslie and I pursued him, but when we reached the street, he had disappeared. We did not know what to think. We had not even been given an opportunity to express our gratitude.

A NEW GENTLEMAN ENLIGHTENED MY LIFE: BASIL

One evening I received a phone call from the states. It was Basil. We spoke for a while, and then he said he would try to come back to see me as soon as possible. I was pleased and curious. I put my plan to escape to Spain on hold. Two weeks later, Basil called again and told me that he would call me once every two weeks until he could visit again. Naturally, Jeno knew about the phone calls, since he was there when they came in. Also, I told Jeno what was going on, just as I would tell a friend. I thought it was interesting that Jeno was jealous of my friendship with Leslie and Coco, but not Basil.

After three months of communicating by telephone, Basil came back. He was so glad to be back that he talked and talked to me. He told me that he had been divorced since 1959, that he had two daughters, one was eleven and one thirteen. The girls lived with their mother and he would see them every other week. He talked so fast that I had to ask him to slow down, as my English was still not very good. I couldn't keep up with him. We danced and enjoyed the champagne. Basil promised to return every night when we opened at 10:00. I was impressed; he was such a charming man. He had wavy hair that was predominantly gray. He had blue eyes and was, all in all, a good looking man. Basil was definitely a man of strong character. I admired his perseverance and was attracted to him for his gallant manners. Basil was staying in the Hotel de Paris. For one week, he came to the club every night. We had one or two bottles of champagne, and then before midnight, he left to return to his hotel room.

One evening, Basil came in visibly upset. He asked me in a stern voice if we could talk. After we were seated, Basil said, "I just spoke with Louis Frosio, the violinist and orchestra leader from the Hotel de Paris. I told him that I am in love with a beautiful blonde lady from the Gipsy Club. Louis looked at me and said, 'You have no chance with her. She goes with no one and is very well respected. Besides, she is married!'"

Basil looked at me and asked, "Is that true? Are you married?"

I answered, "Yes, of course! Don't you see my wedding ring?"

Basil admitted that he had never looked at my hands, he had only admired my legs. I had to laugh, but Basil did not think it was amusing. He had tears in his eyes as he asked me, "Which one is your husband?"

I told him that he would have to guess.

"Is it Leslie?"

"No."

His eyes moved around the room, guessing each of the musicians, and hearing always the same answer. Finally, he asked, "It is not the little man with the cigar, is it?"

"Yes!"

Basil could not believe it. I pointed out that he had never asked me anything about myself. Basil sat there quietly and considered. I was wondering how to handle the situation, and was moved by his apparent sadness. I didn't know that he was seriously courting me. Finally, I told Basil, "We are married, but we don't live like a married couple together. We are more like friends and business partners. It's a long story, but that is the truth. I never discuss our situation with anyone."

Basil's face lit up. "Will you introduce me to your husband?"

I made the introductions and the two men had a good conversation. It was easier for Jeno to speak with Basil because he was more fluent in English than I. I excused myself and went straight to the bar, where I asked Leslie to pour me a nice glass of vodka. I needed it to calm my nerves.

Unfortunately that didn't work, so I had another. Then I returned to the table where the two men were still sitting. They smiled at me and Jeno excused himself. Basil seemed more relaxed and ordered some champagne. It must have been a good conversation. Before leaving the club, Basil approached Jeno and told him that he wanted to invite the two of us to lunch. Jeno said that he had things to do, but that I was free to show him around. I was excited and pleased that Jeno was open to the idea of me spending time with Basil. Jeno suggested that we drive further out of Monte Carlo and discover one of the beautiful restaurants that are in the mountains. I understood that Jeno wanted us to be discreet and away from the prying eyes of Monte Carlo.

It was very enjoyable being with Basil, who was pleasantly amorous. It was obvious that when he wanted something, he pursued it in his own charming way. I was beginning to fall in love with him. It was not the all-consuming love that I had felt for Werner; but it was a stable, soothing, secure kind of feeling, mixed with some excitement. Basil stayed for two weeks and two days. On our last day together, I took Basil to my favorite place, the Cap Estel, which was located between Nice and Monte Carlo. The setting was gorgeous and the cuisine was exquisite. Basil fell in love with the location and establishment immediately. He reserved a room for when he planned to return in one month.

After leaving Monte Carlo, Basil went to Paris France and to Munich Germany. There he participated in an electronics exhibition. I felt lonely and would talk to Coco constantly. But thinking of Basil kept my spirits up. He sent me a letter and red roses every week, first from Paris and then from Munich. One month went by and Basil returned, staying in Cap Estel. I couldn't wait to see him. I drove my car to the hotel, and we fell into each other's arms and kissed. It was a warm welcome. Then Basil drove us in his rental car on a sightseeing tour, exploring the famous Cote d'Azur. We stopped at the charming small fishing village, Villefranche, and had a wonderful lunch at a seafood restaurant. Basil marveled at the fresh tasty seafood. Then he said, "Let us take to road to visit Eze Village. I've heard it is very picturesque.

"It is on the road Moyenne Corniche," I told Basil. I was very glad that I would not be the one driving, because Basil was adventurous and loved driving. From the medieval town of Eze, we had a magnificent panoramic view of the French Riviera. Later on, we had a superb early dinner at the Chateau de la Chevre d'Or Hotel in Eze Village. Then we returned to Basil's hotel in the beautiful du Cap Estel. It was a romantic spot with his own beach and lovely gardens, located on the Basse Corniche. It was late, and I had to hurry to return to Monte Carlo in time to open the club. Quickly I went to my car and told Basil, "If you are too tired, Basil, you do not have to come tonight to the club. I will see you tomorrow for another excursion." It was only a twenty minute drive from Cap Estel.

As was his custom, Basil came to the club around 10:30 and left before midnight. We had a wonderful week together, getting to know, appreciate and respect each other. Basil then had to return to the states to look after his factory in New Jersey.

The Gipsy Club was not the same any more. Basil had brought sunshine into my heart, but now the dark clouds were building up again with full force over Jeno and me, and the Gipsy Club. Our faithful clients would visit when they came to Monte Carlo, but it was not enough. We did not make much money. The Monegasques group came one evening and brought Emil back. He seemed sober, but was unfriendly. I kept my distance. When he approached me, he asked, "Will you go out with me now?"

I quietly answered, "No Emil."

He turned red and demanded that I bring him the company books. "I want to see your bookkeeping!" Emil was the local Finance Minister. Although the club has been open for years, no one had ever requested to see the books before.

I went to speak with Jeno and told him of the request. He became agitated when I said, "I know what Emil will do. He will find some fault with how I have kept our books and he will make us pay. I'm sure I have made mistakes, and he will find them!" I had a bad feeling about how this was going to end.

Jeno was nervously puffing on his cigar. "That is probably true, Brigitte."

The following day, I went to Emil's office with the book. He greeted me coldly and told me just to leave the books with him. A couple of days later, we had to pay a large sum of money. I was ready to leave, but I would not just walk out on Jeno.

Basil was writing now in French. He must have taken a course to learn how to communicate better with me. Between letters and flowers, Basil also called me sometimes at the club. These exchanges served to keep my spirits up enough for me to persevere in my life and work.

It was the beginning of September 1966 when Lucien, the property owner from whom we leased the club, informed us that when our lease expired on November 30th, he did not want to renew it. He had other ideas for the property. Jeno and I looked at each other, both feeling lost and sad. Jeno said, "Now that the property has the good name back because of the Gipsy Club, Lucien can ask a much higher rent from another renter."

"You're right, Jeno. But maybe it is time that we move on, since lately our business has gone down. Maybe it is a good sign." Jeno and I looked for some other place to take over. We found a snack bar location that would be available on the 1st of January 1967. We agreed to rent it, but had no idea what we would do with it.

When Basil called one evening at the club, I just told him that I was sorry, but that I would not have much time to answer his letters. I must have sounded sad, because Basil promised he would come at the end of September. I was relieved. It was close to the end of September when I received a surprise phone call from Basil, he had just arrived at Cap Estel. My heart beat faster and my low spirits rose again. I was delighted when he asked me if he could pick me up for lunch the next day. After a warm greeting, Basil drove us to Cap Estel where we enjoyed a delicious lunch, complete with champagne. Afterwards, we rested in the garden chairs. I admired the lovely garden with its wonderful peacocks and birds. After a while, Basil said, "You look happy to see me, but I see something else in your eyes. Tell me what is going on."

After I finished relating the latest events, Basil's eyes lit up and he smiled. I looked at him crossly and asked him, "Are you mocking me?"

"No, Brigitte! But now I will tell you what I have planned. I want you to come with me to the states and be my wife."

My mouth dropped in disbelief. "But, Basil, you know that I am married. And we do not know each other very well. I am honored, but I will not leave Jeno alone. He needs me now and I cannot let him down. I have wanted to leave many times, when Jeno was established. But now he has nothing! He helped me through a very difficult time, and I am grateful to him for this."

"Brigitte," Basil replied, "I admire your honesty and faithfulness. But you are so young and full of life. I think all of those years you gave to the Gipsy Club should count for something. Tonight, I will ask Jeno to dine with me later this week."

"Oh no," I protested. "He will never accept the invitation."

"We will see. I would like to take the two of you to the picturesque Hacienda, which is nestled between the hills of Menton. I know you will like the area," assured Basil.

The evening came and Basil walked into the club. He requested Jeno to visit with him at his table. I headed to the bar to fortify myself with vodka. When I walked back to Basil's table, Jeno had left and Basil had a big smile on his face. "It is confirmed. Tomorrow night, the three of us will go to the Hacienda for dinner!"

The next evening, the owner of the Hacienda, Jean Claude, greeted us and escorted us to a lovely table by an open fireplace. The Hacienda had four fireplaces where meats were roasted over the open flames. Jean Claude had his own farm, so all produce was fresh from the garden. The wine was brought straight from the barrel. After our wine was served, we ordered lamb shanks. In spite of being nervous about this dinner, I kept a calm demeanor.

Jeno turned to me abruptly and said, "It takes a while for the dinner to be ready. I want you to go to the ladies' room and then maybe outside to talk with the birds. I would like a word in private with Basil."

I turned red at this unexpected request. I feared that he was going to chase Basil away. I had never before seen Jeno take the initiative. I left the table and walked outside to the birds' cage. I spoke to them as I had before. Laurie, my favorite love bird, came right up to me, showing her brilliant red feathers, desiring for me to caress her head. I didn't know when I should go back to the table. At one point, I peeked in the door and saw that Jeno was still talking, while Basil listened attentively. After twenty minutes, I told my heart to calm down and walked serenely back to the table, my head held high. My timing must have been good, because when I arrived, both of the men were smiling. In spite of being nervous and agitated, I was able to compose myself and to make light conversation with the two men.

The meal was excellent. First a rolling tray came by with fresh vegetables and cheeses. Then the main course arrived and then another selection of cheeses. There was an incredible decanter of liqueur that was brought to the table. The decanter, which had been made of olive wood, was so elegant. On the way back to Monte Carlo, there was very little conversation.

Finally, alone with Jeno, I asked him, "What was said when I left our table?" But Jeno would not tell me.

He just said, "You will find out tomorrow. It is Basil who will tell you then."

The next day, Basil picked me up to for lunch at Cap Estel. I was dying of curiosity. "Jeno did not tell me what he said to you!"

It wasn't until later that Basil responded, when we came to our table. "Brigitte, please sit down and have a glass of champagne with me." Then Basil acknowledged that he had felt very uncomfortable when Jeno spoke to him. "I felt like a school boy, looking for a crack in the floor in which to disappear!"

Basil then related their conversation to me. "Jeno said this to me, *'You think I don't know what is going on between you and Brigitte? I let it happen because I love her, she is my queen. I want the best for her. There have been many admirers, but she is very taken with you and I have the least objection to you. Brigitte is young and she deserves better than I can give her. My life is almost over, and I don't need anything, just my cigar. But Brigitte has her life in front of her. I want to see her in good hands.'"*

Basil told me that he had tears in his eyes, he couldn't talk. So he reached out for Jeno's hand and shook it. Basil acknowledged, "Jeno is a great man with a good heart."

"I agree with you, Basil. However, Jeno has been behaving strangely lately." I related Jeno's unfounded jealousies. "But he doesn't seem to be jealous of you," I pointed out. This conversation continued until late afternoon.

Then Basil took me into his arms, "I want you to be my wife," he told me gently but firmly.

"Oh, Basil. That is not so simple. First I have to be divorced. Here in France, only the husband may ask for divorce. Secondly, I really don't want to jump from one marriage into another. I want to get to know you better. And thirdly, you must come to know me better. Then we will know if the marriage will work."

"You are very wise, Brigitte and I have respect for you and your wishes," Basil said.

Thank you, Basil. We have much to think about. I must now talk to Jeno, which won't be easy. I have to catch the right moment."

Basil agreed, "And please be sure to mention to him that I want to take you on trips away from Monte Carlo, so that we can get to know each other outside of this environment. This time, I will cut my trip short so that I can get enough work done to be able to return here in January."

"That would be wonderful, Basil!" I spent the night considering the situation, and realized that I wanted to leave Jeno amicably, and to leave knowing he was set up in a new successful business. Since the Gipsy Club was closing on the 1st of December, and the new business was opening on the 1st of January, 1967, this was a very good time to set things up together for the future. I was thinking that maybe Jeno and I should keep the new business as a snack bar. The snack bar was going to be a more manageable business venture and Jeno should be able to run it by himself, with help from Leslie and one of the staff from the Gipsy Club. Although this new business would not be fueled by passion, it should provide a very good living for Jeno. The time it would take to get things setup and running, would allow me slowly to prepare Jeno to grow used to the idea of my future plans, and help him adjust to life without me.

Next morning, I suggested to Jeno that we should open the new business as a snack bar. "I know, Jeno, it is a big change from working at night to day work. But Monte Carlo has changed, we have to adapt."

Jeno looked at me with sad eyes. "Whatever you decide, Little Mommy, is okay with me."

Before Basil left, Jeno invited him to our apartment for a good Hungarian meal. To my surprise, Coco was not happy about Basil's visit. He went into the corner of his cage, puffed up his feathers and brooded. He wanted nothing to do with Basil.

With only one month before the closing of the Gipsy Club, we began to tell our clients; they were not happy about it. One night a group of Monegasques came in accompanied by the Prime Minister of Monaco. He seemed to enjoy himself and drank quite a lot. A couple of days later he came alone and was very aggressive towards me. He brought back memories of Lotzie, with his reddish balding hair, blue eyes and very white skin with freckles. When he asked me to join him for a drink, which I declined. He asked Jeno to drink with him and Leslie, and complained to Jeno that I would not drink with him. Jeno suggested to him that perhaps Brigitte was not feeling well. The minister asked me directly if that were true, and I replied, "Yes." The prime minister left and we all breathed a sigh of relief. I did not have a good feeling about that man.

The following week, the Prime Minister returned to the club, already tipsy. Again, he asked me to have a drink with him. Although I did not want to, I took a small glass of vodka. I didn't want to give him any reason to cause a scandal. But trouble came anyhow. He asked me to go out to lunch with him the next day. I explained that I was married and I did not go out with customers. I pointed out that he too was married. His face turned red and he informed me, "If I invite you for lunch, you should be honored!"

I thanked him, but told him that the answer was still no. He was furious and left the club. Jeno was worried. Although he was pretty sure that the Prime Minister had not seen me with the Maharajah or Basil, he wondered if Emil maybe had told him about me; and that now he wanted to discover how far he could get with me. I was worried too that he could make trouble for Jeno. Monte Carlo had been Jeno's home for many years now. If I would go for lunch with the Prime Minister, his wife would find out and it might make the newspapers. We definitely could not have a scandal.

I told Jeno about my feelings for Basil; that he wanted to marry me. I also gently said to him that I wanted a friendly parting. Jeno only replied, "We will see."

The situation with the Minister grew worse. He telephoned the club one night, and in a strident tone, demanded to see me. Calmly, I spoke with him and said that we would soon be closing the Gipsy Club. I would then have a quiet private life. He seemed surprised by that and did not have much more to say.

THE GIPSY CLUB CLOSES

The first of December came, and we closed the Gipsy Club. It had been educational to meet so many different people and to learn about them all; from aristocracy to criminals. I was happy to have had the opportunity to live in that privileged world of glamour and high society. I had enjoyed and was deeply moved by the gay and melancholy music, as played by the gypsy musicians. I was also sad, knowing it was time to move on.

CHAPTER 9

Back to Coffee

1967

1ˢᵀ OF JANUARY SNACK BAR OPENS

We opened up the snack bar after much cleaning and many repairs. It was a wholly different lifestyle; back to coffee, which we served in the afternoon with snacks, cheese sandwiches, ham and cheese sandwiches, and an assortment of sweets with tea. We also had a liquor license. So we had gone from champagne and vodka in the evening to tea and espresso in the afternoons. What a change!

I received a letter from Basil informing me that he would be arriving the 20th of January. I was thrilled. Three months had passed since I had seen him. Jeno was not so enthusiastic. I reminded him, "I promised to help you get established here in the new business, and I will never break a promise. But you also know that I am ready to move on."

Jeno said, "Yes, I know," and he gave me a little smile.

I had a surprise for Basil. I had called Cap Estel to discover what time he was expected to arrive on the 20th. I drove to Cap Estel and awaited his arrival. When he saw me, he was so excited that he could barely speak. He was overwhelmed and, with tears in his eyes, he took me in his arms. It was a wonderful feeling both of us shared.

Over a bottle of champagne and a delicious meal, I told Basil the story of the Finance Minister, who charged us all kinds of fines; and the Prime Minister, who tried to put obstacles in Jeno's way. I confided to Basil, "I think that all of the bad things happened at once for a reason."

Basil smiled and said, "That fits right into my plan, because I would like to invite you to join me on a trip to Italy for three weeks. We will fly to Rome and Venice."

"Oh how romantic!" I exclaimed.

"It's about time that I have you all to myself, Brigitte," he told me.

I blushed, and Basil kissed me. "In three days we will leave. Tell Jeno that it is better like this. No one from here will see us."

I thought it a good plan and hoped that Jeno would agree. I explained it to Jeno. After some thinking he approved, and that he was relieved that nobody would see Basil and me together.

Venice was the first stop for Basil and me. We stayed at the Gritti Palace in a charming, romantic suite. Basil couldn't wait to take me in his arms and undress and make love to me. "We have to make up for lost time," he whispered in my ear, before loving me again. Later, we took a gondola through the Grand Canal in Venice, admired historical palaces and visited different places every day.

One day, we went to Murano where there was a well-known glass factory. Basil purchased for me a lovely set of glass candlestick holders. After Venice, we traveled to Rome and stayed at the Cavalieri Hilton. It was breathtaking! Between loving each other and sightseeing, we savored the tasty Italian cuisine and enjoyed a great selection of wine. What a wonderful life it was! Basil stayed for three more days in Monte Carlo, and promised before departing that he would return in April. We would visit more exotic places.

I was delighted, and Jeno could see how happy Basil made me. Knowing that it would take months to process, I asked Jeno to begin the proceedings for our divorce. After hesitating, he agreed to start the paperwork, "I am only doing this because you are so young and should be enjoying a good life."

Days and weeks passed without incident. Our Hungarian friends visited the Snack Bar, choosing to meet there rather than at the Café de Paris. Then the conversation would move into high gear as usual. I was waiting impatiently, counting the days until Basil would return. He wrote often and I answered each letter. He was now quite skillful at communicating in French!

In the middle of April, Basil arrived. I drove to Cap Estel, as before, to meet him. We explored Rome and walked up the Spanish Steps, visiting the Church of the Holy Trinity. On a side trip, we visited the world famous Fountain at Villa de Este.

Then, we flew to Lebanon. I had always wanted to travel there. We landed in Beirut and checked into the Hotel Phoenicia. It is a fascinating country, rich in history, with incredible scenery. The people were extremely hospitable and we had no problems with the language, as many people spoke French and English in addition to Arabic. Most people were Muslim, but there was the occasional church.

Basil and I were adventurous and tried all kinds of food. We had the same approach to travel, wanting to experience the culture and the local food and customs. We went to a traditional Lebanese restaurant and ordered all of the standards, mezzeh, local hor d'oeuvres and arak for our drink. For our first meal, the mezzeh just kept coming, and we sampled them all. We didn't know that we should just take a few from the many choices. We tried everything. It was a feast. But when the main course was served, we looked at each other, embarrassed. Needless to say, we could not eat one bite more. The owner of the restaurant came to our table and asked us if there was something wrong with the food. Basil apologized and told him that we had enjoyed the mezzeh too much, and that we could not possibly eat any more of the meal. Basil assured the owner that we would return the next day and order only the main course. Smiling, the owner sent us small cups of strong Arabic coffee.

Every day we went sightseeing. We didn't hire a guide, instead Basil rented a car and we would buy road maps. I admired Basil's spirit of adventure. We traveled to Baalbek and took many photographs, sitting beneath the six remaining Corinthian columns of the Temple of Jupiter. We stopped at Byblos, a very enjoyable destination, and then Tripoli, which was like going back through history. We visited ancient mosques and Turkish baths, built by sultans in the 14th and 15th centuries. From there, we arrived at the famous Cedars of Lebanon. My head was spinning so much, it was difficult to take it all in.

Back at the hotel, we rested and talked about the exciting sights. Basil told me to look at the map, because we would be driving to Damascus Syria. After breakfast the next day, we left the hotel and followed the road to Damascus. We turned the radio on and enjoyed the local music, which sounded very exotic to us. After leaving Beirut, we passed through small villages, then came the desert.

After some time driving, seeing only sand dunes on both sides of the road, I got excited. "Basil! Basil, Stop! I see a camel's head sticking out of the dunes. Please, let's take some photographs!" We walked through the sand and as we came closer, we saw that the camel was standing in front of a circle of beautiful columns. This is all that was left of a great building. As Basil wanted to take pictures of the camel and me, the owner of the camel approached. He asked me if I would like to sit on the camel.

"Of course!" I exclaimed. But first I needed to be in the appropriate clothing, advised the young man. We followed him with great curiosity. We traversed another sand dune and were astonished to find many tents. We both understood now that we were fortunate to have met the Bedouins. This young man we had followed, entered a tent and came out with some scarves for me. He wrapped them over my clothes and then placed me gently up onto the camel. He was guiding the camel around for Basil to get photographs. Then he helped me down and invited us into his tent.

Our host busied himself with making coffee. Several people walked into the tent and sat down on a cushion, bringing a variety of different musical instruments, ones I was not at all familiar with. The sounds they made were wonderfully exotic and mysterious. I was in heaven. Our host told us he was purchasing carpets from the Bedouins and would then take them to Berlin Germany. From there they would be sent to other countries. I was impressed by our handsome host, because apart from his own language, he spoke to me in perfect German and to Basil in English. We all then conversed in French. Everything was fascinating to me.

The coffee was wonderful. Our host told us that he had put rose petals into our beverages. Hours passed and more people arrived with their instruments and some sweets to share. I told Basil that I would like to purchase the small rug that hung on the tent wall. It displayed a picture of a camel, palm trees and a man praying. Basil agreed that it was a nice rug. All that time we drank more and more little cups of the wonderfully flavored coffee. We left the tent laughing, and I said to Basil, "I think the coffee intoxicated us with laughter and gaiety."

"Yes, Brigitte, you are right. I too feel very relaxed." Basil agreed.

After a while, I remembered the rug. Basil said, "Oh well, if the Bedouin had wanted to sell it, he would have remembered."

We were still laughing when we arrived in Damascus. The route took us right into a busy marketplace. It was impossible to go anywhere with the car. There were cars, trucks, goats, camels and people, all crowded together. Since we were truly stuck, we left the car where it was and asked a policeman where to go to get something to eat. He showed us the way to a little restaurant. We thanked him and told him we'd retrieve the car later. He said not to worry about it. In the meantime, we had a delicious meal of mutton kebabs grilled over charcoal on skewers. Later we found our car, in the same spot, but were too tired to do anymore sightseeing. So we worked our way out of Damascus and drove back to Beirut.

We did one more side trip to the town of Sidon, a beautiful place from Phoenician times. Sidon had been the richest seaport in the world. Our last night we went to a nightclub and enjoyed the belly dancing performance. We returned to the hotel and I thanked Basil for the wonderful trip. Basil kissed me sweetly and I just melted in his arms. Next morning, Basil said, "I want you to come to America as soon as possible." I told him I had already begun the divorce process; and Basil was satisfied. We returned to Monte Carlo to good news. Jeno had actually made a little money the previous month. The Grand Prix Auto Rally had been good for business. The snack bar was well situated along the course. Basil left in good spirits and I felt good too. We had a strong bond between us.

One lovely day, Jeno suggested that we drive to Nice to have lunch. I said, "Okay, but remember Jeno, that I am always afraid to drive the Moyenne Corniche through the dangerous curves." Jeno replied that he was not worried, as he had confidence in my driving skills. It was a beautiful day and there wasn't much traffic. As we drove down the hill into Nice, I tried to slow down, pressing on the brakes. To my shock, there was no response. The brakes were not working! I stamped on the brake pedal as I cried out to Jeno that the brakes were not working. The traffic light at the bottom of the hill turned from green to red. People began to cross the street in front of us. I broke into a sweat, slammed my hand onto the horn and just kept honking while I desperately shifted the car into parking gear. The pedestrians looked up and moved quickly back out of the way. Luckily, everyone made it to safety. Jeno and I were relieved when I steered into a parking space as we finally rolled to a stop. I sat there in silence, still shaking. Jeno jumped out of the car and stomped around, sucking on his cigar and cursing in Hungarian. The police came and took us to the best mechanic in Nice. We had the car towed to his workshop. The mechanic told us to call back in a couple of days. I did not ever want to get into that car again.

Ten days later, we picked the car up in Nice. The mechanic informed us that they had fixed the brakes temporarily, but that I needed to take the car back to the factory in Germany to have the problem permanently resolved. Jeno decided,

"We have to drive to Germany." Jeno bought a map. Then I drove us home and he made arrangements for us to be gone for several days. I was incredulous. What if the brakes failed again? I didn't want to drive at all, much less with a car that was "temporarily fixed".

Two days later, very early in the morning, we began our journey. After six hours, I required a break, so we stopped for lunch. I stretched out on the grass next to the restaurant. My back was hurting and my clothes were soaking wet from perspiration. Thankfully, the roads were very well marked. But I was drained of energy due to my fear of another brake failure and having to maintain a high level of concentration. After a couple of hours of rest, I continued driving until we were almost at the German border. We stayed in a small hotel overnight. Then in the morning, we headed out. Now I had to deal with a heavy fog which covered the fields. The car's bright lights did nothing to help. I followed the rear lights of the truck in front of us. Jeno was in a panic, and my fear was such that I was not far from joining him.

Slowly the fog lifted and we were breathing sighs of relief. Before noon, we approached Munich. I told Jeno that I wanted to get rid of the car, first thing. Jeno agreed to that. At a gas station, we asked for directions to the car factory. When we arrived, the manager of the factory was very friendly and offered to buy the car back. I was relieved. A driver took us to a hotel where I could finally relax.

The next morning, I said to Jeno, "You know, Jeno. The manager from the factory was very eager to buy the Borgward Isabella back. I think he knew that the brakes had a manufacturing defect."

"You're probably right, Brigitte," Jeno responded. "We are very lucky to be alive. I was thinking of the Princess Grace. Something could have happened to her if she had kept the car."

Another troubling thing happened around this time. For weeks, Jeno had been complaining that he couldn't smell anything. He went to a physician who specialized in ears, nose and throat issues. Either the doctor could find nothing wrong with him, or Jeno was keeping the diagnosis to himself. He told me nothing, so I was left in doubt concerning his health.

I wrote to Basil relating to him everything that had happened. Basil called me right away and wanted to return to Monte Carlo immediately. I calmed him down, telling him that everything was fine now. A couple of weeks later, Basil came anyway, just for a week, to see me. After that, he went directly to Paris for business and then back to the states. He promised to return in September.

Business at the snack bar was slow. I let Jeno and Leslie take over, spending most of my time in the apartment, cleaning. Then I would play with Coco. In the evenings, I would go to the Snack Bar and help out a little, but I was hoping that Jeno and Leslie would get used to doing all of the work themselves.

In the beginning of September, Basil arrived. It was a marvelous feeling to be in his arms again. We traveled again to Italy and visited Milano and Capri. In Milano, we wanted to go to La Scala, but it was not the opera season. Basil said, "You know, that means we will have to return when La Scala is open."

"Oh yes, Basil. That would be wonderful!"

We visited the famous cathedral, admired "The Last Supper" by Leonardo Da Vinci and then took our time to enjoy each other. Capri was very busy at this time, filled with fashion designers attending an international convention. Basil looked for a little private beach, so we could enjoy the sun and water. But the beaches were also filled with the eccentric designers. It was time to go home.

Jeno invited Basil for a lovely lunch in our apartment. Basil asked Jeno to relate to him all about the dramatic trip to Munich. When Jeno had told the story of our trip, I finished it by stating that I never wanted to drive again. Basil's only comment was, "We shall see!" Then Basil wanted to play with Coco, but Coco had other plans. He would have nothing to do with Basil, as if he understood my affection for Basil and was jealous.

Basil stayed for three more days, visiting me at the Snack Bar every evening. In the day time, Basil and I had wonderfully intimate and long lunches at the Cap Estel. Later in the afternoons, he took me back to the apartment. On our last day together, Basil told me he would see me later at the Snack Bar. He wanted to bid farewell to Jeno and Leslie. Then he would spend the rest of the afternoon going over paperwork and finish with a nice hot bath. It was close to 7:00 when the doorbell rang. The loud sound drifted through the quiet room, startling me. I jerked up and wondered who it could be. I opened the door and was stunned to find Werner. I could not move or speak. He had a smile on his face, and asked me if he could come in. I stumbled backwards and he reached out to take me in his arms.

In a shaky voice, I said, "No. Don't touch me!" My blood was boiling and I became angry. "I did not hear from you for over a year and all of a sudden you are here?" I was by then fuming. "Sit down," I demanded. "I have something to tell you." I proceeded to pour two cognacs and handed one to him. "Well, Werner, you are too late. I have met a man I adore, and I'm about to leave with him for the states. This time I am moving forward. There is nothing you can say to me." Werner looked stunned. He watched me silently, with sad eyes, as I poured two more cognacs which, without hesitation, we both tipped, bottoms up, and drank. I needed to leave for the Snack Bar, and told Werner I must go.

He offered to drive me there, saying, "I want to come meet the new man in your life."

"No, no. Please do not come, Werner." I showed him the door and he left without another word. I was angry because I felt the same old desire rushing throughout my body. I tried to think what to do. I called Jeno and told him that Werner might visit the Snack Bar. "Think fast, Jeno. What will we tell Basil? I don't want to lose Basil." I fretted.

Jeno asked me to calm down and he suggested that we tell Basil that Werner is my cousin from Berlin. "Don't worry, I will pull Werner aside and make him understand that he has to go along with this."

Nervously, I entered the Snack Bar. Then Basil came in and I sat down with him. He ordered some champagne and invited Jeno and Leslie to join us for a glass. Jeno sat facing the entrance. A couple of people came in and Leslie seated them and took their orders. Jeno suggested we open another bottle of champagne. My nerves began to settle. I was hoping that Werner would not come after all.

No such luck, the next customer to enter was Werner. Jeno sprang up and met him at the door. He spoke to Werner for a few minutes there. Then Jeno came over to the table and tapped me on the shoulder. "Look who is here, your cousin from Berlin! He brought a friend with him."

I rose and greeted them and introduced them to Basil. Werner's friend was a Rabbi, which I found very strange. Basil asked them to have a seat, and Jeno pulled a chair up next to me. There I was, sitting between my present husband and my future husband, with my ex-lover and a Rabbi rounding out the table. It was a most uncomfortable feeling. The palms of my hands were moist and my heart was beating fast. I was thankful that Werner and the Rabbi spoke only in German. Basil did not understand what they were saying, so I translated some banal story for him. Werner said that he and his friend were just passing through Monte Carlo. Tomorrow they would be visiting Nice and then Cannes.

I was relieved when, after a short while, the two left. Basil looked at me curiously and said, "You never told me about this cousin." I made a lame excuse about not seeing him very often. I could see that Basil was not entirely convinced by my explanation, but he let it pass. He must have been aware of the undercurrents in the room while Werner was there. Jeno and I moved the conversation away from Werner and his friend. The next morning, Basil left.

A couple of weeks later, the divorce came through, and Basil sent me an airplane ticket to New York. I was excited about beginning my new life, but was also sad about leaving. When I played with Coco, I cried. My sweet bird must have understood, because seven days before I left, he died.

Jeno accompanied me to the airport in Nice. He had tears in his eyes as he said, "Little Mommy, You know that if things don't work out, you can always come back. I hope that you will not forget me." I made a vow to Jeno that if he ever needed anything, I would help him. We promised to stay in contact. Then off I flew to my new life, my new love and a new land.

CHAPTER 10

America: A New World

In October of 1967, I arrived in America at JFK Airport in New York, and found a porter to help me with my suitcase. There were many people waiting for their loved ones outside the gate, but no Basil. My heart sank. As I waited and waited, I began to get scared, and soon I became very upset. Maybe Basil had changed his mind at the last minute. I didn't know what to think. The porter could see that I was confused, so he took me to the information desk. The lady there was very friendly and asked me if I was lost. In broken English, I told her that I was waiting for Basil Kassa. She made an announcement on the loud speaker, asking Mr. Basil Kassa to come to our location. Minutes passed and nothing happened. I was beginning to panic. "Here I am in New York; and what am I going to do now? So much for my dreams of the New World and a new life." Nothing was familiar; the language, the way people looked, how they interacted. Everyone was going about their own business, in their own way, on their own agenda. I began to think that perhaps I did not really belong here. I thought about asking the lady at the counter when the next flight to Nice was departing.

Just then, I heard my name called. As I turned around, I saw Basil running towards me. Oh, what a relief! Basil was breathless from running. His face was flushed with excitement. He apologized profusely, explaining that he had been waiting for me in the wrong terminal. He took me into his arms and then led me to another part of the airport. There was a small plane waiting for us. I was quite surprised. "Do you live very far from here?"

"Not so far," was his answer. We soon landed at a private airport in New Jersey where Basil had his car parked. Five minutes later, we arrived at his home. It was all lit up! My nervousness began to subside, but I felt suddenly exhausted. Basil opened the car door, lifted and carried me up the walkway to his house. He rang the doorbell! I wondered, why doesn't he just walk in?

The door opened wide. What I saw was shocking. People were standing everywhere, clapping, cheering and laughing. "Please Basil, let me down!" I pleaded. I struggled in his arms. As I freed myself from him, I asked, "Do all of these people live here?" I had thought he lived alone.

Basil answered, "These people are all of my friends. They have come to welcome you." Basil then proceeded to introduce me to all of the people, five couples in all. Much food had been prepared and even more conversation, all in English. I could only catch the occasional word. My head was spinning, I was exhausted; it was simply overwhelming.

Finally, everyone left. Basil escorted me to the bedroom. It was a fast love-making, after which Basil immediately fell asleep. As tired as I was, I lay awake all through the night. I would have much preferred an intimate quiet evening alone with Basil, a chance to cuddle and catch up. For me, this was a strange new world. After two more sleepless nights, I finally began to get some sleep. I told Basil that I wanted to know more about him, so we would take long walks together through the woods behind his home. Basil's house was shaped like the capital letter L. It was surrounded by a beautiful garden painted in fall colors with asters and chrysanthemums. Behind the house, there was a large outdoor fireplace made of natural stones with a grill of considerable size. The marble dance floor was designed like a compass, showing the directions; it was stunning. I discovered a swing between the trees. I sat on it, and taking some fast steps, launched myself into the air. Basil smiled and gave me a push. When I finished swinging, we continued our walk through the woods and came then to the end of his property.

Basil said, "You see the large building, Brigitte? That is a high school."

"Yes, that is the first building which I caught sight of, it's quite a distance from your house."

Smiling proudly, Basil explained, "Yes, I do like my privacy."

We turned around and slowly walked back through the trees. I recognized almost all of the species and realized that I recognized them from my youth. The climate seemed to be very similar to that of Germany.

The next day, Basil took me to see his factory, which had formerly been a blacksmith shop. Basil had purchased it at a good price after he returned home from the war. Because of an injury, he had been unable to continue as a sharpshooter in the military. As a young man, he had gone to Alaska to work in a silver mine. During the winters, he put himself through college. There he learned metallurgy and became an engineer. His specialty was designing his own tools and dies, and manufacturing electronic components. Basil's components were used in televisions, radios, refrigerators and pace makers by the end of the 1950s. Basil introduced me to his employees, most of whom came from different countries in Europe. The tool and die designers were upstairs. Downstairs I saw the big presses that stamped little holes in the components. Basil also made coins. His business was going very well. He sold his components in many different countries. There was another section of the factory where the components were gold plated. Pointing to another stack, Basil told me it was going to be shipped to Siemens Germany. Then he pointed to another stack and said that they were going to France. He also shipped product to Munich Germany. He participated in the Electronic Exhibition in Paris every spring. Now Sony, in Japan, was interested in buying components for their televisions.

"Soon I will have to attend a trade show in Tokyo," he said. I was fascinated. Basil was so talented and intelligent. I praised him and told him how much I admired him. In the beginning, it was difficult for Basil to get the company started. But one day, an executive of Texas Instruments came to see him and asked if he could make a die according to their design. He said he could and gave it a try.

"Little did I know," he confessed, "that it was almost impossible to bend the metal the way the company wanted it. I spent many nights working on the prototype. All of my references stated that it could not be done. I invested heavily in different kinds of metals, made tools to facilitate the process and kept working on it.

I finally finished the part one day before the executive of Texas Instruments arrived in my factory to see what I had done. I presented it to my client, and that was the turning point in my business career. Texas Instruments became my best customer, and others soon followed. Companies asked me to make custom components for them. It was 1955 to 1958 when the electronics industry was taking off.

"Basil, you have extraordinary skills," I noted.

"Thank you, my darling Brigitte. Now, we have completed the tour of the factory and we will visit my secretary, Etta."

Etta greeted me with a friendly smile and remarked, "Now I understand why Mr. Kassa was traveling so often to Europe."

Basil praised her, saying, "Etta is my loyal secretary. When I am not here, she can assume all of the responsibility for the factory." We chatted a while longer, then had lunch and returned to his home.

The next day, Basil announced that he would be going off to work, but that his maid would be with me. She would look after everything and would be making lunch for me. The gardener would be there too, if I needed anything. What a different world this was! I had no work to do, no stress about anything and there were no demands on my time. I didn't even have to think! Finally, I had a man I respected and who would take care of me. I thought back to the encounter with the gypsy woman in my mother's store in Berlin. She had predicted that I would cross the ocean and that my life would change for the better once I reached the age of thirty. I was almost twenty-nine and astounded by how the gypsy woman could have foretold my future so accurately, many years in advance.

I tried to think of how I could please Basil. I knew that he liked me to be in short dresses and skirts to show off my legs. He preferred me in stockings and high heels. So I decided to give him what he liked best. Every evening between 4:00 and 5:00, I dressed up and waited for him with a glass of Seagram's VO mixed with 7Up and a slice of lime. Basil was thrilled and excited. After a couple of sips of the VO, he took me hastily in his arms and kissed me. But mostly he adored and enjoyed my legs. I was amazed as I could not understand what it was that Basil found so exciting about my legs. But, I enjoyed his attention. I was happy with Basil. He resumed his schedule of going to work every day. I spent my time going on long walks in the woods and quickly figured out a different way to get back to the house. I walked past the high school, turned right and walked on the street.

At the corner, I turned right again, and I saw the golf course which was opposite Basil's home. To my surprise, there were no sidewalks as there were in Europe. There, we were used to walking, as not everybody owned a car. The lack of sidewalks did not stop me, however. I walked every day. Occasionally, cars would stop to ask if I needed a ride. I always declined and found my way back to the house.

Then I had a new idea. Basil had a sweet dog named Candy. She was a Great Dane and was an outdoors dog. There was a long fenced-in kennel for her. The gardener, Steve, fed and cleaned up after the dog. To me, it seemed to be a very sad existence for the poor baby. I made friends with Candy and started to take her with me on walks. Candy was lonely. But when she saw me, her sad eyes would light up. I stroked her fine beige fur and then let her out of her yard. She was joyful when we were in the woods. I allowed her to go off without the leash. But when we reached the street, I put the leash back on her. Candy had never seen a street before and was afraid to walk on it. She began to shake as we walked along. Every day I took her a little further along the street until Candy became used to it. By then, we were arriving back at Basil's house. Needless to say, no more cars bothered to stop to offer me a ride.

SILK STOCKINGS

One day, Basil told me that he wanted to show me New York. It was only a 40 minute drive from where we lived. We drove through the Lincoln Tunnel and parked the car in a garage on Fifth Avenue. Out on the sidewalk, I stood still and looked up at the sky scrapers. It was a phenomenal experience to be there; what a total change from Europe, where there might be four or five tall buildings in a city, but not one skyscraper. Here I was, looking up at a forest of skyscrapers. I strolled along Fifth Avenue with Basil who eventually guided me into an impressive department store. It was Saks Fifth Avenue. He seemed to know his way around and guided me directly to the hosiery department. Stockings! Basil asked the sales lady to show us different qualities and styles. He also informed her of my size. How did he know?

Basil purchased six boxes of Christian Dior and four of Berkshire. I could not figure out what I would do with so many pairs of stockings. Then we walked to a well-known shoe store, Ferragamo, where I tried on a collection of fine quality high heel shoes. Basil purchased at least five pairs of shoes there. By this time, I confessed to Basil that I was absolutely exhausted. So we stopped at an elegant restaurant for lunch. Then we left for home.

At home, right away, Basil asked me to try on some of the new stockings and shoes, with a mini skirt. Nothing else. So I did, parading around like a model in front of him. Basil got so excited that he very quickly lifted me up and we landed on the bed. Then everything went quite rapidly, like a flash of lightning with the explosion following. I was amused that my legs dressed up with stockings and shoes had such an electrifying effect on Basil.

"But what about me, Basil?"

Well, I didn't have to wait long. He began to cover my body with his kisses.

Next day, when I walked with Candy through the woods, I was engrossed in thoughts. How different the new world was, everything was broader, taller and intimidating, like the sky scrapers. The people were friendly enough. Life seemed to be moving along more easily. The etiquette was not as formal as in Europe where acquaintances, neighbors and even friends were always addressed as Mister or Missus; or only Mister or Miss. Here people introduce you to others using your first name. I felt a kind of freedom from restrictions. Happily, I walked Candy back to Basil's house.

The next day, we returned to New York. This time Basil showed me the Empire State Building. I told him that my one fear is of heights. "But you must see New York from a great height," he insisted. Yes, it was breathtaking. I made a point of not looking directly down. After that, we went to lunch at a luxurious hotel restaurant and then strolled the streets of New York City, down to Time's Square and back to Fifth Avenue. This time, Basil pulled me into Bonwit Teller to buy some more stockings. Two pairs had been ruined in the passion and excitement of the previous evening. Then we went to the Waldorf Astoria for some drinks. Basil suggested, "Let's go home now and rest a while. We are coming back this evening for dinner in the Persian Room at the Plaza Hotel. There would be excellent food, a great orchestra and dancing." I was very excited about the plan.

Once home, Basil asked me to go to the dressing room. "Open the mirrored closet door and you will find a surprise. I will be waiting in the living room." I did as he requested and was dumbfounded. There in the closet were hanging some beautiful cocktail dresses. Did Basil buy these for me? How did he know my size? What a wonderful surprise. Basil wanted me to choose one to wear out tonight. I chose a green satin dress and loved how smooth it felt. It had a deep décolleté. I put it on and zipped it up. To my disappointment, it did not fit me! The waistline was perfect, but it was made for a woman with a larger bust. I decided to try on another one, choosing a yellow silk dress with flowers. The same thing happened; my breasts were too small! After I tried one more dress on, only to have the same result, I noticed that these dresses were made to order. I called Basil in and informed him, "Look Basil, not one of them fits me. The waist size is perfect, the lengths are correct, but the busts are all too large. You didn't take the correct measurement for my breasts."

Basil sheepishly told me that the dresses were not made for me. "Two years ago, I had a girlfriend for whom the dresses were made. But she left me after a year and married a wealthy doctor. Since then, she was in a car accident and, unfortunately, died. Apparently she was on drugs at the time of the accident. I would not give her the dresses when she left me, as I had purchased them."

All of the blood drained from my face. I was angry, humiliated, disappointed and even a little jealous. In disbelief, I lashed out at Basil, "You want me to wear her clothes because you put a lot of money into them? Would you be longing for her while I wear them? What should I think?"

A myriad of emotions flooded through me. "I will not take these. Tomorrow I would like to return to Monte Carlo," I stated in a firm voice. Basil was speechless and began to cry. He kneeled down and begged me not to leave him. He told me that he didn't understand what he had done wrong. And so we went, on and on.

Finally, Basil told me, "I will do whatever you want. Just please don't go. Please, marry me!"

I began to calm down and started thinking. What *did* I want from Basil?

"I will not marry you here in New Jersey. I don't want to live in the house where another woman lived with you. I don't like the climate, it makes me think of Germany and you know I hate the cold. I have always dreamed of sunshine and palm trees, like I had in Monte Carlo. I would rather go back to that life than to live in another woman's shoes. I also want dresses made just for me. I would like to be married in a warm climate and have our own home. It does not matter how long it takes. It will give us time to get to know each other better."

Basil's eyes lit up and he took me into his arms. "I will do for you everything you want. Tomorrow, we will go and visit my travel agent, Mr. Greenwald, to seek sunshine for you. I agree with you about this climate. I don't like the winters either. Now it is November and we are facing several months of unpleasant weather."

The next day, we visited Mr. Greenwald and made the first travel arrangements.

CHAPTER 11

Life with Basil

GETTING TO KNOW BASIL

First we traveled to Miami, staying at the Hotel Kenilworth where the best suite in the Hotel was named after Arthur Godfrey. It was on the top floor, with a terrace on the ocean side and a view of Bal Harbour on the other side of the building. There were exquisite stores in the area. Basil bought me a long orange chiffon dress with ostrich feathers around the hem. It was very elegant.

Then we went to Lincoln Road, another beautiful section of Miami Beach. There we could walk without having to worry about car traffic. There were lovely restaurants and boutiques; palm trees lined the walkways. We stepped into one store that had stylish evening dresses on display in the windows. The moment we entered, a middle-aged saleslady greeted us warmly. It was obvious that she had met Basil previously. Now I knew where the other dresses had come from. The lady showed us a wide variety of materials and colors, then she made sketches of how the dresses might look. She took my measurements and told us that the dresses would be ready in two to three weeks.

We enjoyed Miami Beach for a few more days and then headed to Arizona. Here the climate was different, warm but dry. We stayed at the luxurious Camelback Inn. One day, Basil drove from Phoenix far into the desert. He would not reveal what kind of surprise he had planned for me. After a long drive, I saw a wooden building that looked like a hacienda. As we came closer, I could read the sign; Pinnacle Peak. And strangely enough, on the next rooftop was standing an enormous statue of a cow. It was very comical. As we entered the restaurant, a large cowboy came up to welcome us, and then proceeded to cut Basil's tie off! I was appalled and could not understand why Basil was laughing. Then Basil pointed upwards. I looked up and saw hundreds of ties hanging from the ceiling. I was speechless. When I looked at Basil for an explanation, he just smiled.

"Now Brigitte, you will learn how good a steak can taste."

"But Basil, you know that I don't like steak. It is always too tough and difficult to chew. It has no flavor," I protested. I was familiar with the steak that was served in Germany and Monte Carlo. It was always chewy. Basil assured me that I would taste the difference. We went outside where the cowboys were cooking enormous steaks on the open fireplace.

The cowboys asked us how we wanted our steaks cooked. Basil placed our orders and we went back inside. When the steaks were served, I could not believe how large they were. It was enough to feed an entire family in Europe. "I cannot eat this whole thing, Basil. You should have ordered something different for me."

Basil laughed and told me that the restaurant was famous for their steaks. There was nothing else on the menu. Steaks, potatoes and vegetables; that was it! I looked around at the other tables and true enough, I only saw enormous steaks with potatoes and vegetables. Not far from our table was a little girl sitting with her family. She was half done with her steak and still eating. I told Basil, "If she can eat it all, so can I," and I picked up my knife and fork. I expected I would need to use a lot of effort to cut into the steak, but to my delight, the knife slid through the meat. It was like slicing butter! And what a tender, juicy bite! I could not believe it, so I took another bit. It was just as wonderful as the first. Bite after bite, savoring each tasty morsel, I finished my steak. From that time on, we kept the tradition of having steaks on Sunday. Basil would cook them on the grill. I would make a salad and vegetable, and we would enjoy a good bottle of champagne with our dinner. We owed it all to Pinnacle Peak!

From Arizona, we went on to San Francisco. We stayed at the Hotel Mark Hopkins, poised at the top of Nob Hill and with a gorgeous view.

However, it was foggy and too cool. So Basil took me to Hollywood. It was warm there, and Disneyland was so much fun. The last stop was Honolulu Hawaii. There we stayed at the Kahala Hilton, where we had a room overlooking the ocean. It was incredibly beautiful. There was also a large swimming pool, a turtle pond and a dolphin pond. Sometimes I swam in the ocean, and other times went into the pool. I loved it all; the climate, the people, the food and the environment, every-thing. With the exotic trees and flowers, I felt as if I was in paradise. Too soon, the last night came. We had a delicious dinner and champagne in the elegant restau-rant at our hotel. On the way up to the room, I felt tipsy and amorous. I thought, "Basil has kept his part of the deal; he bought me new dresses and is showing me the world and taking me to warmer places." We began to undress and, as always, per Basil's wishes, I kept on my stockings and high heeled shoes.

I told him that this time I wanted to spoil him. "Basil, come lie down and relax." I began to kiss his lips and went slowly down to his tender parts. Instantly, Basil jerked away and sprang up, his face was red.

"What are you doing?" he demanded. "Don't do that!"

I was shocked, my immediate reaction was to think of Dario, my first boyfriend, who had been a stiff prude. "You don't like it, Basil?"

"Oh, I do." He answered. "But I am afraid that I will get too excited. No one has ever done that to me before."

My eyes widened in disbelief. "Basil, you were married before, had two children and also you've had girlfriends. You are twenty-four years older than I. And you mean to tell me that no woman has ever kissed you there before?"

His answer was, "No."

I felt compassion for Basil and I told him, "Just relax, and enjoy."

At the end of two months, we traveled back to Basil's house in Caldwell, New Jersey. It was close to Christmas and the snow on the ground made everything look festive. Inside, it was cozy warm. Unfortunately, the snow brought back unpleasant childhood memories of freezing in Germany. It dimmed my contentment. Leaving the lovely tropical climate and non-stop sun didn't make this change any easier.

One day, a large package arrived from Florida, filled with the beautiful designer dresses. Basil could not get enough of me modeling them and, of course, wearing the stockings and high heeled shoes. Once or twice a week, we would go dining and dancing, or see a show in New York. During the day, I had lots of time to watch television, which was my opportunity to learn English.

I would take Candy for long walks through the woods. One day, I dared to bring Candy into the house. She was petrified at being inside and was very afraid of the carpet, never having seen or experienced it before. Even the linoleum in the kitchen felt strange to her; it was gray with a yellow stripe; Candy would only walk on the yellow stripe. That evening, when Basil came home, I was dressed up as usual and had his drink waiting for him. But he was surprised to hear that Candy had been in the house with me. "You brought Candy into the house?"

"Yes, she was lonely out there, and I was lonely in here, so I brought her inside." I felt particularly close to Candy. "Candy is the one I practice my English with."

Basil smiled when he heard that and told me, "You know enough English, and everyone likes your accent." That reminded me of how Jeno had not wanted me to learn French. I wondered if it was Jeno's and Basil's way of keeping me to themselves.

"No, Basil, I want to learn how to speak English well. And I would like for you to buy me a book that I can use to study.

I wrote to Jeno in Monte Carlo and asked him to send me my cookbook from Germany. I explained to Jeno that it was wonderful not to have to think of business or to worry about the next day. I described how nicely Basil took care of me and how he did everything to please me. Unfortunately, that also meant that I had no challenges, and I was fighting boredom. I wrote to Jeno about the full time maid and gardener, and how there was nothing for me to do. My goal was to surprise Basil by learning how to cook.

Once the book came, I selected the recipe for my favorite meal, Rinderrouladen, and wrote out a list of the ingredients, which Basil obtained for me. That night, I presented him with a wonderful meal. It was a new skill for me and an enjoyment for Basil. From that time on, I would cook every second or third day, something different that was maybe Hungarian or German. Soon I did not need the cookbook any more. I seasoned meals to my own taste with aromatic herbs, and I had great success! On Sundays, per our custom, Basil would grill steaks that we would enjoy with champagne. Other nights we would go out to dine in our area or in New York City.

1968

After the turn of the New Year, 1968, Basil asked me when I would marry him. By now, I knew exactly what I wanted. First of all, I wanted to see more of the world. And then I wanted to marry Basil in a warm place. "Basil, I like Florida. What do you think?"

Basil said that it sounded great to him, and added, "And then we will have children. You do want children, don't you?"

"Oh no, Basil," I told him. "I certainly do *not* want children while *you* travel the world on business trips. I want to travel with you, wherever you go. I want to see the world and have fun with you. I also want to find a place in the sun, like an island with palm trees, where we can live. I always dreamed of that when I was living with my aunt and uncle in Germany."

Basil looked a little disappointed. "No children?"

I reminded him that he already had two daughters. "But they are not very close to me," he complained. "My ex-wife has poisoned them against me."

"You see," I pointed out, "that is another reason to enjoy life together!"

Basil was quiet; deep in thought. I explained that we would be a team on the business trips. I would be able to help with several languages. And on top of all that, he would always have me there as a playmate. I am now twenty-nine and I don't want to be a housewife with children; especially with you always traveling around. I saw many men alone, remember that is how I met you!"

Basil's eyes lit up at the word "playmate" and, in the end, he agreed.

In February 1968, we took a short trip to Barcelona Spain, just to get out of the winter cold. That May, we traveled to Bermuda and Florida. We set a wedding date, October 17th, 1968. We planned to marry in Miami.

Married in a Hurricane

The summer was lovely, I enjoyed being in Basil's garden and playing with Candy. On October 15, we traveled to Miami. Basil had once again rented the Arthur Godfrey suite in the Kenilworth Hotel. On the 16th of October, Hurricane Gladys hit Miami. Some water leaked in from the terrace doors. I was terrified, having never experienced such a violent storm. We didn't sleep much that night, but Basil calmed me down. Around 10:00 the next morning, October 17th, we drove through the pouring rain to the courthouse. Everything was delayed, given the weather; but when we left the courthouse, we looked up at the sky and the sun broke through the clouds. It looked like a pathway to heaven. We took that as a very good omen and celebrated our union. Proudly, Basil took me in his arms and said, "Now, how do you feel, Mrs. Kassa?"

"Very Happy, Mr. Kassa!"

The winter of 1968 we spent in New Jersey. Basil bought me a beautiful black mink coat, made to order. He ordered a matching white mink coat, so that I would have no cause to complain about being cold. He also purchased me high heeled boots, so that he could enjoy looking at my legs when I wore the coats.

One day, Basil told me that he wanted to open a bank account for me. He asked how much money I wanted to have in the account. "I don't want any money," I told him. "It is you who dresses me, feeds me and pays all of the bills. Why would I need any money? Besides, I have had to handle money since I was very young. I don't want that responsibility any more. Maybe I am old fashioned in that I want the man to take care of everything."

Basil was surprised, "You don't want any money of your own, really?" he asked.

"That is right," I told him.

"Well, this is the first time that a woman doesn't want money from me." Basil was touched and he embraced me warmly.

1969

On January 1st, we visited Jeno in Monte Carlo, staying at the beautiful Cap Estel. Jeno was thrilled to see Basil and me and greeted us with great enthusiasm. He handed me a letter with my previous name and address in Monte Carlo on it. It was a letter from the Palais de Monaco and was from Princess Grace thanking me on behalf of her son, Albert, who had received a present at Christmas with my name on the card. I looked at Jeno, and then at Basil, who smiled and explained that he had sent a mobile sculpture, the newest toy in the states, to Jeno. He informed Jeno that it was for Prince Albert for Christmas. Jeno had sent the gift in my previous name. With the mystery cleared, I thanked Basil.

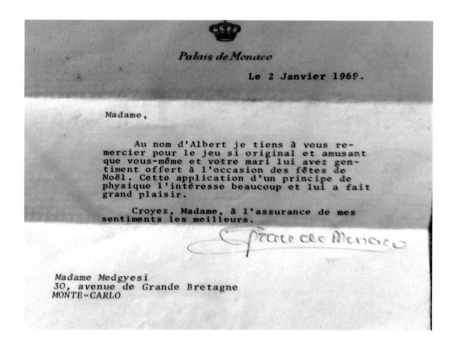

Jeno invited us to sample his newest offering at the Snack Bar, a sweet pea salad. It was around Noon when we arrived and the Snack Bar was closed. It was scheduled to open in the afternoon around tea time. Jeno was anxious to try out his new recipe and served it to us. The first two bites were delicious. But then I felt something crunching between my teeth. I looked over to Basil, who also had a funny look on his face. We both spit the food out into our napkins and discovered that the crunchy substance was glass! I yelled at Jeno, "Do you want to kill us?"

Jeno looked into our napkins and saw the tiny shards of glass. I snapped at him, "What were you doing?"

Jeno explained that the glass bowl he was mixing the salad in had broken when it slipped out of his hand. He had fished out the large pieces of glass and thought he had gotten it all. "I must have overlooked the tiny pieces," he commented without showing concern.

I explained to him, "Jeno, you should never have served this at all!"

He just smiled at me and suggested, "So, let's just go out and dine."

I was amazed at his lack of distress with regard to what he had done. I looked to Basil and quietly murmured, "Strange behavior." Basil and I invited Jeno to get into our car to find a nice restaurant for lunch.

"No, I am not getting in the car with you. I will walk," Jeno stated hotly. Again, Basil and I exchanged glances.

"Fine, we will all walk," Basil declared. We went to a nearby restaurant and Jeno became again his old self. He was charming and happy to be with us.

Later, when Basil and I were back in our hideaway, we discussed what might be wrong with Jeno. I suggested that perhaps he was ill. I remembered when he had gone to a doctor in Munich, but had never shared a diagnosis. The only thing he related to me at that time was that he couldn't sense odors any more. We stayed a couple of days longer, then Basil suggested that we head back home to New Jersey. We were planning a long trip around the world that would be our honeymoon. There was much we needed to do before leaving on that journey. Jeno begged us not to travel too far in case something should happen. Then Jeno said to me, "Little Mommy, don't forget me!"

I assured him that I would be in touch and would send him postcards. Basil invited Jeno to come visit us in New Jersey the following year. That request seemed to calm him down. I felt that Jeno was afraid of something, but I could not figure out what it was. He wasn't giving us any clues.

The day after we flew home, Basil visited with Mr. Greenwald to make travel arrangements. This trip would take us from the end of March 1969 through June 1969. Before leaving, Basil would be working at his factory for two more months to get everything in order before his absence. I enjoyed the time playing with Candy and being a *hausfrau.*

CHAPTER 12

First Trip Around the World

ADVENTURES WITH BASIL

The end of March, we traveled first to visit Aunt Didi and Uncle Max, who no longer lived in Berlin. They now were in Bodensee, on Lake Constance. It was not far from Switzerland. Their house was on a little hill overlooking idyllic scenery. Far off in the distance, but within view, was the silhouette of the Switzer Alps. On the bottom of the hill was Lake Constance, where little ripples of water were glittering in the sun.

My aunt and uncle immediately opened their hearts to Basil and he responded in the same way. Aunt Didi was the perfect hostess. She whipped up all kinds of marvelous dishes. We also enjoyed drinking champagne together. Basil told them how impressed he was with me, paying them the compliment of raising me so well. This was a lovely boost to my aunt's ego. She then told Basil how she was raised in an upper class family in Hungary. She knew it was difficult to live in Germany, where people were so rough and unrefined. She went on and on. Uncle Max and I exchanged glances, knowing that she was talking about Uncle Max's family, all of whom I loved dearly.

To distract my aunt, I dragged her away to see all of the beautiful clothes that Basil had purchased for me. Since it was March, it was still cold. I wanted to show off my mink coats and other lovely winter clothing. Aunt Didi told me, "I know that now you are all grown up. But to me, you will always be my little Spatzchen."

Later that afternoon, we all took a long walk through the woods.

Am Bodensee with Aunt Didi

We came to a farm where there were several sheep grazing. Aunt Didi walked right over to pet the baby lambs. We called to her to come back, but she refused. So Basil went to join her. The ram, however, was not happy to see people in his field, touching his babies. Uncle Max and I called to Basil and Aunt Didi, suggesting that they leave. Basil came back to where we were standing, and looked back just in time to see the ram charge Aunt Didi. In the blink of an eye, Aunt Didi was airborne! We worried that my aunt was hurt, but it was so very comical that we burst out laughing. She was alright, as we thought, only her pride was damaged.

After an enjoyable stay, we made our farewells and left for Milan. Basil had not forgotten how disappointing it was when we last visited Milan, with opera season over. Now we had come at the right time. Basil bought tickets and said, "Now Brigitte, I would like to see you in the white mink when we attend the Opera La Scala!"

"Oh, Basil, I would love to," I answered. We attended La Scala and spent a romantic week exploring Milan.

ISTANBUL TURKEY

Next stop was Istanbul Turkey. We stayed at the Hilton. For two days we had a guide to show us around. What wonderful scenery to enjoy as well as the classic Byzantine architecture. The atmosphere was sophisticated with an exotic flair of the East. The Turkish people are extremely cordial and internationally minded. We enjoyed a wide variety of delicious Turkish foods; my favorite meal being dolma; grape leaves filled with ground beef, pine nuts, rice and spices. We were visiting the old section of the city with museums, mosques, the Aya Sofia and the Blue Mosque. We visited the bazaar where our guide walked on one side of me and Basil on the other. They were protecting me from the Turkish men who were notorious for pinching women. As much as my companions tried, I still got pinched. It was an uncomfortable sting on my bottom. When I jumped and turned around, no one was there!

We appreciated the incredible array of hand-made items for sale at the bazaar. Then we went to Topkapi Palace, dating from the Ottoman Empire. We were able to see the harem section, admire the stonework and exclaim over the wealth of jewelry. It was mysterious and fascinating.

One day we took a ferry to the Bosporus, and visited the Prince's island. No cars were allowed there; the only transportation was a calash carriage pulled by miniature horses. We savored the local cuisine and had lots of fun.

One night after we returned from sightseeing, Basil told me to put on my black lace dress. He had a surprise for me. When we came downstairs, Basil led me to a lavish jewelry store. The salesman greeted Basil as if he knew him. We were served Turkish coffee and had a light conversation. Then the manager pulled out a case. Set on black velvet was a gorgeous diamond necklace. I was speechless. The manager explained, "This necklace once belonged to a princess who lived in the Topkapi Palace. The diamonds were hand cut, it is an antique from the Ottoman Empire."

Basil took it out of the case, put it around my neck and said, "Now it belongs to *my* princess!"

I had tears in my eyes and couldn't speak. I just kissed Basil and held him close to me. We had another cup of the strong Turkish coffee. The manager had more items to show us. Now he brought out a ring that matched the necklace. I tried it on; three carats and rose cut, also cut by hand. Basil asked if I wanted the ring too.

"I would love it, Basil. It is exquisite. But it is too much at one time. We will come back and maybe get it at a later time. I don't want you to spend all of your money at the first stop of our trip."

Basil was pleased. He took me in his arms and said proudly, "Now my princess, we will have a marvelous time together." I was overwhelmed with happiness and touched my magnificent, precious necklace and answered, "I thank you my charming prince." We left the jewelry store and dined and danced that evening until the nightclub was closed. I loved Turkey, but was looking forward to our next stop.

INDIA

The flight to India was very long. But I didn't mind it because most of our travel was on Pan Am Airlines first class. It was luxurious, I was able to relax throughout the flight in complete comfort. I closed my eyes and dreamed of the India I had seen in the movies. The palace would be richly decorated with silk fabrics and gold gilding. The Maharajah of Jet-Pour, my very good friend from the Gipsy Club, and his wife with her entourage, would be clad in silk trimmed with gold. The Maharani would be wearing precious jewelry. In my dream, I saw the Maharajah presenting Basil and me to the Maharani. I even envisioned myself sitting on a richly decorated elephant, gliding through the jungle. My dream was interrupted by Basil who was offering me a glass of champagne. He had been chatting with the couple seated behind us on the plane. I preferred to read or watch movies, rather than to chat with strangers. But Basil was more of a *people person*. I still had the address and phone of the Maharajah. Basil and I had spoken about surprising him with a visit. With anticipation, I provided Basil with the Maharajah's contact information and asked if he might send him a telegram.

Our flight arrived in Bombay at 4:00 am. As the taxi drove us to the hotel, an awful stench drifted in the window of the cab. We peered out of the window, but could see nothing in the dark. As we got closer to the city, the smell intensified. It began to get light, and we could vaguely see piles of what we thought was garbage, begin to move. Horrified, we watched as people stood up and began to walk. Further on, we saw raggedy looking people emerge from large PVC pipes. Before we reached the city, we had to wait for a couple of cows to pass. Our hotel was named the Taj Mahal after the monument. It was the finest hotel in the city.

As soon as we were comfortable, I called the Maharajah. To my surprise, a lady came on the line. I gave her my name and she said, "I do know who you are, but to my regret, I must give you sad news. The Maharajah died one year ago. I am his wife. I would very much like to meet you and your husband. I will send my car to pick you up tomorrow for lunch." I thanked her and hung up the phone. I could not understand how this could happen.

Basil saw my confusion and sadness and took my hand. "Let's explore the hotel and have lunch," he suggested. I was truly stunned. It was inconceivable that the Maharajah had passed away. It is not anything I could have imagined. Basil attempted to distract me by guiding me through the halls of the luxurious hotel. He suggested that we go outdoors for a walk, as fresh air would be helpful. As soon as we stepped out of the door of the hotel, we were swarmed by ragged children begging. Basil gave them some money, which was the wrong thing to do. More beggars came, some without legs, sitting on cardboard which moved on wheels. Some of the children had runny eyes and looked very sickly. They all pressed upon us; it was a very unpleasant situation.

We returned to the safety of the hotel and asked for a guide. Very shortly, a Sikh guide was at our disposal. He spoke excellent English and took us on a tour, chasing the beggars away. He advised Basil not to hand the beggars any money; that we would never get away from them once that was done.

In the evening, we had an excellent dinner in the hotel, with Basil doing his best to lift my low spirits. After dinner, as we approached our room, we saw a man lying in front of our door. He sprang up when he saw us and told us that he would be there all night in case we had a wish for anything. We went into our room, thinking that this was a strange custom. After a while, we were curious and opened the door to see if he was still there. Yes, he was, sound asleep on the floor. Basil suggested that he might be there to protect us. That was the first time I smiled. "Oh Basil, the poor man is so thin that the wind could blow him over."

The next day, the Maharani's car arrived to pick us up. She was living in a residential area. The chauffeur escorted us to her flat. We passed at least eight to ten servants on our way in. The Maharani greeted us warmly. She looked a little like the Maharajah, with a round face, dark brown eyes that sparkled, and a round mouth with full lips. We had drinks and then lunch. She told us that her husband had truly enjoyed his time in Monte Carlo. "Especially with you, Brigitte. His last thought was of you as he died, holding an ashtray from the Gipsy Club in his hand," she recalled. He had suffered a fatal heart attack when he was only forty-five years old.

The Maharani invited us to join her for the evening. We went to a night club where we enjoyed a show. The Maharani squeezed my hand and told me, "You should have married my husband. I would have liked very much to have you here with us." Then she kissed me. I was pleasantly surprised. So it was true; the Maharajah, or Jet as he wanted me to call him, had truly been courting me in Monte Carlo! I thanked her for her generosity and kindness. During the evening, the Maharani asked us if we would like to see the palace in the Pink City, where the Maharani and Maharajah had once resided. We declined the invitation. It would have meant a short flight, and I didn't want to see the palace now that the Maharaja was gone; it would be too sad.

The next day, Basil and I went through the beautiful shops in the hotel. In one of the stores, we picked out material to have Saris made for me. We did some sightseeing with our Sikh guide and even braved going out without him in the late afternoon. When we returned to the hotel that evening, we had to step over the people who were sleeping in the street. I was grateful that I had not fallen in love with the Maharajah. I would not have been able to live there knowing of the poverty that surrounded me.

ISRAEL

The next stop of our trip was Israel. We stayed in the luxurious Hotel Caesarea, located between Haifa and Tel Aviv. Basil had a client there who sold and distributed parts from his factory. Basil must have contacted him earlier, because a young couple greeted us as we arrived at the hotel. Ben and Ruth had drinks with us and the two men made arrangements for the following day. They were a lovely couple whom Basil had known for a long time from a distance. This was the first time he met them in person. The next day, they came to the hotel. Basil and Ben talked business while Ruth took me to their house and showed me around. Afterwards, we all drove to Kibbutz, an Israeli collective farm. Here they grew vegetables hydroponically. They also had many cows that were milked by machines which were technologically advanced; and the barn was incredibly clean. It was impressive. With Ben and Ruth as our guides, we were able to see parts of the country that no typical tourists ever visited. Modern garden citrus orchards lay adjacent to ancient sites.

It felt strange to be in the Holy Land. We went to Old Jerusalem, which was enclosed by a forty foot wall. We saw churches, mosques and temples. It was amazing to see so many religions represented in such close quarters. When we went to Nazareth, I hopped on a donkey and rode for a while. Ruth and Ben showed us the Sea of Galilee and the complicated irrigation systems that allowed the Israelis to grow fields of oranges. Across the sea, we could see the Arabian side where there was only desert. One day we went to Tel Aviv and asked, "Why are there large white containers on the roof tops?" Ben explained that they were water containers that the sun was heating, so that people would have hot water.

"What a great idea," Basil and I said at the same time. We all became good friends. Ben and Ruth shared a secret with Basil and me; they told us that because they lived so close to the Arabian border, they both worked for the government as spies, mostly at night. They lived two lives, one that everyone knew about and the other kept secret. Just before we arrived, they had experienced a dangerous situation in which the Arabs were shooting at them as they fled an area they were not supposed to be in. Ruth lost her shoes. The next day, a patrol came by and asked if they had seen a child escaping from the other side of the border. Ruth's feet were so tiny, that the patrol was sure the shoes belonged to a child. We had to laugh, but at the same time we recognized that Ben and Ruth were living a dangerous dual life. We remained for three weeks in Israel and had a wonderful stay.

THAILAND BANGKOK

Next on our itinerary was Thailand. We traveled directly to Bangkok, where we stayed at the Hotel Siam Intercontinental. Everyone we encountered had a cheerful smile. They seemed almost childlike in their small stature. We were fascinated by how rich and colorful all of the temples and palaces were. The city is interlinked with canals and the main river, Chao Phraya. We enjoyed a ride through the floating market.

PHILIPPINES MANILA

We moved on to the Philippines with a brief stop in Manila. It was a very busy city where we took rides in the unique and colorfully decorated cars. We stopped at the open kiosks on the streets and tasted marvelous roast suckling pig. We agreed that the crackling skin was the very best part. The people were helpful and polite.

TAIWAN FORMOSA

We made another short stop in Taiwan Formosa. It was a lovely island with friendly people who were excellent hosts to travelers. We stayed in the Grand Hotel outside of Taipei on a hill overlooking the city and river. The rooms were decorated in a very grand oriental style. The grazing water buffaloes were impressive, massively large animals. We were able to stand right next to them on the side of the road. There were no fences separating us from them; but the buffaloes were disinterested in travelers. Only one of them looked over at us and then, after a moment, went back to grazing.

We continued to wander around the area and found a Chinese restaurant where we were served genuine Cantonese food and learned to use chop sticks. In the evening we dressed for the dinner at our elegant hotel. Basil ordered for both of us. After a short wait, a waiter served us a dish filled with caviar. I had never seen such a presentation. There was light beneath, illuminating upward, then ice and finally on top, the dish filled with beautiful gray pearls of caviar. After dinner, Basil teased my imagination with the news that I would have another surprise the next day.

HONG KONG

Next morning, Basil said, "We are flying to Hong Kong today and you will meet a Chinese man whom I befriended at the Hotel de Paris in Monte Carlo. The landing in Hong Kong was very scary. It felt as if the airplane was flying between houses and that the wings were about to touch the sides. We both held our breath as we landed safely. When we looked around us, we realized we were not the only ones who had been afraid. Once outside the terminal, there was a man holding up a sign with our name on it. He was the chauffeur from our hotel, and guided us kindly to a Rolls Royce. Astounded, I asked Basil, "Is this for us?"

"Of course my darling, we are celebrating our honeymoon first class!" The luxurious Mandarin Hotel was most impressive. Our suite was fully decorated with original art work. From our balcony, we could see the harbor. There was so much hustle and bustle going on, it was difficult to look away. It was almost like watching an ant colony at work. The combination of skyscrapers and small bungalows, the rows of big ships and the junks, they all jostled for the same space. There were cargo ships, liners from all over the world, ferries going back and forth, sampans and batwing junks with traders or fishermen. It was exhilarating to observe the colorful city with all of the busy movement and commotion.

The following day, I met Basil's friend. His name was Teddy Yip. He and Kim, the lady who accompanied him, greeted us warmly. Kim would be our guide. Basil and Teddy reminisced about times together in Monte Carlo. Basil told Teddy, "After your departure, I met Brigitte, and now she is my wife!"

"How wonderful, Basil. Tonight you will be my guests."

Teddy was of small stature. He had brown eyes, a little mustache around his lips and smiled a lot, radiating energy. I liked him immediately. Kim took us to a variety of shops, from European department stores to cubby holes on the side streets. We were passing many tailor shops. Then we walked up to Cat Street which was lined with antique stores. At lunch in a small Chinese restaurant, we even managed to eat the noodle soup with chopsticks. Later, we met Teddy's wife, Sue, and had a lovely evening together. They lived in Repulse Bay, a beautiful residential area.

The next day, Kim took us over a ferry crossing to Kowloon, a densely populated peninsula with workshops, small factories, shops and apartments. We boarded a rickshaw for our sightseeing pleasure and then entered a Dim Sum Restaurant, where the waitresses sang out the items on the menu and circulated with samples in small bamboo baskets for the guests. We were sampling several small dishes each, and had no idea what we were eating. At the end of the meal, the number of bowls on the table determined what we had to pay for the meal. Basil and I had the same outlook on life, taking much pleasure in savoring the new and unfamiliar cuisine.

By the third day in Hong Kong, we were learning our way around the city. Basil was in heaven. He had found a first class shoe store that made shoes to order. Basil had many pairs made for me in multiple colors, but in the same style. He even had some made for himself. I felt uncomfortable about it, but it made Basil happy. Then he found a dressmaker who created Cheongsam dresses. He ordered several made of exotic brocade materials for me, along with a couple of traditional American style outfits. We both chose the colors and styles. We then returned to Cat Street, where we purchased three wooden carvings covered with gold leaf, which we planned to hand transport on our journey home.

We became the best of friends with Teddy and Sue, as well as with Kim, whom, we later discovered, was Teddy's mistress. She was from Canada, and very much in love with Teddy. Teddy was quite the entrepreneur, importing everything from pigs to cosmetics to China. His son owned the Hotel Estoril InterContinental in Macao, where Teddy escorted us for some pampering. Teddy had his own race car team which competed internationally in events including the Indianapolis 500. Our friendship continued on for years; many times we would return to Hong Kong.

We purchased souvenirs in each country we visited; from small items like shoes and dresses to furniture, which we had sent directly from the stores to Basil's home in New Jersey. At the end of our three week stay, we decided to buy a lovely craft table and two end tables. The furniture would someday decorate our dream house which was not yet on the horizon but definitely on our minds.

TOKYO JAPAN

The last stop of our honeymoon trip was Tokyo Japan. We stayed at the deluxe Hotel Okura, where we enjoyed a view of the lovely Japanese gardens. The restaurants in the hotel presented a variety of different foods with Sukiyaki becoming our favorite dish. Even the simplest fare is a work of art in Japan. The next day, Basil had an appointment with a manager of Sony, who was interested in Basil's products. Basil was asked to participate in the electronic exhibition that would be held the next year. Sony was already a very good client of Basil's. One of the executives invited Basil and me to his home in Gifu-Hashima. We boarded the Bullet train for the trip, which in itself was an adventure. The train was super clean and very comfortable. The countryside flew by. When we arrived, our hosts greeted us cordially. It was interesting to see that the gentleman wore western apparel and the lady wore traditional dress, a kimono, with high wooden sandals. Before we entered the house, we all removed our shoes. Instead of being seated in chairs, we knelt on cushions on the floor. Every day we absorbed and learned new things, it was all so fascinating. But by now, it was already June. Our three wonderful months had passed and it was time to fly home.

CHAPTER 13

My Life of Leisure and Luxury begins at 30

We were back from our wonderful and inspiring world tour. It was like having Christmas in June continuing throughout the summer. We received packages, cartons and even heavy wooden cases with handmade brass and copper work from Turkey. Carved wooden furniture arrived from Hong Kong. In the lighter parcels, there were dresses from Miami, and shoes from Hong Kong which were wrapped up in fine tissue paper. Basil was especially thrilled with the new shoes and dresses. His excitement was contagious; I was very happy to model them for him and to be his playmate. Basil worked very hard and his business was flourishing. The beautiful summer months passed while I played with Candy during the days and learned English from the television.

One evening when Basil came from work and was greeted, as always, with his favorite drink, he told me that he wanted for me to have bigger breasts. He explained that I would look even sexier. Then he demonstrated the exercises to make it happen. I looked critically at my breasts and thought that maybe there were a bit small. But I could not imagine how, from these peculiar exercises, they would get larger. But I said, "OK darling, I will add these movements to my daily routine." Well, after some months of exercising, my breasts did get a little fuller, and Basil was satisfied.

"Now Basil, I have one request. Could we make love naked just one time?" I explained to him that I might get more excited that way. Basil hesitated, and then said that would be alright. The next night, Basil was not too excited. He missed my legs in the stockings. He was not aroused by naked legs. Afterwards, he said, "Tomorrow, I want you to put your shoes and stockings back on!" I was disappointed. I wanted to be loved for myself, not for my legs in stockings and feet in high heels.

During the day, when I was alone, I tried to figure Basil out. I recalled that one time when I touched his hair in affection, he did not like it. It seemed he was a very visual man, and that was the only way for him to get aroused. I remembered how Werner could trigger my arousal by his voice and touching me. I missed that level of eroticism which seemed to have more to do with us, not what we were wearing.

Basil was a very good and generous man. I needed to live in the present, knowing that I was the lucky one, to have experienced such a deep loving feeling for someone. Looking back, I could see the different types of love I had been given. I had the heart breaking love with Werner, then the friendship and companionship love with Jeno, and now I had the love of a man who gave me security and showed me the world. What more could I want?

1970

On Valentine's Day, Basil bought me a car, a Chrysler Dodge Dart. "Oh Basil, this is very generous of you, I thank you! But don't you remember that I never want to drive again? Remember how I felt after my accident in Monte Carlo? You promised that we would look for an island in the sun. I won't need a car there!" I exclaimed.

Basil told me to calm down, we would travel soon looking for that island. In the meantime, he wanted me to learn how to drive in the USA. Basil was sure that I was bored.

"But, I'm not bored," I protested. "I cook sometimes and I love to play with Candy."

But Basil got his way. I was used to the narrow roads in Europe. It was OK to drive around where Basil was living. But at first, it was very scary for me to drive on the highways. One evening, after days of practice, I was able to drive home from New York City. Basil said, "I am proud of you, that you finally overcame your fear of driving in the states."

"Thank you, Basil. But I prefer you are in the driver's seat for long distances, I really don't like to drive."

Basil was smiling, "Don't you worry, my darling. I love to drive, and now I'd like to tell you what I am thinking about. How would you like to invite your Aunt Didi and Uncle Max to come to visit us?"

"Oh Basil, that is a wonderful idea! How noble of you!" I was moved by Basil's attention to me and to what I desired.

It was a great pleasure to see my uncle and aunt again. They were just like me when I first visited New York City. They stood on the sidewalk and stared up at all of the tall buildings. After a lot of sightseeing, Basil invited them to Florida. We stayed at the Hotel Kenilworth in the Arthur Godfrey Suite. Aunt Didi was very impressed, and proud of me. She said, "Well, the little sparrow has made it!"

Basil showed them how much he adored me. Every night we all got dressed up to go out to eat at Miami Beach's finest restaurants. We enjoyed the dinners and entertainment, enjoying a thoroughly wonderful time together.

We soon received news from Jeno that he had closed the Snack Bar. I had known his interest in the business would not last long. He wasn't used to doing things all by himself. Basil invited Jeno to come to visit us. Jeno was pleased to receive the invitation and three weeks later, he arrived. He looked the same, but soon we noticed some strange behaviors. At first he acted normally, cooking several fantastic meals for us. I got some cooking tips and learned how to make new dishes.

One day, when we were walking and sightseeing in New York City, Jeno stopped abruptly and said he would prefer to stay in the city, in a little hotel. We looked at him as if he were crazy, "But why? Is something wrong?" we asked him.

"Oh no, everything is fine," he responded. "It is wonderful, and I appreciate your hospitality, but the three of us cannot be together in Basil's house or walk together on the street. They will harm you, Brigitte. They will think you are Mata Hari, a German spy."

Basil and I exchanged looks and smiled, "Jeno, you are making jokes." But no, Jeno was serious. The more we teased, the more agitated Jeno became. His face got redder and he puffed harder on his cigar. He insisted that he would stay in New York City. We all returned to New Jersey to get Jeno's suitcase and then drove back to New York. We went to a section of the city that was populated with many Hungarians. We knew of the area because Basil would go to Mrs. Herbst's Bakery to purchase her delicious strudels. We found a small hotel, and Jeno was again happy. We told him that we would visit him every day, and would pick him up and drive him around.

The next day, when we went back to pick Jeno up, the hotel clerk told us that Jeno had moved to a smaller room. We knocked on his room door and Jeno was reluctant to let us in. I told Basil that Jeno seemed paranoid. "Remember Basil, in Monte Carlo, he would not get into your car and so we all walked to the restaurant?"

Now, he was fine traveling in the car with us, but not anywhere else. After a week, Jeno wanted to go back home. "I just wanted to see you, Little Mommy, and to make sure everything is all right." I assured him that everything was very good.

Two months later, Jeno sent Basil a letter asking if Basil would help him financially. He claimed that he had no money. When Basil mulled over the request, I urged him to send the money to Jeno, pointing out that he willingly facilitated the divorce and didn't get anything out of it. We both had told Jeno to let us know if he needed any help. Basil agreed with me and said he would send Jeno some funds every month.

Three months later, Jeno's Hungarian friends wrote to us to tell us that Jeno had cancer, he was getting injections for it. He was constantly asking for me. Reluctantly, Basil agreed that I should go to see Jeno. I promised to talk to Basil twice a day, and I cooked several dinners for him to enjoy while I was gone.

I took a room in a small hotel, not far from Jeno's apartment. It was strange to be in the apartment now, it seemed so small. Jeno lay in his bed. He didn't look sick, but I could tell that he had lost weight. He was thrilled to see me. We drank some port wine together and talked about the good times in the Gipsy Club. I visited him daily and helped to take care of him. It was difficult to get him to eat. He had no longer any sense of taste or smell. I cleaned the apartment, and then walked about Monte Carlo visiting old friends. But it no longer felt like home to me. I did not belong here anymore.

Two weeks passed in this fashion. Then one morning, Jeno's friend, Bela, called to tell me not to go to the apartment. He had taken Jeno to the hospital early that morning and didn't want me to see the apartment splattered with blood. Bela said he would contact a cleaning service to take care of the mess. Then he offered me a ride to the hospital. I scolded Jeno when I first saw him, "Why did you not call me?"

Jeno told me that he didn't want to wake me up. I called Basil to let him know what was going on, and that I could not do anything more for Jeno. It was time to return to New Jersey. Basil was thrilled to have me back home. For three weeks we enjoyed being together. I was again Basil's fashion model, he was the photographer. It was one of his hobbies.

Bela sent us a telegram informing us that Jeno had only a couple of days to live. We immediately made the arrangements to travel to Monte Carlo to see him one more time. Once there, we hurried to Jeno's room. "Where is Jeno?" Basil asked. We looked at the two patients in the room, and neither one of us recognized Jeno. Then I pointed to the small childlike body of a man who was curled up in a fetal position. There were tubes administering morphine in his feet. The doctors were no longer able to use other veins to give him relief from the pain. It was Jeno!

I touched Jeno and he looked up at me. His eyes were enormous. "Mommy, take me home. I don't want to be here any longer." I promised to take him home the next day, but knew that he would probably not live through the night. I couldn't sleep much that night. At 7:00 am I sat up abruptly and told Basil that Jeno had passed away. Soon after, the hospital called to tell us that Jeno had died. I took care of the arrangements, sold the furniture through an auctioneer, cleaned the apartment and went to the bank to close his account, which was still in both names. All of the money that Basil had sent to Jeno was sitting in his bank account, so I gave it back to Basil. After the funeral, we returned to New Jersey.

CHAPTER 14

Second World Tour

SEARCHING FOR AN ISLAND IN THE SUN

We traveled again, first to Hong Kong where we visited our friend Teddy Yip. We purchased more furniture. Then we went to Singapore, which was extremely clean. There we enjoyed the sightseeing. Next was Indonesia. We stopped in Jakarta and then went on to the Isle of Bali.

In Bali, the InterContinental Bali Beach Hotel had just opened. It was spectacular. The stone and wood carvings were amazing. Flowers were everywhere in total profusion. The fragrance from the frangipani scented the air all around. The people were delightful, small in stature, and always with bright smiles. They wore colorful clothing and flowers in their hair. We were fascinated by their dances, all of which told stories. One performance in particular that I enjoyed told of a young man who danced through fire. You could see the embers of the wood glowing and sparks were flying out. To prepare him for this feat, he was hypnotized by a priest.

We went through little villages and rice fields. We saw young boys tending to the animals. Our guide took us to the areas where very few tourists came, so there was a mutual fascination between the villagers and us. One village was most interesting. As we drew close to it, we saw a stream spilling from the top of the hill. Up there were topless women who were bathing. Then further along, downstream, the men were bathing. At the foot of the stream, young boys were washing the animals. It was such an efficient use of the water. In the village, people made baskets. We saw one man carrying fifteen baskets. You could only see the baskets! It looked as if the baskets were walking! The women prepared food using mortars and pestles, all by hand.

Then our guide took us to another part of the country where artists worked on stone carvings. There were several sections of the Artisan Colony where stone and wood carvers worked. The masters would take on young boys as apprentices to learn the art.

The boys would sleep right next to them in the working area. The folklore is that when the king was thrown out of Indonesia, he took all of the artists with him to Bali. We bought several stone statues that were later sent to the USA, as well as eight wood carvings.

On another day trip, we visited other villages. At one place we could see no houses, but only a huge wall. The guide told us that the people lived behind the wall, it was supposed to protect them from evil spirits. When we walked to the other side of the wall, children greeted us and showed us their temple where offerings were displayed. Everyone seemed very happy, there was no begging.

On the way back to the hotel, we stopped at a restaurant where they were roasting a small pig on a spit. It made for a delicious feast. I admired the decorations in the restaurant, all made using frangipani flowers. That evening Basil had a surprise for me. "Tomorrow we will fly to New Caledonia, maybe you will find your island in the sun, my darling!"

I was hopeful and excited. We were scheduled to stay for three days in Noumea, the capital city. New Caledonia was French and very isolated. Basil assured me that I would like it. When we landed, I immediately felt the warm breeze and smelled the fragrance of flowers. I liked it instantly. It was a dreamy, flower filled, South Pacific island with heavenly beaches. We had a lovely hotel room, modernized with all of the facilities for comfort. Our balcony was surrounded by blooming flowers.

"Oh Basil, I could live here. It is paradise!"

"I agree, my darling, let's rent a car and explore New Caledonia!"

We drove around sightseeing. Since we spoke French, it was simple to communicate and locate the locations we were interested in. The white beaches were gorgeous. We enjoyed a great diversity of seaside and mountain scenery with lovely colorful native villages. The restaurants featured a superb French cuisine along with local specialties, Tahitian, Indonesian, Vietnamese and African dishes.

Three days later, we took a half hour flight to Isle of Pines. There were only ten thatched roofed cottages and one restaurant on this small island, which is a part of New Caledonia. The sand was pure white, very crystalline. The water was an incredible combination of colors, shades of blue, green and turquoise. Best of all, there were very few people. We could see our own footprints in the sand the next day. We looked at each other and simultaneously said, "This IS paradise!" There were many varieties of birds; parrots with brightly colored feathers, parakeets and mynas. Even Basil was impressed with the many species. One day we discovered a cascade of water and cooled our feet in the natural shower. It was all magical.

The next day we came across a field of orchids growing. But when I bent over to pick one, something moved. I yelped, "Basil, please come quick, pick me up! Something moved! I think it's a snake!"

He picked me up and carried me piggy-back to the road. Then I yelled again, "Put me down! Put me down! There is a wild man coming!" A man who looked like a head hunter was approaching. He carried a machete in one hand and a sack with something in it in the other. Could it be someone's head? Basil was calm and conversed with him in French. Eventually, he photographed the "wild man" with me.

After going back to our cottage and relaxing, we agreed that we both would enjoy living there. The beauty and serenity of the place appealed to us. And most especially, the trip to Noumea with its variety of restaurants and things to do, was only a small airplane ride away. Next day, we took a jeep to explore the inland. The owner of the lodge, Maurice, told us to follow a small trail. It would take us to the native village. Enthusiastically, we headed out. After a thirty minute drive, we saw straw huts, but no people. However, we heard singing. The people were all in the church. We realized it was Sunday and so decided to wait quietly until the service was over. We really wanted to meet the locals.

Not much later, the door to the church opened and we were astonished to see that all of the people who came out of the church looked like wild savages. Their skin was a deep black, and they had very bushy orange hair. The children ran right up to me, laughing and circling around me, trying to touch me and to pull my hair. I didn't care for this attention at all. They had obviously never seen a blond before. Basil was taking movies from outside the swarm that kept pressing closer against me. As my discomfort grew, I tried to figure out how to get away from this crowd. I devised a plan, they would get away from ME! I would shock them! I made an awful face, then hissed and shrieked loudly like a witch. With my hands up in the air, I made threatening gestures. The people immediately backed away. The circle that had held me prisoner, opened up. I ran to the jeep with Basil following. We jumped into the car and drove quickly away.

"Why didn't you help me?" I breathlessly demanded of Basil.

"It was just too funny! And I was busy filming you," Basil chuckled. We both agreed that it had been a distinctly uncomfortable situation. We asked Maurice why all of these people had orange hair. He told us that the island had originally been a French prison colony. Many of the released prisoners stayed and mingled with the natives, producing a unique looking population.

The next day, Maurice provided us with a basket containing food and wine. Our plan was to canoe to a nearby island and enjoy a picnic. There were several very small islands in the area. Once we arrived at the island of our choice, Basil tied the canoe to a tree, spread out the blanket and unpacked the food for our lunch. Maurice had prepared a whole chicken, a baguette and a bottle of wine for our dining pleasure. In the middle of our lunch, Basil sprang to his feet and, in a serious voice commanded, "Don't move, you must sit very still." He broke off a big branch from a nearby tree and began hitting at something. I jumped up to see what he was killing; it was a tiny black snake. I hollered that I would run to the water, but Basil said, "No Brigitte, this is a water snake and very poisonous. In twenty minutes you can be dead if this snake bites you." I stood very still while we watched more snakes come pouring out of holes in the sand. As I watched, Basil killed eight snakes. We then quickly picked up all of the provisions and our belongings, jumped in the canoe and paddled back to the Isle of Pines. So much for our dream of paradise! No one had mentioned the danger.

We cut our stay short and headed back to Noumea on the little plane. There we ran into another obstacle; no hotel room was available. All of the rooms on the island were filled. Where were we to sleep? The police offered us a jail cell in the station and we had to laugh. Basil asked if there wasn't something else. Then the police told us we could go up the hill to a guest house, Monte Coque. Apparently this "Rooster Mountain" had no telephone, so the police did not know if there was an available room. Since we had a car, we drove around looking for it. We had almost given up when a man we encountered told us to look for a sign very low to the ground. Monte Coque was up a small, single lane road that had no barricades to keep cars from going over the edge. By the time we made it up there, it was almost evening. The room was available! It was very basic with only a bed and the toilet room at the end of the corridor. We had an outstanding meal and a spectacular sunset. Then our host informed us that it was time for us to go to our room as she was about to shut the generator off for the day. We had a kerosene lamp in the room, which we lit so that we could undress and retire. We were both exhausted. I climbed into the bed. When Basil dropped onto his side of the bed, I was unexpectedly catapulted into the air. I shrieked in alarm and pain. Both of us had injured our backs. When we pulled up the sheet, we saw that there was no mattress, only iron springs. Incredible!

Basil took the sheet and lay on the floor to sleep, while I took the two pillows and carefully lay on top of them in one place on the hard springs. Somehow we managed to fall asleep, because we were awakened by a muffled snoring sound at daybreak. We looked up and peered just outside our open window, and spied a big pig, snuffling around. We looked at the pig, the pig looked at us, then Basil and I looked at each other and laughed. What could possibly happen next?

TAHITI

With great optimism, we continued on our adventure. The next stop was Tahiti, in French Polynesia. We landed in Papeete, the capital. At the airport was a sign in French that informed us that the porters were not working and that no tips were allowed. The porters were all sitting there and would not move. Basil had to go to the bathroom and asked around to find where one was located. The porters were unfriendly, but finally one pointed and said, "Outside, around the corner." I waited and waited, becoming more worried by the minute. When Basil finally returned, he told me that there were no bathrooms, only a cement wall that he "baptized". They had only begun to build a bathroom, but it was not done yet. Now we were standing there with our suitcases. Basil flagged a taxi and the driver helped us with our suitcases. We told him that we wished to go to Bora Bora.

The taxi took us down to the waterfront, where we were to meet a seaplane, which had not yet arrived. We were told that it should land in a couple of hours. We asked the driver to take us around and show us the area while we waited for the plane to arrive. It was a small island, with only one main road. The beaches were black, some lighter than others, and they were covered with small coral stones. The vegetation was very lush, and the ground was fertile; bananas, sugar cane and beautiful flowers were growing everywhere.

After three hours, the sea plane arrived. As we stepped in the plane, perspiration began to run down my legs. It was a hot day, and we were crammed into a small area. The plane took off and we flew a short while to a stop in Moorea, another small island. The pilot informed us that there was a typhoon building, and he put the plane down into a protected area. It was difficult to breathe in the "tin can". The pilot opened the door and one by one we climbed out for a few minutes to get some air. Finally, we took off for Bora Bora. When we landed, several small boats drew near to the plane. Several inches of water was standing in the bottom of each of the boats. Three other couples and ourselves were offered assistance onto the boat benches and our suitcases were tossed to the wet floors, where they promptly began to float. I removed my shoes so as not to ruin them.

When we made landfall, we walked in mud until we reached the lodge. We were shown to our room, put our suitcases down and wasted no time in finding a restaurant. There we had a delicious meal and drank a lot of champagne. We barely could finish before the wind began to howl. We knew that the typhoon was approaching, so we carried a bottle of champagne to our room, knowing that everything was going to be closed down until after the storm had passed.

The typhoon then hit with full fury. The wind howled and rain poured down, with some coming into our room. We put the chairs on top of one bed and our suitcases on top of the other. Then we climbed up on the chairs, sat down and sipped champagne while we waited out the storm. Coconuts were being tossed around by the waves which came increasingly closer to our little hut as they continued to grow. At one point, coconuts came rolling into our room! After our adventure in Noumea, we only thought that things could improve. How wrong we were.

After two days of gale force winds and rain, the weather cleared. However, there was no communication with the mainland until the fourth day. We decided to go swimming, but were kept out of the water by the giant sea urchins that were everywhere. There was not much to do, so as soon as communication was reestablished, we checked out.

Back to the states, we had a short stop in Honolulu Hawaii. We had had enough adventure to last us for a while. On the Pan Am flight, I picked up a travel magazine. There was an article with photographs of beautiful sandy beaches, and it reminded me of my goal. After all of our recent experiences, I did not say anything about it to Basil. I figured that he would not be open to new ideas at this particular moment. I tucked it away for later viewing.

1971

Come January, after months of relaxation for me and work for Basil, I pulled out the travel magazine I had saved and showed to Basil an article about a small island with pure white sand beaches in the Caribbean. It was not so far away, only a bit over an hour by air from Miami. LACSA was the airline that flew the route. It piqued Basil's interest and he decided to show the article to Mr. Greenwald, our travel agent. He told us that we would not want to go there. "Nothing to do and it is not well known for tourism."

Well, that was just what I wanted to hear, I was very excited. It was exactly where I desired to go! So Basil made arrangements for us to travel to visit the place. Since LACSA was a Costa Rican airline, we stopped first in San Jose, Costa Rica. The vegetation and climate were wonderful. But the contrast between the wealthy and the poor was striking. All of the houses had iron bars protecting the windows and doors. LACSA then took us to our next destination.

GRAND CAYMAN, CAYMAN ISLANDS

We arrived at the end of January on Grand Cayman Island and exited the plane with about twelve other people. We rented an apartment right on the beach. When we stepped out onto our terrace, it took our breath away. The white sand was very fine. There were no people in sight. We were drawn to the beautiful blue-green Caribbean Sea with warm waters that felt heavenly when we immersed ourselves.

Basil reminded me that we could not stay long; this was just a first peek at the island. He said, "I have a long business trip and an exhibition coming up. You, my darling, will be my assistant!"

"Oh Basil, that is wonderful. I love to help you!" Paris, Japan, India and Korea, these were all of the stops on our upcoming trip.

We rented a car so we could explore the island and drove around for four days. The people were very friendly, and this time we asked more questions about the local dangers, and the flora and fauna. Everything appeared to be perfect for us and we promised each other that we would return as soon as possible.

CHAPTER 15

Combining Work with Pleasure

SALON DES COMPOSANTS ELECTRONIC

In April of 1971 we found ourselves in Paris staying at the Hilton Hotel. It was wonderfully exciting to see Paris again. When I was living in Monte Carlo with Jeno, we had visited Paris a couple of times. Basil was also not a stranger to the city. He had participated in numerous electronic shows before. So it was easier to find our way around. I was amazed when Basil rented a car and was driving like a Parisian, sometimes it was scary. The next day was the opening of the electronic show. For me it was an exciting new experience. I was full of anticipation to see Basil's work displayed. We entered the large hall of the exhibition. It was not long before Basil pointed in the direction of a booth. "There it is! I can see the name of my company from here!" It read; Richfield Composants pour Transistors.

A very charming couple greeted us. Basil presented me to Guy and Yolande. "Guy is my representative for components in France; and his lovely wife, Yolande, is keeping Guy company."

I complimented Guy for the attractive display in the large show cases. Guy and Yolande admired how well I conversed in French. We made a good team, the four of us, and we were very successful in our work. The exhibition lasted five days. After that, we were exhausted and rested for a couple of days. Guy and Yolande showed us their favorite places in Paris and the surrounding areas. We were pleasantly surprised and honored that this young French couple would open their hearts to us. We enjoyed their company very much and became close friends

ISTANBUL TURKEY

After Paris, we made a short stop in Istanbul. We wanted to see if the beautiful diamond ring was still in the jewelry store at the Hilton Hotel. The ring matched my unique and exquisite necklace; which Basil had purchased for me the first time we visited Turkey. But to our disappointment, the ring had been sold. Basil said, "Let's enjoy ourselves and have a stroll down the main street to Taksim Square. There are many clubs with entertainment."

"Oh yes, Basil, that would be wonderful. I would like to see a show with belly dancing. It reminds me of Lebanon." We did not have to look very long. One club advertised a variety of performers and among them, some attractive belly dancers. Inside the club it reminded me of a theater. The seats were arranged in rows, each row as you moved back was a little higher than the one in front of it. We were captivated by the performance, when suddenly I felt some hard, cold metal sliding down my leg. Then it stopped and was leaning against my leg. I took a quick glance and did not move. It was a rifle which had probably come from the row above us and had probably slipped down from the inside of one of the men's trousers. I told Basil in German, "Look at me and then take a quick look down at my leg, but make believe you see nothing out of the ordinary, and then act as if you are concentrating on the show." Within seconds, the rifle was picked up and the men left. I am glad that we both had the common sense to stay calm; otherwise it could have become a dangerous situation. At the end of our stay, we asked our guide where we might buy caviar at a good price. He took us to the black market. While we remained in the car, the guide went to his source. He returned with three good size containers.

We returned to the hotel and I became worried and said to Basil, "I hope it *is* caviar. You know they could have put sand instead of caviar into the containers." Basil opened them to see, and we were both relieved that we had indeed purchased caviar.

TEHRAN IRAN

Our next stop was Tehran. We stayed in the Royal Tehran Hilton Hotel. It was very luxurious and located just outside with city with a superb view of the Elburz Mountains. For breakfast we ordered only tea, with lemons and toast. Then we took one container of caviar out of the refrigerator and had a royal breakfast. We visited the ancient city of Rey, built in the Median Empire. We saw people washing Persian rugs and drying them in the open air on cliffs. We strolled around in the streets and observed the daily life of Iranians in the city. Some people were getting haircuts or playing games. It seemed to be a very unhurried life. We enjoyed the hospitality of the people, we enjoyed the food and especially an ethnic specialty, the chelo kebab.

NEW DELHI INDIA

New Delhi was a business stop for Basil. We made a day long tour of Agra in order to visit the Taj Mahal. On the way back, we saw a figure in a field tumble to the ground. Vultures quickly began circling. People were dying of hunger before our eyes.

1971

TOKYO JAPAN

In May, we stayed again at the deluxe Okura InterContinental Hotel. It was Basil's first time to participate in the Electronic Exhibition in Tokyo, and he had great success. After the show, the director of Sony invited Basil to accompany him and explore Tokyo at 9:00 pm. We prepared ourselves and went downstairs to meet our host. There were five men from Sony waiting for us. After the polite bowing and greetings, they told Basil that I was not invited to go with them.

"Why not?" Basil asked.

"It is not customary," they answered. Basil insisted that I would go with him, that he never went anywhere without me. The men conferred with one another in Japanese and reluctantly agreed that I could come. We first went to the Ginza District and took an elevator to the top floor of a building. As the door opened, two well-dressed doormen greeted us and ushered us to another door. When they saw me, they told me that I was not allowed to enter. Basil spoke up, saying, "This is my wife, and I would like her to be with me."

One of the doormen said, "We already have too many women."

I spoke up for myself, "I will do everything the men do. May I go in now?"

Finally, the doormen decided to let me enter. The hostess greeted and led us to a table. Almost immediately, a group of girls came and sat with us. The girls ordered drinks for the table. I also had my own girl. The host danced with some of the girls and they asked Basil and me to dance too. When we sat down again, there was a new set of girls to sit with us. Young girls came and went, ordering more drinks with each move. The Japanese hosts seemed to take pleasure in this process. Basil and I looked at each other and agreed in French that we would soon leave. After the third change of girls, we made our excuses to go. The bill was very high, each glass ordered was $10.00 US and no one had ever even finished a drink. We couldn't understand what the Japanese men found enjoyable about this set up.

The next day was another successful day at the show. Basil received even more orders. Later on, during the show, Basil received another invitation to go out in the evening. The very same scene in the same nightclub was played out again. The only difference this time was that everyone bowed to me and welcomed me in. The ladies greeted me happily, probably thinking that I was the one bringing them new customers. Who knows, did I make a change to their tradition of not admitting women?

KYOTO JAPAN

Kyoto was an absolutely elegant city which reflected the beauty and tradition of a bygone era. The most impressive sights were Nijo Castle, the Imperial Palace, the temples and the gold and silver pavilions. We admired and walked through the masterfully designed rock gardens.

SEOUL KOREA

The last stop on our trip was Korea. Basil had a client in Seoul, where we enjoyed the natural unspoiled landscape. The people were friendly, inviting us into their homes. This gave us the opportunity to learn more about the Korean culture. I was placed on a cushion among the women, while Basil was seated with the men in the next room, also on a cushion. The meal was delicious, consisting of a mixture of charcoal broiled meats and vegetables steamed to a delectable flavor and consistency. The dining ceremony was long, but we enjoyed all of it. I was once again grateful for all of the experiences Basil was sharing with me. We had all of our souvenirs crated and sent home. We arrived home in mid-July. Having been gone around three months, Basil had lots of work to do. And he had received many new orders from the exhibitions. I was happy to be home again with Candy; and each day a new shipment was likely to arrive containing more of the treasures from our travels. The year 1971 went by quickly and Basil and I were living in harmony.

CHAPTER 16

Exploring Grand Cayman

1972

We returned to Grand Cayman, flying from JFK to Miami. On the flight, we renewed our acquaintance with a stewardess, Veronica, whom we had come to know through our many trips. She was from Finland. On this trip, we had a very pleasant conversation and exchanged telephone numbers before the end of the flight. She was stationed in New York City.

When we reached the island, it was still wonderfully undisturbed. Basil rented a car so that we could tour the island. We visited a small community named Hell. We discovered the blowholes in the iron shore. We boarded a glass bottom boat and viewed an amazing variety of fish through the floor of the boat. Next day, we accompanied a fisherman who caught fish and gathered conch. He told us that he would make for us our first ceviche, raw fish cured in citrus juices. We carefully observed how he cleaned the conch, and then marinated it in lime juice and spices as we sat on the beach watching. Then he announced, "I will make a fire to cook the fish." I helped collect sticks for firewood.

Basil proposed, "Let's go swimming now, while he is cooking the fish."

"Oh Basil, this lifestyle where people can cook on the beach is simple and beau-tiful." After enjoying a great time in the crystal clear, warm ocean, we had a tasty meal on the beach in the sun. We were staying at the Pan Cayman House in an apartment with two bedrooms and a terrace facing the fine white sand of Seven Mile Beach. Soft waves were rushing to the shore as we watched the Caribbean Sea with the colors of water changing hue daily from dark blue to shades of green.

In the evening we went to one of the two hotels, the Royal Palm, where we enjoyed a satisfying Caymanian meal. After dinner, we walked to the beach where we sat together on the sand. It was not unusual for locals to join us there; bringing their instruments to play calypso music. Every day, we loved it more. Maybe this was the island we were looking for. We liked the people, the environment, the food and the climate. We were inspired to walk Seven Mile Beach. Basil suggested, "We start here at the Pan Cayman House and walk in the direction of George Town. Maybe something will catch our eyes."

"That is a wonderful idea, Basil. I really like the island." We walked quite a while before we saw a *For Sale* sign. It was a property of considerable size and located on the beach. We walked inland from the beach to the roadside. Basil estimated that it was about three acres. Later, we visited a real estate agent and requested that she look into a property we had seen for sale. She told us to come back the next day. When we returned she informed us that three people owned the property. She had only been able to contact two of them. The third owner was currently in South America. She explained that since there was no local work, the men went away to sea to find a means to support themselves and their families. They would often be gone for long periods of time. Consequently, the island was inhabited mostly by women, very old men, very young men and children. The agent promised to stay in contact with us.

In March, we traveled to London England to visit a customer. To our surprise, Veronica was staying in the same hotel. She was tall, beautiful with thick blond hair and a warm smile. I enjoyed the female companionship. Basil reveled in taking two beautiful blondes out to dine! We all became good friends.

When we returned to New Jersey, Veronica had left some messages on our answering machine. She let us know which weekend she had off. Then we would pick her up from her apartment and drive back to our house. Basil would cook steaks on the grill. I would prepare the salad. And Veronica would open a bottle of wine or champagne, which she contributed to our feast. She told us stories about some of her trips and about her roommate, Heidruth, who was German and also a stewardess. Veronica continued, "But she has a peculiar way of handling a long dry spell of dating. She compensates for her frustration by eating a gallon of ice cream every night to feel better."

We had to laugh. I asked Veronica, "Is she obese?"

"Oh no, Brigitte. She is an attractive woman, about my age, mid-twenties."

I remarked, "Heidruth is an unusual German name, as is her habit. I hope to meet her one day."

The weekend passed by quickly. We had fun and exchanged more interesting stories.

In July, I began to feel extreme pain in my abdomen and had unusually strong menstrual periods. Basil took me to a doctor who spoke to Basil, but not with me. Basil didn't tell me what the doctor had said. He simply whisked me away to Florida, saying that I would feel better any day now. We stayed at the hotel Kenilworth, as usual. I did not feel better. I couldn't sleep at night from the pain and would stay up watching television. I tried drinking Basil's Seagram's VO straight, thinking it would help to subdue the pain. But it didn't help, nor even make me feel tipsy.

One evening, I was sitting down and Basil gently put his hand on my abdomen. I screamed out in pain. I told Basil that I needed to see another doctor; something had to be done. That was when Basil informed me what the New Jersey doctor had told him. The doctor advised him that I needed surgery. Basil was afraid I wouldn't be able to have sex after that. The doctor had assured Basil that "the playpen stays", but Basil didn't believe him. I looked at Basil in disbelief.

"So, you let me endure this pain because you think that you won't be able to have sex with me anymore? How selfish!" I was deeply disappointed in him.

We flew back to New Jersey for me to have the operation. The doctor removed one of my ovaries, leaving the other in. He told me that if I had had the operation when he first diagnosed the trouble, they would have been able to save both ovaries. It was a very difficult operation and I remained in the hospital for ten days. Veronica came to visit me one day and told me that Basil still believes that I will not be able to be as playful as I was before the operation.

Sadness accompanied my disappointment. I had time to think while I was in the hospital and pulled myself together, putting myself in Basil's shoes. For him, I always was his beautiful playmate. He had put me on a pedestal. He liked to show me off, like a trophy; and now the trophy was damaged. Basil couldn't cope with the situation. My insight gave me a better understanding of his predicament; that in Basil's point of view, he loved me and would give me as much as he was capable of giving. I determined myself to accept, and adjust to fulfilling his expectations.

After the hospital stay, Basil hosted a large party for the local Chamber of Commerce, and asked me to attend. It was July. Everything was set up outdoors in the shade of the tall trees by the fireplace, where Basil was preparing the steaks. I was barely able to walk, but did not complain. I spoke with some of the men, and remained as long as I could; then excused myself and went back into the house to rest. I simply sank onto the couch, with extreme pain. I put my hands a little bit above my abdomen and prayed for help. Suddenly, I felt as if rays of heat were touching my abdomen where I touched, and gradually a pleasant warmth was reaching my wound. It was amazing, the pain began to subside right then. It took me two more months to fully recuperate.

At the end of 1972, we returned to Grand Cayman. We asked the real estate agent if she had been able to locate the third owner of the land we were interested in. Regretfully, she had not. The serenity of the island brightened up our lives, and we were enjoying being with each other. Later on, we met a couple at the airport who told us about a smaller island a half hour flight away from Grand Cayman. We asked a lot of questions about it and they gave us the information and to whom we should write for more

CHAPTER 17

Realizing My Dream: Finding Little Cayman

1973

In February we received a letter from Miss Eleanor Bodden whose return address was *365 Under the Almond Tree, Little Cayman, Cayman Islands*, B.W.I. We were thrilled. Miss Eleanor told us to bring food with us to the little island.

After landing in Grand Cayman, Basil asked personnel how we could fly to Little Cayman. It took him a while to find helpful information. Basil told me, "So now, we are staying for two days in Grand Cayman. There will be a plane, which flies once a week, to take us to Little Cayman."

"That is wonderful, Basil. We can relax now in the sun and enjoy the water." We returned to the Pan Cayman House and stored our food in the refrigerator. On the third day, we boarded a large DC-3 and were surprised that only two other gentlemen were joining us, but lots of supplies were loaded into the plane. We introduced ourselves to the two men and asked many questions. They were friendly Caymanians, telling us that they had relatives living on Little Cayman. One of the men had a small cottage there, but both were living and working in the states. They just came to visit and bring supplies to their relatives. We flew for about thirty minutes, then the plane landed on a grass air strip. Excitement rushed through my body with the thought of our new adventure. About ten natives greeted us. I was dressed as usual, in a mini dress, high heels and stockings. My heels sank into the sand, making it difficult for me to walk.

A small skinny woman greeted us, introducing herself as Miss Eleanor. Then came another woman, Miss Sissy, who greeted us; she too was very slim, both were nicely dressed. Miss Sissy spoke very quickly, presented us to her brother Joe

Grizzel and told us that everyone just called him Uncle Joe. He was tall, slim and much older than his sister. I would have said he was around eighty years old. He had a mustache and mumbled something, barely moving his mouth. I was able to understand him, although luckily, Basil could not. Uncle Joe looked at me and with an amused gleam in his eyes, had turned to his sister and said, "She, (meaning me), doesn't belong here in her high heels. The mosquitoes will take her away."

I laughed, telling him he was right. I liked him right away as I could tell he would always to speak his own truth. When Basil asked me what Joe had said, I smooth-tongued his remark, "Uncle Joe said I am very pretty and the mosquitoes will take me away." Basil laughed at that. Miss Eleanor called to us and pointed to an old truck. She invited me to jump in and drive; she would direct us to the cottage we'd be staying in. We drove on a small white, sandy road, passing a building on our right which had not been painted. To our left was a lovely cottage, which was painted white and blue. The eaves were decorated with blue lattice wood-work. The drive had taken only five minutes when Miss Eleanor announced, "This is Blossom Village."

"What a nice name," I remarked to Basil.

There was a small old building that served as a store. Miss Eleanor told us that we could buy groceries there, if there were any. We stopped at a cottage with a patio in front. "That is it, said Miss Eleanor. "Mr. Kassa, the generator house is right across from the cottage, where you will find the written instructions."

We both thanked Miss Eleanor and entered the cottage. First, I placed the food inside the propane powered refrigerator. Then I unpacked our suitcases. The cottage was simple. There were chairs and a small kitchen table upon which sat a kerosene lamp; the other room was a bedroom. Basil returned from the generator house, and I asked, "Look, Basil. We don't need the generator all of the time, only for lights, taking a shower and using the bathroom.

"Yes, Brigitte, that is fine with me." We changed our clothes and walked to the little store. We saw the almond tree. We asked the gentleman who managed the store if there were 365 people on the island. He was amused and told us that we would be lucky to see all ten of the residents. We three laughed together. The next morning, we found an array of fruits on our doorstep; bananas, papayas and mangoes. Every morning, someone was dropping some fruit or vegetables off for us, but we were not able to thank them. The person who brought them was remaining anonymous.

Uncle Joe's house was right across from the little store. One day, he offered to show us his land. "That is a wonderful idea, Uncle Joe," I said. Basil and I were very curious, and anxious to see how the natives were living on the little island. We walked for over half an hour; then, crossing the middle of the airfield, we stopped in front of a very small trail. Uncle Joe began to cut branches away with his machete. The vegetation was very thick, sometimes we had to turn sideways just to squeeze through the wilderness. Suddenly, a wide clearing opened up in front of us. Uncle Joe proudly showed us his plantation. We were amazed. I touched the leaves of the tall banana plant. All kinds of vines were creeping on the ground, some were curled around the trees. Uncle Joe explained that the vines were cassava, yams, watermelons and sweet potatoes. The trees were papayas and mangoes; and all along the beach were coconut trees. I pointed to a row of plants, "Look Basil, Uncle Joe even has corn growing."

Basil was surprised, "In the states we harvest corn in the summertime."

I said, "Here it is winter now, but the temperature is like spring or summer in the states."

We walked back to Blossom Village and then along the sandy road. After fifteen minutes, we saw a FOR SALE sign. It was a large parcel of land. We both sat down in the sand, looking out to the sea. As always, the colors of the water were fascinating; the combinations of blues, greens and turquoise. I let the white powdery sand run through my fingers and felt peaceful, free and light, and so close to nature. I turned to Basil and said, "I finally feel at home. We don't have to search any more for a different island, Basil. The locals are the friendliest people we have met. We can be self-sufficient. I will grow vegetables and plant fruit trees. We will catch fish, conch and lobster. Once in a while, we will fly to Grand Cayman or Miami to go out in style, and return with provisions. This is the island that time forgot. It will be our little paradise."

To my delight, Basil agreed. "It is a great parcel of land, I would say it is about three acres and is protected by an off shore reef." Basil wrote down the phone number on the sign and we returned to Blossom Village. We stopped in to see Miss Eleanor in her pretty little island home. We called out her name and she responded, inviting us inside. It was so cluttered, we had to turn sideways to get by a table that was covered with porcelain dishes which Miss Eleanor said she had never used. She had a knife in her hand, which she was using like a fork, to eat some fish. I had to smile, she made me think of a pirate wench, from two hundred years before. With the other hand, she pointed to the next room where the radio phone was located. Basil parted the screen covering the doorway, it was made of strands of aluminum soda pop tops. We seated ourselves on a well-worn red velvet sofa and Basil placed the radio phone call.

The following day, the two owners of the land came by boat from the neighboring island, Cayman Brac. After some discussion, they agreed with Basil on a price. Basil told them that he would send them the payment once we were back in New Jersey.

Now we needed to do some research. What would we need to make a new life here? There was just a tiny store that sometimes had supplies to sell, mostly canned goods. We began to prepare ourselves to become more self-sufficient with food supplies by learning how to fish from the locals, using a hand line, and to fish with a baited line trailing behind our slowly moving boat; which was trolling. We had great success, every day we caught a fish or picked up conchs. I learned quickly how to clean fish, just like a native. Conch were more difficult; very slippery. Sometimes the locals would bring us lobsters which Basil cooked. There was no electricity. There were no doctors. And obtaining fresh water was a chal-lenge. We would have to build a large cistern to catch the rain water. Basil began to make a list of what to bring back to Little Cayman. We asked the natives what they would like for us to bring to them. Uncle Joe's answer was, "I do not need a thing." He was too proud to ask us for a favor. But we knew that he liked chewing tobacco. The women were requesting basic provisions, like flour and sugar.

It was heaven. When the sea was very calm, it looked like glass. From afar, it even looked gray; but from the boat, we could clearly see the bottom of the sea and a wide variety of colorful fish passing by. One day, we cruised around inside the reef; then headed for Owen Island and dropped anchor. There we lay in the sun and played together in the warm water. "Oh, Basil, Thank you! I am so happy to live a simple life here; it would be my dream come true."

"I am happy too, my darling, because you are. I also feel good and secure in the water here by shore, it is not deep. Alas, I never had the opportunity as a child in New Jersey to learn how to swim.

"I think that everything has its own time, and there is a reason why we could not buy land on Grand Cayman. There, the waves came right to the shore. It was wonderful to go into the water, the bottom was smooth and sandy. Here on Little Cayman's south side, we have the protection of a reef. Yes, we do have turtle grass growing in the water, but I don't mind it; I walk right through it. Here on Owen Island, we have a large area with white sand, on the beach and in the shallows. I think we have found the perfect island for us!"

Basil agreed. I told Uncle Joe that we wanted to settle on the island. His responses were all negative. "The sand flies will bite you. The mosquitoes will eat you alive. The more he spoke against it, the more positive I felt that we had found our ideal island paradise. Uncle Joe did not know me yet. I liked to have challenging subjects to debate and was looking forward to our daily dueling discussions.

After two weeks, the weather suddenly changed. The sky grew gray. The color of the water changed to a pale green, dotted with irregular shades of purple. Some of the spots were even darker where the coral and seaweeds were established. Big waves were rolling over the reef and breaking into white foam. We could see the rain coming. It looked as if a tall, gray wall was rushing to the shore. Now we could not even see the reef or the shore. Everything was gray. Gusts of wind were hurling the rain against the windows. After four hours, the rain eased up. We could see the reef again with the white wave crest. The colors of ocean were changing from light green to turquoise and blues now. Behind the reef, it was a solid deep blue, and the sky turned light blue. Spectacular!

Back in New Jersey, we looked for a jeep to ship to the island. Then we made a plan to build a small house. It would be our first island house, with a garage and an efficiency apartment. Our plan was to live there while building our new home. While the garage and apartment were being built, we would continue to rent the same cottage in Blossom Village.

In March we returned to Little Cayman. Apart from our Caymanian friends who welcomed us at the airport, there was a newcomer; a four legged one. The dog accepted us, but was barking furiously at the plane. Everyone accompanied us to the cottage. The women were happy with the useful gifts we had brought for them. Uncle Joe's eyes lit up when we gave him the chewing tobacco. His remark was, "You are a case." I figured that this meant he was pleased. This time we made the acquaintance of Captain Edward Bodden and his wife, Miss Lila. From the airport, we walked about fifteen or twenty minutes along a small path to Captain Edward Bodden's cottage. Both he and his wife were in their eighties and tall and skinny. His nickname was Captain Woody. He had single-handedly cleared the land which was used as the runway for the airplanes. He proudly showed us a medal that the Queen of England had given to him in recognition of his fine work. Captain Woody was almost blind. His son wanted to take both of his parents to the rest home on Cayman Brac, but neither would accept that fate. They wanted to live out their lives on Little Cayman. Their son was living in the states, as so many Caymanians did. But he visited often and helped his parents as much as he could. Captain Woody showed us the local well; which was not far from his house. He told us that during the hurricane of 1932, a tidal wave came onto the island and people survived because of this well. We were just ready to end our visit with him and Miss Lila when another woman appeared, carrying two buckets. This was Miss Naida, the post mistress, who lived close to the airport. She asked Captain Woody for some water, since there had been no rain for some time. We watched him fill the bucket for her by lowering it into the well and pulling it back up. Miss Naida was very slim, much like Miss Eleanor. She was in her sixties, with dark hair. Her legs were bowed. She took the two buckets and prepared to walk back to her house. But Basil took the buckets from her and we all walked together to her home. She had a house similar to Uncle Joe's and Aunt Sissy's home. She thanked us and informed us that she had four sisters, all living in the states. They all wanted her to join them there, but she was not yet ready to leave the island.

We returned to the cottage we had rented from Linton Tibbetts, a very successful businessman living in the states. He owned several lumberyards in St. Petersburg, Florida. Mr. Tibbetts was born on Cayman Brac. As most Caymanians, he worked hard, learning in early childhood to become a seafarer on the ships where men made their income. Later in life, some men made it to captain of the ship. Others learned about ship building on the islands and became masters in that field. Uncle Joe was a master of building catboats. After the hurricane in 1932, many had to leave the Cayman Islands; most who left moved to Jamaica. There they continued teaching their skill in ship building. Uncle Joe told us that he became ill in Jamaica. He had cancer and was sent home to die. But instead, his wife died. We were astonished when Uncle Joe told us his story. We could not imagine him being sick or feeble. His face was weathered, his body was strong, tough and hard like iron. His character was consistently stubborn. He went every day out rowing his boat to catch fish or to lift out a few conchs, which he shared with his sister. Miss Sissy was the cook and the baker. Uncle Joe carried firewood and food supplies on his shoulders from the airport. He would not accept any help from us;

and was able to walk faster than we could. Uncle Joe showed me how to open the coconuts with a machete. He also taught me how to choose the best coconuts to plant on our property.

One morning we took the truck, which came with the rental cottage. We wanted to explore the north side of the island. We lingered at the Salt Rocks to watch the waves crashing onto the iron shore. The water was gushing irregularly very high up into the air, resembling a row of fountains. The sea was deep blue with white caps; a spectacular display. Then we drove further on and observed how the land and sea views were changing as we drove further east from our cottage.

Our truck began to slow down, and finally came to a standstill. Basil tried to start it again and again; he checked the fuel gauge which indicated that we had enough. I guess the old truck was tired of us driving her so far from the village. I said to Basil, "Let's go, we will have to walk back, and it is quite warm already."

We did not bring water with us, but luckily I had brought along a machete. After more than one hour of walking, we were thirsty. I asked Basil, "Look for a coconut tree, one with a green coconut!"

Ten minutes later, Basil said, "Look Brigitte, there are a couple of coconut trees, but we have to cut a way to them through the bush."

"Very good, Basil. Here is the machete."

Basil chopped a small path, the trees were loaded with coconuts, only I could not reach them. Basil was taller and was able to chop a bunch down. Now it was my turn to show off my newly learned skills; opening a coconut and finding the sweet refreshing water within. I did pretty well and didn't spill too much. Basil was content, and I was proud of myself. We took two coconuts with us, just in case we became thirsty again. One hour later, we arrived in Blossom Village. We were tired, but happy that everything went well.

Next day, we had a visitor, a good looking young man. We were surprised to see such a young person here. His name was Franklyn Bodden, but he asked us to call him *Frankie*. He was younger than I, maybe in his mid-twenties. Tall and slim, black hair and brown eyes, Frankie had a very charming smile! His skin was tanned from many hours in the sun, but like all of the islanders, his body was firm and strong. He told us that he had been born on Little Cayman and worked on ships from when he was very young. Two of his three brothers were living on Cayman Brac; one brother, Billy, had a small grocery store there. The third brother lived on Grand Cayman.

Basil told Frankie that we wanted to settle down on Little Cayman. Frankie was delighted and informed Basil that he had worked in construction and had knowledge and experience operating and repairing heavy equipment. This information impressed Basil, who told Frankie that when we were ready to break ground, he would let him know. When Frankie left, we counted the people from Little Cayman who were still living on island. They were; Frankie, Captain Edward Bodden with Miss Lila, Uncle Joe and his sister, Miss Sissy, Miss Vaida and Miss Violet. That was it! Miss Eleanor was the store keeper. Miss Rilly and Jack were born on Cayman Brac.

One day, Basil said, "My darling, we have had a wonderful time, but now we must leave the island. I have to go back to work."

"Oh Basil, I understand. I too had a fantastic time, and this trip was very educational."

In April of 1973, we attended the annual Electronic Exhibition in Paris; which again was a great success for Basil and our friends, Guy and Yolande. Basil was happy to see me in my beautiful dresses again, with stockings and high heels. We enjoyed being with our friends. Basil told them that we would love to have them come to be our guests on island when we were established. Guy and Yolande were pleased, and very curious.

Back in New Jersey, Basil worked hard. I prepared pleasant evenings for him. In the day, I played with Candy. Sometimes I cooked, and I studied English to become more fluent.

In July, we planned our return to Little Cayman. This time Basil invited my Aunt Didi and Uncle Max to the Cayman Islands. I thought this was a very generous gesture and thanked him for it. But I didn't think that they would enjoy being on Little Cayman. Basil smiled broadly, "Oh yes, we are all going to visit Little Cayman together, I am curious about their reaction."

"Basil, I think you will be disappointed." I sadly remarked.

We picked them up from JFK Airport and drove to New Jersey. We gave them a warm welcome with time to recuperate. Five days later, we all flew to Florida. As always, we stayed at the Hotel Kenilworth in the Arthur Godfrey suite. Basil was in his element there. He spoiled us with elegant dining every evening. My aunt adored Basil and was at ease with the refined lifestyle. I know my uncle would have preferred simple meals in more casual settings. But he did observe everything with great enthusiasm. Basil was a thoughtful host; every day we went sightseeing to different places. Basil had two sisters living in Florida. We were visiting one of them, Marie. She was close to Palm Beach. My uncle and aunt were captivated by the beautiful tropical scenery which included long stretches of orange groves and other tropical fruit trees. Marie was overjoyed to see her brother, and to meet my aunt and uncle.

A couple of days later, we landed in Grand Cayman. My aunt and uncle could not get over how beautiful the Caribbean Sea was. Uncle Max remarked, "In Germany, near us, there are countless boats cruising around in the sea."

Aunt Didi added, "And the beach would be crowded with people." Both were very good swimmers, and enjoyed the wide open spaces on Grand Cayman.

Mr. Ebanks took us fishing again and we dined, as before, on the beach. Uncle Max loved it, expressing his contentment with a smile. Aunt Didi remarked, "I liked the fish and conch, but I would rather sit in a restaurant and eat." We all chuckled, and the next day Basil took us to a hotel where we had a good meal inside the restaurant.

Next we flew to Little Cayman. A delegation of ten Caymanians joyfully greeted us. The three of us watched Aunt Didi closely, curious of her expression and reaction to the welcome. She didn't say anything, only her eyes widened. We took the old truck which was waiting at the airport and offered Aunt Didi the front seat with Basil. Uncle Max and I climbed into the back. Linton's cottage was a duplex; my aunt and uncle were right next to us. Aunt Didi sat down, looked at me and said, "Brigitte, did you lose your mind? Why in the world would you want to live here in the wilderness? I don't understand you. Why did you not choose a beautiful location in Florida, which is civilized?"

Now we all had to laugh. I knew that Aunt Didi would say that. I replied, "My dearest Aunt Didi. I love the pristine Island, surrounded by the warm Caribbean Sea. For me, this is a challenge. I am glad that island life is not for everyone. Maybe if I had not had the glittery life in Monte Carlo in my younger years, or the life I have now with Basil, traveling all over the world first class, then I would have chosen Florida. But I feel at home here and close to Mother Earth. I know that Basil will always want to travel. You see, Aunt Didi, I still will have both worlds. I also know that I will always want to come back to my paradise."

Aunt Didi was thoughtful. Then she said, "Well, Little Sparrow, I remember now; when you were living with us, you must have been ten or eleven years old, you would always say that one day you would find an island with palm trees, sand and sunshine. That was your goal, to settle on an island in the sun."

The next day, my aunt was in a better mood. We all walked the beach and then went swimming. My uncle liked Little Cayman right away. He and I were planting coconut trees together. Aunt Didi pulled some weeds. Basil added more things to our list. We needed a generator. Then we had to look for a refrigerator and freezer, kerosene or propane; and this was just the beginning. We left Little Cayman in good spirits. First we stopped again in Grand Cayman. We stayed for a couple of days in Florida. Then we flew back to New Jersey where my uncle and aunt thanked Basil and me for the marvelous time they had, after which my aunt and uncle boarded a plane for Germany.

On October 10, 1973, I obtained my citizenship for the United States of America, passing the test after attending night school classes to learn the American constitution.

CHAPTER 18

Intermission

CLOSURE TO MY PAST

We were back in Basil's home in New Jersey. The first thing that Basil said to me was, "Brigitte, I like Little Cayman, but you know that this was not my dream, it is yours. I am willing to please you and to build a house there for us to live in. You must promise me not to become a complete native. I want you to be dressed up in the evenings for dinner with your stockings and high heels. I want you to promise to travel with me, whenever I feel like it and for however long I want to be away from Little Cayman."

I thought fast; my dream was so near to being fulfilled, and I wanted to have a home to call my own. "Of course, Basil. After working in the sun all day, I would like to change into some sexy outfits. I also want to be your travel companion and your playmate."

Basil was delighted. Then I remarked, "I think that you are afraid of getting bored on Little Cayman. But now think about how much pleasure you will get out of being able to build your own house." Basil's eyes lit up and with a boyish smile he said, "Yes, I was thinking that I would need a tractor and a crane." I was glad that the conversation stimulated Basil's interest in the *big toys* he would have to play with. Happily, Basil said, "Now, put your high heels on and we will enjoy the dance floor outside."

Next day, Basil began to work long hours to fill the orders for his clients. Over the weekends, we were looking at the advertisements in the newspapers to find a vehicle for Little Cayman. We were lucky. Basil purchased a purple Jeep Renegade. This was our first purchase for Little Cayman. Basil stored the Jeep in his garage. The months were passing by quickly and Basil made his preparations for the exhibition in Japan.

The end of October, 1973, we stopped first in Alaska where Basil wanted to show me the college where he had put himself through school and where he had learned his skill in metallurgy. He was moved to stand in front of the building again after so many years.

In November, 1973, we traveled to Tokyo for the exhibition. Like last year, the show was a great success for Basil. This time we prepared ourselves to politely reject the invitations from Basil's clients for expensive evenings out at the night club, which did not appeal to either of us. Instead, we had excellent meals together in a variety of fine restaurants. After the exhibition, we took the train to visit Nagaya, the home of the famous Noritake China wave. Then we went back to Kyoto. It was lovely, most impressive for the gold and silver pavilions, the rock gardens, the castle and the temples.

By the end of November, we were back in New Jersey, where I received news from Germany that my father was very ill. His lady friend wrote to me that he wanted to see me and that she needed some help taking care of him. He needed full time assistance; he could not be left alone. I told Basil that I would like to visit my father for a couple of weeks to help them out. Basil made the travel arrangements and drove me to JFK for my journey. Basil held me tightly in his arms and I saw tears in his eyes. I know Basil did not like to be separated from me. We promised to talk with each other daily.

I arrived in Berlin and took a taxi to a small hotel located five minutes from my father's apartment, which was in the very same complex where I had once worked for him. The store was there, but now had a new owner. My father was in bed, but did not look to be extremely sick. He had been diagnosed with cirrhosis of the liver. He was very happy to see me and even climbed out of the bed to welcome me. His lady friend, Ida, cooked a hearty meal for the three of us. I enjoyed the home style cooking, but my father ate very little. In the course of the dinner, I watched my father refuse alcohol. Now that was something I had never seen before. He claimed it no longer tasted good to him. For several days, I would sit by his bed and we would chat amicably while Ida was able to get away and do her shopping and other chores.

After a few days, I saw some of the strain drop away from her shoulders. While I was there, I decided that I would look up Werner. I felt I needed closure to our relationship. It had been fifteen years from when I had first met him. I wanted to find out if my attraction to him was still the same. I hoped that my desire would no longer burn so hotly. I telephoned him. He was very surprised to hear from me. It had been seven years since our last encounter.

When he arrived this time to pick me up, he was driving a Jaguar. I felt my heart going faster, but was not overwhelmed with emotion as I had been in the past. Werner drove me around Berlin and then to see his apartment in an upscale section of the city. We also drove to his summer cottage, a very simple cabin made of logs. He lit the fire to warm up the cottage and I kept on my mink coat. I thought that Werner would take me in his arms the moment that we arrived at his cottage.

All the way there, I felt that something was not right. Werner was very different this time. He kept himself busy doing things around the cottage, not even making eye contact with me or initiating conversation. Then he picked up the telephone, making several calls to friends and colleagues. He seemed to be nervous and preoccupied, paying no attention to me, his guest. Werner looked the same, very handsome, but this Werner was a very different man from the one I had been so in love with. I felt something lift out of my soul. I suddenly felt free of that imprisoning passion. I took my coat off and looked around the cottage. Werner continued to talk on the phone. Finally, I thought to myself, "That's enough of this act," and I put my coat back on. I looked directly at Werner to get his attention and gestured that I had had enough and was ready to leave. Werner hung up the phone and in agitation, I bellowed at him, "What is wrong with you? I come all of the way from the states and you don't have the courtesy to acknowledge me? That is not the Werner that I loved for so long."

Werner rushed over to me and tried to explain. "I am sorry. I am very nervous and I don't know how to handle this situation. It is embarrassing for me. You know, Brigitte, you are the only woman I have loved deeply. But something has happened to me."

"Why don't we talk then?" I suggested.

In a worried voice, Werner said, "Please, Brigitte, tell me about yourself and your life first. Maybe it will calm me down."

I told him about Basil, reminding him of our last meeting in Monte Carlo. "You met both of my husbands. Now, Basil and I live in New Jersey, but we have recently purchased land on a small island in the Caribbean, where we plan to move. I am looking forward to our new life there."

Werner asked me, "Are you running away from something?"

"No Werner," I replied. "I am going forward to something." I explained how I had found a peace in my heart and had now found the place where I truly belonged. "But what about you, Werner?" I asked. "Are you still selling Mercedes Benz cars?"

Werner told me that he was now in the automotive import/export business, buying and selling cars in the states.

"That is great! And are you married now?" I asked.

"No, and I will never marry again," he answered. "But I do have a girlfriend. We met on my travels to the states. She is a stewardess for Pan Am. I have to go to New York every month. She is one of a kind. She told me that she went without a man for over five years and used to eat gallons of ice cream every week to make her feel better."

My eyes grew round and I began to smile. "Don't tell me that her name is Heidruth!" I chuckled.

"Why, yes it is! How would you know her name? Are you psychic?" Werner was shocked that I knew of her. I explained to Werner that my girlfriend was Heidruth's roommate, and she had told me about the strange habit. Then I told Werner which restaurant in New York was our favorite, "The Sign of the Dove".

"Oh Brigitte, that is my favorite restaurant too!" It was hard to believe that we had been in the same places for the last few years. Although our ways had run parallel, we had never chanced to run into each other.

"But what is your real problem, Werner?" I asked. Werner was reluctant to answer at first.

Finally he said in a soft voice, "I cannot make love anymore. Next month, I go to the Mayo Clinic."

"Oh Werner, that is so sad. It probably has something to do with your nerves. Maybe it is an aftereffect from the concentration camps. You are in your best years. I hope that the doctors can do something for you.

Werner told me that Heidruth was sure that *she* was the problem, not him; and that it made everything more difficult between them. A silence came then between us. He whispered, "The only person in the world is you. If it does not work with you, then I am truly in bad shape."

I looked at him and wondered if he was making this all up. But then I remembered how different he was now. I felt truly that he was suffering. I went to Werner and he helplessly fell into my arms. I caressed him. His thick wavy hair was hiding the scars from the concentration camps. I looked deep inside myself and decided to love him. I hoped that his desire for me would overcome his problem.

Slowly, I kissed his body, but nothing was happening. Werner covered me with his warm loving kisses, and I was aroused right away. But that was not the purpose. His tender part would not react.

I said to Werner, "I want you to just relax, close your eyes and remember the wonderful times when we were together in your little rented room in Berlin. That is when passion was our ruler."

I murmured stories from the past while I kissed and caressed him. After a long while, there was a slight reaction. Suddenly though, he shriveled up. I told him not to worry and rested comfortably in Werner's arms. After a while, deep feelings were arising from my inner-self and without saying a word, I kissed his body.

Slowly, I transmitted my feelings to him. I could feel his acceptance as he gave me his trust and love. Finally, Werner was relieved, and he was so happy! He held me close and told me, "A love like ours does not exist anymore."

I agreed, and said that a love like ours only comes once in a lifetime. Finally, I was released from the passion that had held me for so many years. Now my heart was filled with serenity. I was at ease with Werner.

He thanked me, "You came at the right time and showed me that there is hope." Werner then opened the refrigerator and brought out some Wiener Wurstchen, (Vienna sausage). "I am hungry!" We shared a meal and then we drove back to Berlin. With a final hug and kiss, he dropped me off at my hotel.

CHAPTER 19

Groundbreaking in Little Cayman

Early in 1974, Basil decided to retire and to sell his company. He was happy with our private life and looking forward to our next adventure together. In February, we made another trip to Little Cayman. Frankie had a bulldozer shipped from Cayman Brac and was ready to begin the work. Basil asked him to dig a well for sweet drinkable water. Then we needed a very large hole for a sizeable cistern. Frankie dug several holes, looking for water, but did not find any fresh water. Everything we found tasted a little salty. So Frankie started to dig the cistern hole. In the evening, he took us out on his boat to look for lobster. Frankie told us that the best place to find lobster was right on the reef. The lobsters came out at a certain time of the night. We had flashlights, but Frankie used a torch made from the mesh and husk of a coconut tree. When we arrived on the reef, Frankie sprang out of the boat and walked along the reef. Basil drove the boat, following him. In a very short period of time, Frankie had caught two large lobsters and tossed them into the boat where they landed on my feet. I squeaked and pulled my legs up. I didn't want to get pinched! Frankie laughed and told me that they wouldn't harm me. They were afraid too. We placed the lobsters into a large basin of seawater overnight. It was a fun adventure to search for and catch the lobsters, even Basil enjoyed it.

The next day we decided to check on how much progress Frankie had made on digging the hole for the cistern. We drove the green truck over to the property. The hole was quite deep. Basil turned the truck around to drive back to our cottage, and whoops! The truck went down into a large hole in the ground. With some difficulty, we crawled out of the truck. Luckily, there was heavy equipment that we could use to pull the truck out of the hole. It turns out that Frankie had refilled all of the holes he dug while looking for water, except this one. We all had a good laugh about it. While Frankie was busy digging the cistern hole, Basil figured out how much water storage we needed. He decided we could use 50,000 gallons; that should be enough. We traveled to Grand Cayman and met Mr. Flowers who had a small cement factory and also made concrete blocks.

Basil gave him the measurements of both of the cisterns and of the little house, which was going to be built on top of a cistern. Mr. Flowers worked up the numbers and told us that he could have the blocks ready for us by the end of October. Basil was okay with that. Then he ordered lumber from the states. It was due to be delivered in October. Now Basil wanted to travel again.

In April, we traveled to Honolulu Hawaii, back to the luxurious lifestyle, staying at the Hotel Kahala Hilton. Then we visited friends in Maui, staying with them. It was nice to see them, but I was longing for Little Cayman. We made a one-day trip to Molokai, an island almost completely unspoiled. It was once the location of a leper colony. We admired the lush vegetation; exotic flowers grew in abundance all over Hawaii.

Hong Kong was our next stop. It was wonderful to see our best friend, Teddy, and his family again. As always, he was an excellent host. This time he took us in the Hydrofoil boat to Macao. Teddy's son owned the Hotel Estoril in Macao. He and his wife greeted us warmly and invited us to a superb Cantonese feast. Teddy and his family insisted that we stay at the hotel as their guests. We had a great time in Macao, the sightseeing was breathtaking. There were white colonnaded, Portuguese mansions. We took a pedi-cab ride through a bustling shopping district crowded with Chinese merchants. We visited quiet Buddhist temples. In the evening, Teddy introduced us to a Chinese gambling casino. Afterwards, we visited a Las Vegas style casino. The contrasting cultures were all there, side by side; Macao like Portugal, China and then Twentieth Century Cosmopolitan.

LITTLE CAYMAN

In October 1974, we arrived on Little Cayman, back to nature again. We had gone from one extreme to another. How exhilarating it felt. We waited for the cement and concrete blocks to arrive from Grand Cayman. Basil hired four men from Cayman Brac to help with the work. The men were very happy to have work. We rented a native house which looked similar to Uncle Joe's house for our helpers who worked two weeks at a time, then went home to the Brac over the weekend by boat.

The cement finally arrived and was brought on a freighter, the Katherine. The freighter moored off of Bloody Bay Wall on the north coast of our island. Basil and the four men had to use a pontoon boat to bring the cement from the freighter to land. Then they unloaded the cement bags from the pontoon, carrying them on their shoulders to the truck. It was not easy, walking over the rocky coral beach. One man even took two bags of cement at a time on his shoulders. Basil helped also with the unloading. I was proud of him and how strong he was. We had good work men and made progress. Uncle Joe and I planted coconut trees. Then I told Basil that I would like to plant some fruit trees. Basil was pleased.

Basil and I traveled to Florida to purchase a variety of fruit trees. We filled gasoline barrels with fresh water and spaced them between the fruit trees. The water came from Mr. Linton's cistern on the property where we were staying.

1975

By January 1975, the floor of the garage had been poured. Then the walls went up. One day, Miss Eleanor came looking for Basil on the construction site. Basil had an urgent call from the states. He went with Miss Eleanor to her house and was connected with the manager of his former company. Basil had sold his factory and agreed to be a consultant for five years. He was urgently needed to correct a mistake that someone had made. He had to leave immediately. Basil called to Grand Cayman to find someone who would act as a foreman while he was gone. He found a man named John Cash who was willing to do the job. John arrived on Little Cayman on a small charter. Basil then flew out on the same airplane. Later, from Grand Cayman, Basil flew to Miami and then on to New York.

The first two days, John showed up for work at 7:00 and worked with the rest of the men until 5:00. I was on the jobsite all day, every day, taking care of my plants and starting my garden. The third day, John came to work late, looked around and went back to his cottage, Ball's Landing. In the afternoon, he returned, smelling of alcohol; and then left again. I started to write down the times he showed up and left. One day John invited me to dinner. Out of curiosity, I accepted. I told Uncle Joe that I planned to meet with John. He became very upset. "You cannot go alone to meet with him. This is a bad man! He is a no-good alcoholic." Uncle Joe was very clear on how he felt about John Cash.

I tried to calm him down, "I know he is a bad man. I figured that out. I have been keeping track of how much he has been slacking off."

I went to dinner at John Cash's cottage; we had a decent meal. When he began to drink after dinner, I got up, thanked him for dinner and walked to my cottage. It was early, so I looked for something to read. I found a perfect little book and sat down to read by candlelight. It was so intriguing and amusing that I became engrossed in it. At one point, I heard someone come by and then some strange noises. I blew out my candle and moved the curtain to take a peek. There was Uncle Joe in his long johns, walking back and forth on the sand, mumbling to himself. He was all agitated, muttering, "Where is Brigitte; she should be back by now! Where is she?" He continued to pace back and forth.

I was very quiet and watched him with suppressed laughter. Finally, Miss Eleanor yelled out from somewhere, "Uncle Joe, be quiet!" He muttered again to himself and finally headed back to his house. I laughed so hard that I had to put a pillow over my mouth. What made this incident more humorous still was that this episode here on island fit right into the book I was reading, Don't Stop the Carnival.

Basil returned and I showed him the log book in which I had written the hours of John's work. Then John approached Basil requesting to be paid for his work. Basil informed him, "You did not work as you were supposed to," and Basil fired him on the spot.

John sputtered, "It was your wife who spied on me!"

"Of course it was her, she kept track of your hours for me," Basil responded. After getting what pay was due to him, John left Little Cayman.

Basil told me that he had ordered lumber from the states three times and it had never come. The lumberyard claimed that they had sent it, but it had never arrived on Little Cayman. "Where is my lumber?" he wondered. Soon thereafter, Basil went with one of the men on his boat to Cayman Brac for supplies. There was a little store there owned by Frankie's brother, Billy Bodden. Basil came back with an angry face.

"What is wrong?" I asked.

"Well, all of our lumber landed on the wrong island, Cayman Brac. I saw all kinds of people with houses being built with lumber that has my name on it, *BASIL KASSA*. The ship captain had no idea which island I was on. So he just dropped it off on Cayman Brac!"

In his fury, Basil turned to me. "Are you sure you still want to live here?"

Without hesitation, I answered, "Yes!" In truth, I found it almost comical. I reminded Basil that the natives were all descendants of buccaneers and pirates.

What did he expect? Basil was deep in thought before he replied, "If you really want to live here, then I will build a big house for us. Do you remember your promise, Brigitte?"

"Oh yes, Basil. Every evening after work I will dress up as you wish, cook dinner and be your playmate afterwards."

Basil added, "And you must be patient when I am taking lots of pictures of you."

I agreed to all of Basil's terms. He was satisfied with my response. Then to lighten up our conversation, I teased Basil. "Now Basil. You are very popular! Everyone on the Brac knows your name!"

Basil stopped the work that was being done and told the workmen that he needed to make arrangements to have the lumber delivered to Little Cayman. We went to Grand Cayman where we met the Governor Dennis Foster. Basil told him of his plan to build a large home on Little Cayman. The Governor was delighted and welcomed us. We also met Captain Charles Kirkconnell and his family, and the Thompsons, the Scotts and many other influential Caymanian business people. They all welcomed us with open arms, and invited us to their homes. Basil enjoyed the great respect shown for him by the Caymanians. I too was proud of Basil.

Next we traveled to St. Petersburg, Florida, where we met Linton Tibbetts, owner of Cox Lumber. He was also our landlord. He laughed when Basil told him the story of the lost lumber. Then he said, "You should have come to me first." Now that we had a good connection, Basil ordered the lumber for the little house. On the same trip, we went to Sears Roebuck and purchased a sofa bed, along with a propane refrigerator and a freezer. They would all be shipped together with the lumber to Little Cayman.

We arrived in New Jersey to find that Candy, Basil's dog, was very sick. She did not want to eat and was only skin and bones. Just days after we came home, she died. This sad loss was just one more bond to our home in New Jersey that was severed.

We made plans for the main house. First we looked through House Beautiful mag-azine. Then we put our ideas on paper. We wanted it to be spacious, with two bedrooms and two bathrooms. We agreed that we wanted a large living room in the center of the house in the shape of a hexagon with a cupola. There would be a good sized kitchen too. Basil crafted a three dimensional scale model of the house out of cardboard. I placed the model furniture in the rooms. With all exact measurements, we knew how the furniture would fit everywhere. It was exciting.

We traveled to Tifton, Georgia where we bought a 5-in-1 tractor and a diesel generator. One day, Miss Eleanor called us in New Jersey. She informed us that the lumber had arrived. We immediately headed back to Little Cayman. Now we could finish the little house.

Back to New Jersey. Basil found an architect and gave him the drawings; explaining to him exactly what we wanted. After a month, we had our detailed house plans. We went to Miami and visited one lumber yard after another, taking our plans to get estimates. Then we went to cement factories to get estimates for cement and blocks. I admired how Basil had calculated everything in detail. I told him he is a genius! Basil said that we never could build a house as beautiful as we imagined if the building material came in bits and pieces or didn't arrive at all. To ensure safe arrival, we drove to West Palm Beach to charter a landing craft. All of the building materials would be shipped directly to the site of the landing craft.

Back home in New Jersey, it was time to think about selling Basil's house. First we had to decide what to take to Little Cayman with us. That would be a lengthy list. There was the New Jersey house furniture, then all of the fragile and unique items purchased during our travels, our tools and vehicles; everything we would want on our island paradise.

One morning, something strange happened. Basil had just awakened and gone into the kitchen. Suddenly, I had an unmistakable feeling that someone was standing very close to me. I opened my eyes and saw Jeno, standing in front of my bed, with a bright yellow light surrounding him. My body was fully paralyzed.

Gazing at me intently, he softly spoke, "You see Little Mommy, I told you so."

I was in total shock; unable to move or even to speak. In my head I started begging, "Please Jeno, go away! I am scared! I don't want to see you!"

He moved away from my bed and walked right through the wall. After a while, I felt the life come back into my body. I arose and walked into the kitchen where Basil was standing at the window, peering curiously outside. "You will never believe this," he remarked, "I just saw Jeno coming out of your bedroom wall. Then he walked towards Candy's yard and disappeared into the woods." So, Basil had seen Jeno also!

"Oh Basil, you too!" I related to him what had just happened to me. Basil had never been a believer in the supernatural, but now he was forced to admit that it might exist. I never was able to figure out what Jeno was trying to tell me. The meaning of his message is lost.

Basil sold his house, but the economy was not good and he didn't come out of the sale with the full value price. However, the profits from the sale of the factory made up for it. We were now prepared to move forward to our paradise.

CHAPTER 20

Pioneering: Redesigning Our Life

We arrived on Little Cayman to find our small house waiting for us to move in; but not quite yet ready. All of the appliances from Sears Roebuck had been put into the garage. It looked like a gypsy camp, nothing was connected. This was quite a change for us from Basil's palace to a two car garage attached to a one room efficiency and a porch. The season had been dry and our large cistern was almost empty. I needed water for my struggling plants, so we bathed and tried to wash most of our dirt off in the sea. The soap wouldn't foam. We tried using two pails of fresh water, one for us and one for the dishes. I would clean the dirty dishes and pans in the sea, scrubbing the frying pan with fine sand, to conserve our fresh water supply. Then I would use a little fresh water for the rinse cycle. The used water would finally be distributed among the plants. We made a fireplace close to the beach, then I fried fish, cooked lobster or wrapped seasoned fish in aluminum foil for steaming it over the fire. Our meals, accompanied with available vegetables, were absolutely delicious. In the evening, we had a record player for our music listening entertainment, or we would read. In the evening, we ran the generator until 8:00 or 9:00 pm. I had a good collection of books on natural healing and home remedies.

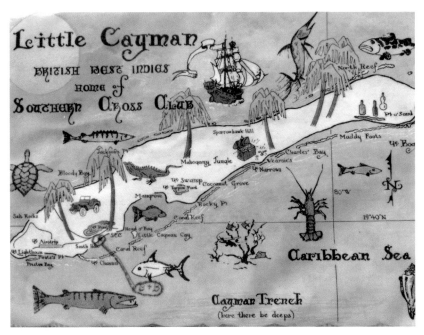

One evening, I read that *Ivory* soap will suds up with sea water. We started a new shopping list with that brand of soap at the top. For myself, I made a long list of herbal medicines. What annoyed me the most were the sand flies, which we call no-see-ums. They bit me under my feet, in my hair and everywhere in between. I swelled up at each bite site. Basil also was bitten, but not nearly as much as I. Even the mosquitoes, for the most part, ignored him. They would fly in between 5:00 and 7:00 pm, cocktail time. You could hear them coming every evening. If we did not begin running quickly enough into our house, we would become their cocktail. The natives closed up their wooden shutters to keep them out, and made torches using the husk of the coconut trees. The smoke helped to drive them away. We also tried using the home made torches, but the smoke turned everything on the porch black. For two hours, we could not see the sky which was obscured by a large, living, black cloud of mosquitoes. After 7:00, the cloud disappeared and the sky was illuminated again.

Frankie stopped by one day to tell us that the vessel, the Soto Trader, would come by and bring us fuel from Grand Cayman. We needed to meet it at the Southern Cross Club around 2:00 pm. The Southern Cross Club, SCC, was established in 1956. It was simply a clubhouse with small round cottages on either side of it. Members came to visit, flying their own private airplanes to the island a couple of times a year. Miss Eleanor informed us that Sears Roebuck was the main shareholder. SCC also had a generator. On island, there were three more cottages with generators, but the people only came occasionally to visit their Little Cayman homes.

At 2:00 we were at the shore waiting for the vessel to arrive. She moored close to the reef at 4:00. Frankie and a couple of men from Cayman Brac boarded the barge from Southern Cross to meet the vessel, which was moored close to the reef. The gasoline drums and propane cylinders were loaded onto the barge, which sailed to SCC and unloaded them right onto the beach. Now it was up to us to push the fifty gallon gasoline drums from the beach to our vehicle and onto the trailer. That was some very heavy work. There were men helping us. I was able to push the propane cylinder close to our Jeep. When we finally finished, it was dark. All five drums of gasoline and four propane cylinders were ready to ride home with us. We had accomplished some very hard work, and felt satisfied. So we celebrated our success with a bottle of wine.

The next day, Basil connected all of the appliances; the refrigerator, freezer and stove to propane cylinders. Then he pumped the gasoline by hand from the drum into our Jeep. Frankie stopped by and showed us how to transfer the diesel fuel into the empty drums, which were in the generator house. Basil had left the diesel drums on the trailer, so they were higher than the drums in the generator house. Frankie took a hose and put one end of the hose into the elevated diesel drum. He drew the diesel fuel up to his mouth and with a swift gesture, he put the hose into the empty diesel drum. A steady flow of diesel filled the drum. Basil watched as Frankie rinsed his mouth with water. Then Basil stated, "I don't think I will follow that method of transfer for the diesel."

Frankie grinned and responded, "Well, Mr. Kassa, that is the only way I know of."

Basil turned to me. "Let's go to Miss Eleanor's house. I want to place a call to the states, Tifton, Georgia, where the tractor is. It will soon be shipped. I will ask them to add one drum of hydraulic fluid and two hand pumps to the shipment."

We thanked Frankie and left for Miss Eleanor's place. She was not in, so we looked all around for her. Finally we went to the sea, and there she was, diving in her dress holding a harpoon in her hand. We called to her, but she didn't hear us. So we observed her for a while. Finally, she surfaced and waded out of the water; harpoon in one hand and the catch of the day in the other. Her dress clung to her skinny body. She was a sopping wet sight! Although she was thin, her inner strength enabled her to cope with the tough environment of the island. When she saw us, she gave us permission to make our call.

On our way home, we stopped at Miss Rilly's and Jack's place. They were both from Cayman Brac, but preferred to live on Little Cayman. Miss Rilly was sitting in front of her home, cleaning large boiled land crabs. We greeted her, and she proceeded to demonstrate to us how she prepared them for a delicious dinner. She picked the meat out from the claws and seasoned it. Then she stuffed it back into the crab shell and baked it. Later that day, Miss Rilly brought us some of her tasty, spicy baked land crabs. We thanked her. These crabs were plentiful in the evening. In fact you had to chase them out of your way. First I was afraid of them; they looked as if they came from another planet. Now I enjoy watching them. When they sense danger, they lift the big claws in front of their eyes for protection. The eyes stick out like a pair of antennae on the crab's head. Before she left, we asked Miss Rilly to make a list of supplies she would need from the states. We would bring them to her after our next trip. She gave us a big smile and went back home.

One evening, Basil said, "I am satisfied that the refrigerator and the big freezer chest are working fine. But most of all, I am happy that the stove is connected to a propane cylinder; now you are able to cook inside the house and to wear your sexy outfits as you promised."

"With pleasure, Basil. In fact, I will change right away and prepare our dinner!" I felt peaceful and in harmony with the environment and people of the island. My cooking was quickly heating up the small room. Basil helped set the long wooden table inside the screened porch. It was cooler there and we enjoyed our dinner with a bottle of wine. Afterwards, we went into the sea to cool off. There was a full moon which illuminated the island. An incredibly beautiful evening; with so much moonlight, you would think that it was daytime! The White sand sparkled and the moonshine reflections threw a silvery glitter over the surface of the sea. It was romantic. We were grateful and felt very blessed to be able to be so close to nature.

Basil added more items to our already long shopping list. As I looked over them, one item caught my eyes. "What is an inflated bed?" I asked Basil.

"Well, that's what we will be needing; when it is so hot, we'll be able to sleep out on the porch. It will be large like our bed in the house. I just have to pump it up. You would not know, Brigitte, you never went camping, or did you?"

"No, Basil. But I am curious, and also like learning and trying new things."

Before leaving for the states, we made our rounds and asked all of the islanders what they would like for us to bring back to them. Then off to Miami we traveled. After settling down in our elegant hotel, Basil rented a car and we traveled to West Palm Beach. There we checked on the landing craft which Basil had chartered. We wanted to see how much construction material had been delivered for our main house. Progress was slow, not much had arrived. Next we stopped at the cement factory and the lumber yard to look after our orders. In the evenings, we went to fine restaurants, and sometimes we visited chic nightclubs with entertainment and dancing.

Basil was looking for a second generator in case ours broke down. He told me that it was not so important right then, but when we were building the main house, we would need a stand by. Then we went looking for furniture that would fit in our hexagonal living room. The last week, we moved from our hotel to a simpler one. It was a Holiday Inn, which was closer to the airport. Basil spoke with the manager and told him that we would be visiting Miami every three months for a couple of weeks. We would like to stay at the Holiday Inn, if it would be possible to keep our food supply in the freezer until we leave for Little Cayman. The manager approved Basil's request, so we purchased all of the essentials. Then we packed it into cartons. We never could have done that in the elegant hotel.

When we were ready to depart, Basil called Grand Cayman to charter a small airplane to transport us to Little Cayman. When we landed on our island, we had a big surprise. We both shouted in the same moment, "Look!" There were private planes parked on the grass field. Basil said, "Maybe these are owned by members from SCC."

Miss Eleanor had mentioned that the SCC is a private club whose members come with their own planes.

First we put the meat and other perishable foods into the freezer chest and refrigerator. The rest of the boxes were left in the garage, next to our room. The Jeep had to remain outside. Then we relaxed. Basil had his favorite drink, *Seagram's VO* with *Seven Up*. But we didn't have a lime. We talked a long time with satisfaction over all we had achieved. In the evening we went into the sea and soaped our bodies with an Ivory soap bar and Ivory liquid. Happy to say, the Ivory did work in the ocean water.

Next day we started to unpack our suitcases and cartons. While we were organizing our island home again, a gentleman stopped by to visit. He introduced himself as a member of the Southern Cross Club. He said that some Caymanians told him that we planned to settle on Little Cayman, build a grand house and make it our permanent home. Basil confirmed it, and enthusiastically shared our plans. The gentleman returned to the club and spread news of us among the other members. This awoke their curiosity and they extended an invitation to us for dinner. They requested that we dress elegantly, it was a club rule that members dressed for dinner. Basil smiled as that was certainly to his taste, and I knew I would enjoy it too. I put on a long dress and high heels which sank right down into the sand. Basil donned black slacks and a dressy shirt. We fit right in! The ladies all wore long dresses, and some of the men even wore tuxedos. After a superb dinner, the Caymanian helpers began to play music. Everyone removed their shoes to dance in the sand under the stars. We had a ball, becoming friends with some of the members. They asked Basil why we didn't just keep the little house as a vacation home. They couldn't understand why we would want to live our life on this little island. One gentleman admitted, "I would not last for long here."

Basil laughed, "It actually was Brigitte's goal to live on a small island and to survive challenging living conditions while enjoying a truly natural setting.

The members looked at us, probably thinking that we were a little crazy. But then one man smiled and said, "You are an eccentric couple."

Members visited SCC a few times every year, and they always invited us, "the eccentric couple", to join them for dinner. I believe that curiosity had a lot to do with their interest in us. They wanted to know, over time, if we were still in love with each other and our island life.

We persevered through to the wet season and welcomed the rain water; enough fell to almost fill up our fifty thousand gallon cistern.

1976

Our first Christmas on Little Cayman was approaching. We invited some Pennsylvania friends to join us to celebrate the occasion. Otto, a professor, and Carol, a teacher, met us a few years before in a restaurant in New Jersey that featured live orchestral music. They were excellent dancers and we all had enjoyed sharing the dance floor together. They expressed curiosity about Little Cayman, so accepted our invitation and flew to Grand Cayman. We flew in to pick them up on a plane we chartered for our guests, for us and for lots of supplies. I had decorated our little efficiency room, especially the porch, for the holidays. We arranged for our guests to sleep inside on the bed while we slept on a sofa bed from Sears which we set up on our porch.

Uncle Joe was the first person to pay us a visit. He was happy to sit between Carol and me, and soon fastened his eyes on her abundant cleavage. Then Uncle Joe's sister, Miss Sissy, came by. She could talk and talk without ever having to take a breath. I called her "The Living Computer" as she remembered all names, dates and how long people visited. It was amazing what she was capable of recalling. She was in her sixties and wore eyeglasses. Uncle Joe was in his eighties and he could still read without glasses.

After the holiday, Uncle Joe decided to go out on a mission to find some good firewood. He didn't want the sea grape wood, which was easy to get. No, he wanted to search the north side of the island. Down a trail into the bush, to where he had more land, there was ironwood growing. It burned well for a very long time, like coal. We asked Carol and Otto if they would like to come with us, to explore.

"We would love to!" they declared. Basil gave each of us a large basket to hold the wood we gathered. Uncle Joe reminded Basil to bring his chainsaw, because the wood was very hard to cut. There was a small trail that crossed the island from the south to the north side. Uncle Joe, the oldest in our group, walked over the rough terrain so fast that it was difficult to keep up with him. With his machete, he cut the bush back so we could follow. After an hour of walking, he pointed to some trees that were growing on a downward slope from where we were standing. The trees were very twisted and gnarled, but beautiful. Uncle Joe showed Basil which branch should be cut and Basil began to saw away, but with much difficulty. The wood was so hard and dense that the chainsaw began to smoke. Basil paused to allow the chainsaw to cool down. He gave me the camera to film him when he started to cut again.

Carol and Otto were to pick up the pieces of wood that Basil had already cut and put them in the baskets. I caught Otto in a moment of disgust. He didn't notice that I was filming him while he grumbled out loud, "Pick up the wood," and in a fury, he threw the wood towards the basket. I caught it on film, turned my back and hid behind a tree to laugh. It's lucky that Basil was sawing and no one noticed me laughing. I composed myself and picked the wood up. Otto and Carol were sitting on a log and grumbled that they refused to help anymore; they had had enough. They couldn't understand why we would help Uncle Joe in the intense heat. They had no compassion and were definitely not cut out for island life. Shortly after this, they returned home; we never heard from them again. But we did have a good story to tell.

Miss Sissy made a long lasting fire from the hard ironwood in her caboose. She cooked food and even baked bread on the large open fireplace. A caboose is a kitchen separate from the house. I tried to bake bread too, but it turned hard as a stone. I left the baking then to Miss Sissy. We gave her flour, sugar and whatever she requested. We exchanged goods and tools with all of the Caymanians. In return, they brought us eggs, tuna and sometimes turtle meat.

1977

Excitement was in the air. Miss Eleanor hurried towards us and hollered, "Mr. Kassa, Mr. Kassa! Your tractor is coming over on the barge in one hour!" We were thrilled and rushed to the landing place. Everyone on the island was anxiously awaiting the arrival of our tractor. The barge landed and brought the equipment; all in parts! It had to be assembled. Basil called Tifton Georgia and confirmed that it had arrived. But now he needed someone to come to the island and help him assemble it. Basil made plans with the factory and they promised to have someone fly down as soon as possible. Days later, a young man arrived. His name was George, he was to be our mechanic. Basil was happy to have his help in assembling it. The tractor was called a 5 in 1 because it was very versatile. It had a front bucket to load, forks to lift, a back bucket to dig holes and a crane on top. Basil and George fastened the iron chains around the branches of a sea grape tree. Then they hoisted some heavy parts up from the ground to begin assembly. It was difficult and heavy work. Finally, the tractor was ready. Joyful and with a bright smile, Basil drove the tractor around and around on our property. Now, Basil owned a big and useful toy, which kept him happily occupied.

I was very pleased too, for now we had enough water in our cistern to keep everything growing well in that virgin soil. My fruit trees were looking great. The vegetable plants were already producing. I had sweet and hot peppers, tomatoes, watermelons, pumpkins, corn and herbs growing. Every season, I added more variety. We were growing more self-sufficient. Household appliances were working well; that made our lives easier. Now we didn't hunt for fresh seafood every day. We alternated with a variety of foods; we had meat, soup, pasta or seafood. What luxury. I felt a deep satisfaction in myself, and was ready daily to accept the challenges that came my way. I asked Basil if he was also content with our island life and home. "Oh yes, Brigitte, especially now that I have my tractor. It's easy to clean up our property and the beach with it." Basil had pushed the weeds and debris into a large pile together. Then he burnt it all down. But after the rainy season, the weeds came back, and they had multiplied. In particular, the nasty sandburs were growing in abundance. We asked the islanders how to get rid of them. They smiled and advised, "Only by hand."

We hired Jack, Miss Rilly's husband. She told us, "Jack can work for you, but only four days in a week. The other days, he and I are going fishing and collecting whelks." Whelks were snails; you could find them on the rocky north shores. We had seen Miss Rilly walking with a heavy, full bucket of them on her head.

Basil offered, "Please let us know when and where you will go for the whelks. I would like to help you with my tractor to carry the buckets." Miss Rilly was pleased and thanked Basil. It would take her a whole day to walk to the north shore, pick the whelks, walk back home and then cook them.

Next day, Jack came to our house. Jack was deaf, and he could only speak a little. He was very slim and strong, like all Caymanians. I touched his shoulder, he turned around and smiled. I talked to him very slowly, so he could read my lips. I asked him to show me how to weed with the machete. Jack cut under the sandburs with the machete and then pulled the whole weed out. Even the roots had burs. I brought a garbage container where we threw the weeds. I was weeding with Jack, and also using a machete, but was working with leather gloves on so that the burs could not prick me. The sandbur is a rough, prickly seed capsule on certain weeds. Basil carried the debris with his tractor to the dump. He also helped the islanders with their heavy chores and delivered a load of coconuts to Uncle Joe, to feed his chicken. We earned the trust and respect of our good neighbors; Basil, by helping them with the tractor and me, by working side by side with them.

One afternoon, we smelled smoke. It was coming from the village. Alarmed, we jumped into the Jeep. The smoke was rising and flames were reaching out towards the papaya trees. There was Uncle Joe, clearing the bush away with his machete.

Basil took a fast turn back to the house for his tractor. I ran into the house and grabbed the camera. It is lucky that there was no wind, and most of the vegetation was green. Basil cleared a stretch of land and stopped the fire from spreading. We asked Uncle Joe what he was doing, but we never did get a solid answer.

Christmas was approaching. This time Basil invited our friends from Paris, Guy and Yolande. We traveled to Miami to pick them up. We were also able to shop for food and supplies while there. This time Basil bought a suckling pig for the Christmas feast. After we had gathered all of our provisions, we stayed for a few days in Miami to enjoy the dining and dancing with our friends. The small plane which Basil chartered from Grand Cayman to Little Cayman was packed very full; it was a tight fit to get all four of us and our purchases on board. I had decorated our porch for the season before leaving for the states, so it would be ready. Basil had cut a gasoline drum to make a fire pit for the roasting pig. A couple renting Linton's cottage was also on island. Danny and Betsy were invited for our feast too.

Basil pierced the pig for the long spit. The men took turns rotating the spit as the pig roasted. It took hours. Yolande and I set the table and made the side dishes. We were ten people for the holiday dinner; it was a feast for all to remember.

Danny was an excellent fisherman. He enjoyed shore fishing and would go out every day, giving what he caught to the villagers. Betsy would spend her days lying in the sun and enjoying the water. Guy and Yolande enjoyed everything about Little Cayman, especially the sun and the beautiful water. One evening, Guy came running out from their bathroom, hollering in French, "You should not play such jokes!"

We looked at him and then each other, "What joke?"

"I was sitting on the toilet, ready for number two, and something bit me on the behind!" Guy exclaimed. "You put a pinching toy in the toilet!"

"No!" we protested. Then we all crowded into the tiny bathroom to see what had bitten Guy. It was a large bullfrog who wanted out of the toilet. How were we going to get the frog out? I wanted to catch him, but he sprang out and landed on the wall. Finally Basil closed the door to the bathroom and chased him around until he caught him. We all ended 1977 with a good laugh, trying to imagine how Guy had thought we would play such a trick on him; a biting toy frog that hides in a toilet!

CHAPTER 21

The Remarkable and Memorable Event

1978

In March, we began preparations for building our main house. Basil hired men from Cayman Brac. We installed a rock crusher. Our helpers told us that we had to drive to the north side of the island to get the rocks. Basil drove his tractor, I drove the purple Jeep with a trailer and the helpers drove a small farm tractor with a trailer. Our men showed us which rocks to pick to mix with the cement. I too helped gather the rocks, and I cooked two meals a day for all of our workers. It took weeks and weeks to get ready.

We took a short trip to West Palm Beach Florida to check on the progress of our shipment. All was ready to ship on the Inagua Wave landing craft.

Back on Little Cayman, Basil had to fill in the dock area with a large mass of rocks to make it smoother. The coral rocks that were indigenous were very sharp. Basil purchased another piece of land located near the airport. He cleared it with the tractor and planned to use the area for storing the vast amounts of building supplies that would be arriving.

UNLOADING THE LANDING CRAFT

In May, the ship arrived on Little Cayman. A reporter from Grand Cayman was there to document the historic occasion with photographs. The news was out that we were the first non-Caymanian settlers on Little Cayman. We brought heavy equipment and building materials from the USA. People came from Grand Cayman and Cayman Brac to observe the dangerous operation. I took photographs to document everything. The landing craft was moored at Salt Rocks. Basil needed his tractor for transporting the materials. I was especially worried when he took on a very heavy load. The tractor once tipped to the side with one wheel of it was suspended in midair. It was intensive, long and hard work. Basil unloaded trusses, lumber, cement blocks, cement bags and machinery. Our new fiberglass cistern was floated in by a boat.

Basil hired more men from Cayman Brac. I had one helper, his name was Bonnie. He weeded and cleaned conchs and fish with me. I went in a boat to Owen Island and was able to lift over fifteen conchs out of the water in about one hour. Then Bonnie and I prepared the catch for everyone's meal. Most of the time we had between six to ten men working for us. Sometimes, I cooked whole chickens or made a delicious pot roast or ham for all of us.

Basil used his tractor to transport most of the building materials to the new piece of land near the airport. The materials which we needed first were brought to our place. Basil brought over the 25,000 gallon fiberglass cistern and then a load of PVC pipes. He began to dig a long large hole where the cistern would be placed.

Just previous to this building phase, members of the private Southern Cross Club had sold their shares and it became public. Now SCC was a fishing lodge with guests. The visitors were curious and watched as Basil lowered the cistern into place. They applauded his success. Basil was proud and had fun with his project. Now we had a convenient place to go out in the evening, sometimes for dinner, sometimes only for drinks. We were always nicely dressed, with me in high heels. Sometimes the employees from SCC played island music, which we enjoyed very much.

Now Basil and the helpers were working on footings, foundation and flooring. One day, I asked him if I could learn how to drive the tractor. "I could take the weeds and all of the other garbage to the dump. It is more important for you to be with the men."

Basil was happy to instruct me; I learned quickly and enjoyed practicing my new skills. All of the work was a challenge and gave me a good measure of pride and joy. I knew that Basil felt the same way.

1978 Christmas ended in contentment. We made a short trip to Miami to stock up on food supplies and were anxious to continue our work on the main house.

1979

In January, the ground work was ready for a concrete floor. We had a two bag cement mixer which two men operated. They first mixed two bags of cement with water, sand and gravel. Then the men poured the ready mixed cement in the front bucket of Basil's tractor. Basil carried the cement and emptied the bucket onto the foundation. Two men scraped the rest of the cement out of the bucket. Other men floated and distributed the cement with rakes. With Basil's help using the heavy equipment, it was a fast and smooth operation.

One day, Miss Eleanor came walking quickly, calling to Basil that he had an urgent call from New Jersey. Basil hollered back, "I cannot stop now. I'm pouring cement and must finish this part." Basil had already finished the guestroom and then he completed the rest of the kitchen floor. It was late in the afternoon when Basil finally stopped the work and went to Miss Eleanor's house to contact New Jersey.

He returned with an unhappy face. The new owner of the factory that had been Basil's called him saying that his problem was urgent; they needed Basil to come help right away. Since he was still the paid consultant, Basil reluctantly agreed and said, "I already called Grand Cayman. The small plane will pick me up in the morning. Now Brigitte, get on the tractor. I must show you how to load sand to take to the men mixing the cement."

So it was time for me to learn another new skill, and very quickly. Basil told me that I could also transport the newly mixed cement to the edge of the foundation once it was ready. "But never touch the back bucket. It is too dangerous and you could kill a man if you swung the wrong lever. The men can carry the cement in the wheelbarrow to the middle of the living room foundation."

Luckily, it was the weekend for the men to go home to the Brac. I knew that when they returned, they would ask me to use the back bucket. It was much harder work for them to move the cement in a wheelbarrow. I had to learn how to use that back bucket, whether Basil allowed it or not!

The next morning, Basil left for New Jersey. I got into the Jeep and drove past the SCC where there was a small house owned by an American. I knocked on the door and a young girl answered it. I had met her before. She previously worked with the Smithsonian Institute and was here now to study bats. Her name was Martha, but she was nicknamed Ooky. She was eighteen years old, originally from the Carolinas. I explained to her what I had in mind and she was happy to help me.

The next day; Sunday, I picked her up. I jumped up on the tractor and asked Ooky to stay far away from it. Then I tried to operate the back bucket, practicing the maneuver until I was sure of my abilities. I asked Ooky to write every maneuver down for me, each shift, each gear, each little move. Then I drew out a design of the process. After that, I drove the tractor to the cement mixer and practiced moving the tractor and swinging the bucket this way and that way. I pasted the directions and diagram on the boom of the tractor so that I could easily read it.

It went very well! I invited Ooky for lunch and then we went swimming. It was a wonderful day. I asked her to come on Monday morning to take some pictures of me demonstrating my new skills.

Monday came, and just as I had expected, the men asked me, "Please try to work the back bucket, Mrs. Kassa."

I dutifully answered, "But I promised my husband not to touch the back bucket. He said it's too dangerous for me."

"We know that, but all of the loads of cement would be too heavy for us to carry with the wheelbarrow. And, the process would be too long and the cement would dry out and the floor would not be even! Please, you can do it."

I smiled and said, "Okay! Let's do it!"

The men applauded and cheered me on with their confidence. Everything was running smoothly. I could easily read the instructions which I had glued onto the tractor. In the middle of the work, a man passed by and stopped. He was a guest of the Southern Cross Club. He observed us working and said, "Why are you working here? This is a lost island. You should come to work in the states where you would make lots of money."

I pretended to consider his advice seriously, and then just smiled and said, "I'll think about it."

After the gentleman left, we all burst out laughing.

Basil returned. The first thing he did was inspect the flooring. He became furious. "Who poured the living room floor?" he demanded.

"It was me," I answered in a worried voice.

Basil then got even more upset. "I told you not to use the back bucket!" He ranted and raved, on and on.

Later, when he was calmer, I explained that Ooky had helped me and we had written down the step by step instructions. I had done everything again and again, practicing so that I would work absolutely safely through the process. I was very proud of what I had accomplished. I had poured the cement onto the entire 36 foot hexagonal area all by myself! But Basil was still unhappy. Maybe his pride was hurt or he was worried.

The walls were going up and the house was beginning to take shape. It was time to make the framework for the six columns. Basil instructed the men to build a wooden mold and to cut the steel to size. They were working to get everything ready for the next stage, which was pouring the cement for the columns.

To our surprise, only half of the crew showed up the next morning. We asked where everyone else was. A young man, Bobo, answered. He informed us that the rest of the crew had left last night because they didn't know what Mr. Kassa was planning to do. It was too much for them to comprehend. It looked like a castle, and, when it was finished, Mr. Kassa would surely put Mrs. Kassa inside and lock her up! We did have a good laugh over that. What a fantasy!

I explained to Bobo and the other men present that it actually was *my* idea to find a quiet island where we could live. "My husband likes to travel and would have preferred to live in a more comfortable place. Please tell the other workers this."

Basil interrupted, "Please tell the men that Mr. Kassa loves his wife and would never leave her here alone." Then he continued, "It is true that my wife had the idea to settle down here on Little Cayman. Now I too have fallen in love with the island. I am thrilled to have the opportunity to put my knowledge and skill to work and build our home. It will be a great achievement to have built this house." Basil paused a moment and then encouraged them, "You know that I am always ready to chip in and help when needed. Now, let's get back to work!"

The remaining men poured cement into the molds. It would take two months for the cement to set and cure. Basil told the men, "We will begin again in May, and I will hire more people."

From that time on, we worked for two and a half to three months on building, and then took the same number of months off. It was a good arrangement.

Now we were alone again, and Basil had his sweet revenge. I had to pose for pictures in the heat of the day with high heels and stockings on. I didn't mind it. I tried to please Basil. It was amazing how quickly it evoked his passions. Afterwards, we went into the sea. We had two weeks on island to ourselves; and then we traveled again. In April, we visited our Paris friends. Then Basil rented a car and we made a tour de France. We stayed overnight in castles, vineyards and in the country. It was absolutely marvelous!

Then we flew to Germany and visited my Aunt Didi and Uncle Max. As always, we all had an enjoyable time together. My aunt was a wonderful hostess and excellent cook. We had a lot of fun and laughter with the wine and the great cuisine.

On the way back to Little Cayman, we stopped in Miami to check on our lumber. The staff at the lumberyard confirmed that everything was as Basil had ordered. Basil then asked a manager to recommend two good carpenters. It was an economically rough time in the states, and therefore easier to find people interested in the job. Basil interviewed several men and asked two of them to come to Little Cayman for three months.

Back on Little Cayman, it was the middle of May and very hot. Most of the crew returned to our island to work. Basil hired more men from Cayman Brac. The work went forward, "full steam ahead". The house began to take shape. The master bedroom was covered with plywood and tar paper. One day I was weeding with Bonnie. He usually talked to himself, but this time he was angry about something and actually threw his machete toward an imaginary figure. So I stayed behind him, as far away from the imaginary figure as possible.

I was cleaning around a coconut tree when something suddenly crawled up my leg. I screamed and threw my machete into the air. I pulled my boots off, my jeans down and Bonnie came running.

"Mrs. Kassa! Mrs. Kassa! Are you alright?"

Bonnie must have thought I had heat stroke or something. I shook my jeans vigorously and a good sized scorpion fell out. Bonnie cut the tail off and looked at me with concern. My knee was already beginning to swell. I went into the little house and soaked the sting in vinegar, which helped.

August was very humid and hot. One afternoon I was weeding with Bonnie. I perspired so much that the sweat ran down my body and my clothing absorbed all of the moisture. It looked as if I had just come out of the shower. I felt so dizzy, and then passed out. When I opened my eyes, I saw Basil and a couple of men standing over me. They said, "Mrs. Kassa, you must take a salt tablet." Basil was ready with a glass of water and the salt tablet. After I swallowed it, I felt much better.

The cement columns were now dry and ready to be connected with a shrink ring. I admired Basil for his ingenuity. With the crane of his tractor, he lifted the wheelbarrow filled with cement up onto the shrink ring. Johnny, who was standing on top of the shrink ring, poured the cement from the wheel barrow into the mold of the ring. Basil called to me, "Brigitte, life me up with the bucket. I want to inspect Johnny's work."

I brought the camera for Basil from the little house and ran to the tractor. Basil climbed into the bucket and I lifted him up. He took some great photographs and was satisfied with the men's work.

The next morning, as I was washing the breakfast dishes, I heard a loud bang and a scream. I ran towards the main house where the men were calling for me with great fear.

"Miss Brigitte, come fast, an accident has happened."

All of the men were standing in a circle and looking down at something. "Oh my God!" I cried. My heart almost stopped. There was Basil, lying on the cement of what would be the living room. I bent down and he whispered that he was okay. Thank goodness, he was alive! I looked around and saw his ladder, broken and lying in pieces on the floor. Basil had brought that ladder from his factory in New Jersey.

Bobo told me, "Mr. Kassa wanted to check to see if the cement had hardened in the shrink ring. He climbed the ladder. When the ladder collapsed, Mr. Kassa fell to the ground."

Basil had fallen sixteen feet! All of the men looked at me as if to ask, "What should we do now?" I told them to bring me a sheet of plywood. I went to get a bed sheet and put it onto the plywood. Then the men lifted Basil up onto the plywood. We decided to move Basil to the little house. The men followed my instructions and set him down on the porch.

"Now, please continue with your work," I told them. They left quietly with down-cast spirits. I leaned close to Basil and whispered to him, "God was with you. You might have split your head open." I brushed his hair aside and gave him a kiss. "I will go to Miss Eleanor's and phone the hospital on the Brac to see what the doctor suggests we do."

First I went to the kitchen and drank two glasses of cognac. Then I went to Miss Eleanor's house and called the hospital. The doctor said that we needed to get Basil to the hospital for x-rays. "But let him rest flat for now."

The next day, the entire population of the island visited Basil. They all believed that it was a miracle he survived such a great fall. I put a pillow under his head. So far, I could not see any injury; no blood or bruising. He could move his arms and legs, but his back was hurting terribly. The sea was rough, so we could not go to the Brac by boat. For four days, Basil lay on the floor. Then he tried to get up. With some help from the men, he could stand. Moving slowly, with much pain, he was able to maneuver around. On the sixth day, the sea calmed down and two men carried Basil to a boat. It was a small craft with an outboard motor. They navigated to Cayman Brac.

Surprisingly, Basil was home by lunch, with a disappointed face. "The doctor could not help me much." Apparently, the doctor wanted to take an x-ray, but the machine was completely corroded and broken. The doctor gave Basil a corset to support his back; that made Basil feel a little better. Then he advised Basil to get a check-up in the states. Every day, Basil felt a little bit better. The pain was still there, but not as intolerable as before. Ever since that accident, Basil could not sleep through the night in the bed. He would need to lie on the floor.

We finished this phase of the work on the house and then shut down the operation. We asked the crew to come back in two months. Basil and I went to Miami where he looked for a doctor. He thought he needed a chiropractor. Basil made an appointment and the chiropractor first took an x-ray. It showed no serious damage, but the doctor said that Basil's back "looked like an old ship covered in barnacles". Then he gave him another corset for support, saying it was all he could do. Basil never took pain pills, nor were they offered to him.

Uncle Joe too had a small accident. He fell through his rotten chair, on which he had been standing. He hurt his leg and had to walk more slowly. But that he did not want. He left his house in the village and moved in with his sister, Miss Sissy. Now he was much closer to our place and could visit whenever he wanted. He took great pleasure in criticizing our "slow" progress on building the house.

"The bedroom is too big; the iguanas will sneak in and sleep with you."

"I do not think so, Uncle Joe. You forget, we will have doors." I replied.

We teased each other until one day, Uncle Joe said, "Brigitte, I want you to come with me. I need some wood to build a cat boat."

"Okay, Uncle Joe!" I took the tractor and off we went.

Uncle Joe pointed out where to stop, "Right here! Close to the mahogany tree."

We both chopped a path through the bush with our machetes. Uncle Joe looked for a special kind of tree which is curved like a bow. It would be for the bow of the boat. After a while, he found it and cut the tree down. Then we both carried the tree out and put it on the tractor. We selected and cut some more pieces of wood and then drove back to Miss Sissy's place. Uncle Joe said to me, "You are a case!" That meant he was very happy with me.

A couple of days later, I visited Miss Sissy and Uncle Joe. He was sitting on the ground sharpening his tools on a wobbly grindstone. It was precious! He really had the intention to build a cat boat. This time when I teased him, but he didn't pay any attention to me. His concentration was all on his work. I talked to Miss Sissy a little bit and then walked back to tell Basil what Uncle Joe was doing. "It's remarkable! Uncle Joe must be well into his eighties by now. I will take a photograph of this scene to imprint it on my mind." And so I did!

Christmas 1979 was celebrated with my Aunt Didi and Uncle Max on Little Cayman. I knew my uncle liked our island life. The first thing he did was to inspect the coconut trees which we had planted together four years previous. He was astonished by how tall they had already grown. My aunt was more agreeable than before. I showed her my fruit trees, which were bearing fruit in abundance. Then, as we walked towards my vegetable garden, we saw the tractor coming into the driveway. Basil was driving, and Uncle Joe was proudly sitting next to Basil. The

big surprise was in front of the tractor. The cat boat! Uncle Joe's great achievement. It was a gift from Uncle Joe to us. A great gift!

CHAPTER 22

Surviving the Elements: Hurricane Alan

1980

In May, the second landing craft, the Inagua Sands, arrived. This time the craft came inside the South Sound of the island and landed by the cemetery. There was soft sand and the unloading process was not nearly as dangerous as the previous time. Basil unloaded another generator for us. Now we had two, our main and a backup. Then he unloaded pallets of shingles and more roofing material. Now he smiled broadly; he had bought a crane in Miami. He said to me, "Brigitte, you drive the tractor with a load, and I will take the crane to lift the big tank for diesel fuel off of the boat." Everything went smoothly. Most of the material was transported to the property near the airport for temporary storage, and out of our way.

In June, the Emanuel II arrived at the Salt Rocks. Basil drove the Crane and I drove the tractor. To make the transfer of materials safer, Basil would lift a load with the crane directly off of the ship, without driving onto it. And I was ready to receive the load in the tractor. But the first load that Basil put onto the tractor nearly turned it over. It was too heavy! I learned quickly that I needed to put the arm of the back bucket out and fill it with rocks for counterbalance. I went back up to where the men filled the back bucket with rocks for me. I wondered why Basil had not instructed me on how to operate the tractor in a safer way before putting that load onto it. But now it was okay, and I took some loads up the little hill.

People came to look at our house and complimented Basil on how strong and well-built it was. Even the police and building inspector were impressed. Only Uncle Joe criticized it. "Why did Basil leave a big hole in the middle of the roof?" he asked. "Your old man does not know how to build houses, the rain will pour in.

The master bedroom is too big. It could sleep six people and a couple of igua-nas!" Then Uncle Joe pulled out his chewing tobacco; mumbling to himself as he shuffled away. We had a good laugh; we enjoyed his comments and were very fond of him. The work progressed more quickly now. Basil lifted the plywood with the crane. One side of the roof was already covered with shingles.

HURRICANE ALAN

Early in August, the sky darkened, and the clouds grew and glowed a strange mix-ture of gray and pale yellow. The sky was eerie; disturbingly quiet. The barometric pressure was dropping. Uncle Joe came by, moving much faster than we had ever seen. He spit some tobacco out of his mouth and hollered, "You had better stay in your little house, bad weather is coming!"

We agreed and got busy preparing for a storm. With the tractor, Basil picked up the wooden cases that held all of our treasures; our furniture, china, cloths, liquor; everything that was fragile and valuable and he started to place them under the roof of the main house. We did our best to protect it all from what was coming. The workmen helped with the project while gusts of strong wind blew leaves and sand into the air.

Then it began to rain; it was pouring! The men ran back to their house, we ran into our little house, and the storm became a hurricane! Since we had no communica-tion with the outside world, we were unaware of how awful it was going to be. We could hear the waves crashing on the shore and the rain bombarding the roof all night as the storm rolled over us. It was terrifying. In the morning, it stopped. We tried to open the door but could not. A tree had been uprooted and barricaded the door. I found the machete for Basil and he began to chop away, but could not go far. Soon after, our crew came to help us out. Everyone was okay; even the house where they were staying. Basil began to clear the fallen trees. Some of the branches split our cases open, but luckily the contents were not destroyed.

Later, we drove the tractor around to check on our neighbors, making sure that everyone on the island was safe. Most people had tree damage, and Basil was able to help remove debris. Uncle Joe commented, "Now you see what can hap-pen. Do you still want to live here?"

"Of course I still want to stay here." I told him.

Then he said to me, "You are a case." That was a rare compliment from him.

Later we learned that hurricane Alan was a Category 3 and had hit Little Cayman in full strength. The storm was a big setback; it took a long time to clear away the trees and fix the damage on the little house.

CHAPTER 23

Serious Accident: Basil's Brush with Death

We hired more men from the Brac. There were some interesting characters among them. One of the men talked constantly, interrupting the work of the others. His nickname was Captain Blood. He would stand, leaning on his shovel, and talk away. When I politely asked him to go back to work, he replied, "The days of slavery are over."

I answered, "I am much younger than you and work much harder. My husband is paying you well."

The rest of the men agreed with me and commented, "Captain Blood was born lazy."

Basil started watching him after I told him of our conversation. By the end of the week, Basil fired him, paid him his wages and sent him back to the Brac. He was the only slacker in the bunch. There was a good carpenter in the group who wanted to be paid two dollars and twelve cents per hour. Basil decided to pay him two dollars and fifteen cents. He got all upset, his face grew red and he demanded the two dollars and twelve cents. Finally, Basil agreed to pay him what he requested. We looked at each other and turned away, as we wanted to avoid letting him see how amused we were. He was a strange character.

Bonnie was a constant talker, and he occasionally let the machete fly in frustration. But he was harmless and a good person. I grew used to him and just made sure to be always out of the way when he was agitated. Everything went well for a while.

One day, Basil came hurrying back on the tractor from the inland. He had left to get the trusses and was driving alarmingly fast. Bobo was sitting next to Basil who was holding a roll of paper towels to his head. Blood was running down his face! Although Bobo was a very dark man, he now looked pale and gray. Basil climbed down from the tractor and said, "Brigitte, you have to sew up my head injury."

First I cleaned it with water. Then I took the shower hose and head from the bathtub and sprayed the fine streams of water to cleanse his hair. I looked at the wound carefully. Unexpectedly, blood spurted out of his head, like a fountain. I was stunned, and informed Basil that I would not be able to sew it up.

"It is very serious, your blood is coming out like a spray!" I observed how it would spray, then stop, and then spray again. I asked Bobo to drive the Jeep over to Miss Eleanor's house. "Tell her she must call Grand Cayman. An emergency plane has to be sent here."

I took one of my feminine napkins and tied it around Basil's head, like a scarf. One man brought ice, which I put into a plastic bag and set on top of the napkin. I then drove Basil in my car to Miss Eleanor's. She had good news from Grand Cayman. The communications center told her that there was a plane in the air headed for the Brac. They diverted the flight to Little Cayman first to pick Basil up. I called the Brac hospital so that transportation would be ready at the Brac airfield, waiting for Basil's arrival.

We stood at the grass airfield and waited. I finally had time to ask Basil what had happened. Sheepishly, he said that he had picked up some material from our land near the airport. He went back to look for his water jug, which had been missing for several days. He saw it sitting under the trusses at the storage area. He pulled his jug out, and all of the trusses fell on his head!

"Oh Basil, I am so sorry you are hurt because of the water jug!" We later learned that he had split the main artery open. We waited for ten to fifteen minutes, hoping all the time that Basil would not faint. The plane landed; there was one empty seat for Basil. He climbed on board with the feminine napkin and ice pack tied to his head. Later on, I called the hospital and asked Dr. Fraser how my husband was doing. He assured me that everything went well, and added that Basil's head had required 26 stitches. He would be allowed to come home the very next day. What a relief it was! I told everyone on island the good news. This was the second time that Basil escaped death. The accident did not diminish his spirit, and he soon bounced back with new energy and enthusiasm to continue his project and his life.

ANECDOTE 1

TWENTY-FOUR HOUR HAPPY HOURS

We had a new district officer who was from Cayman Brac. He was a good looking young man, middle thirties, always polite and friendly. It seemed to us that he didn't need much sleep. We would often hear his truck pass by at 4:00 am. His purpose was to check the coastline for unauthorized vessels off shore. We knew he carried his *life support* with him at all times. Sometimes he enjoyed a little bit too much of this life support, and his truck drove its own way, getting stuck in the soft sand or on hard rocks. Then he would come to Basil, after hours of walking, and ask for help to free the truck with Basil's tractor. One time, after heavy rain, Tarpon Lake overflowed and flooded the road. Our officer made his rounds and became stuck in the middle of the road, with tarpons swimming around his truck. It was hilarious.

On another lovely day, Basil said, "Let's take a drive to Salt Rocks and have a picnic."

"That is a wonderful idea, Basil!" I prepared some tasty snacks and filled our basket. I also packed some cool drinks. We were sitting under a row of sea grape trees in the shade at Salt Rocks. A truck stopped and our district officer came and sat down with us. Suddenly he sprang up and went down to the waterfront. Then he walked slowly back with his head bent down as if searching for something. Then he went behind us to the sea grape trees.

After a short while, he returned to us and asked, "Did you see anything suspicious?"

"No," we answered.

"Well, come with me and I will show you, you are sitting in front of forty garbage bags of Ganja, you *look* like guards." He said.

"What?" We looked in disbelief at the dark green garbage bags piled up under the sea grapes.

The police came from Grand Cayman and placed four of the bags by the government house outside along the telephone booth. Next day, there were only two bags there. By police order, thirty-six bags were burned over a period of three days; and the sweet aroma lifted the spirits of all islanders, as we became uncharacteristically cheerful. Our officer informed us that Little Cayman was a drop off point for drugs. For now, his happy hours would cease, as he took care of his official duties.

SPIRITS OF THE PIRATES

Miss Leoni, who took care of my animals when we traveled, asked if she could have our boat. "I needs the boat, Mr. Kassa, to go fishing."

"Okay, Miss Leoni." We helped her put the boat into the water and off she went. Days were passing, then weeks. After a month, we wanted our boat back. So I went to Leoni and spoke her language.

"Miss Leoni, we needs our boat, we want to go fishing."

"You really needs it?"

"Yes, Miss Leoni."

"Okay then, you can have it back," she said.

I thanked her and I drove our boat back home.

ANECDOTE 3

KINGSTON BIGHT

Kingston Bight is a lovely and romantic spot on Little Cayman, with a panoramic view of the pristine Owen Island in the middle of our sea; the south coastline on one side and the reef on the other. It belonged to the Bodden brothers. Most of the property was owned by Billy, Frankie's older brother, who was living on Cayman Brac with his family where he had a small store. The brothers decided to build a fishing lodge. Two of the brothers with their families stayed on Little Cayman. With hired help from the Brac, they completed the lodge. To our surprise, the first guests were from Europe, some from Germany and some from France. All of them were experts in fly fishing. They came to the right place. Little Cayman had plenty of bone fish, and the brothers were excellent fishermen and guides, it was their second nature. The brothers' wives served tasty Caymanian seafood. But the trouble was, the Europeans did not speak enough English. In the daytime, it was okay, they enjoyed the sports fishing. The brothers asked us to come over in the evenings to translate some of the questions their guests had. We were very happy to do that, and had a lot of fun conversing in French and German.

New Year's Eve came and one of the brothers asked Basil if he could buy some French champagne from us. Basil sold the champagne for the same price he had paid. In the evening, when we were visiting Kingston Bight, the guests were not happy. They wanted to celebrate the New Year with a lot of champagne. But the brothers had raised the price per bottle to three times as much as they had paid Basil, and refused to accept less. We paid the brothers the same price we had sold it for, and took our champagne back.

Then one of the brothers placed bottles of liquor on the tables; whisky, rum, vodka and gin. The ambiance lightened up with the liquor in the bottles going down. Unexpectedly, one of the brothers returned with fast steps and red face, hollering loudly, "Move! You cannot drink anymore!" and he swiftly took away the bottles from the table. The guests stared at us, we too were perplexed. We asked for an explanation, telling the brother that their guests were paying for the liquor.

"Today, they cannot drink anymore, because then there is nothing left for tomorrow," he explained.

We thought he must be making a joke. But, no, he was serious and upset. We were uncomfortable translating such a ridiculous response to the Europeans. Not only were the guests disappointed, so were we. Here the brothers had a goldmine in their hands; but they did not understand how to successfully manage it.

CHAPTER 24

An Extraordinary
Architectural Achievement

1981

In January, we finally moved into our castle. After living in our one-room efficiency with a porch for six happy years, it was overwhelming. So much space; we exuberantly walked from one room to another. Then Basil took me in his arms and we danced from one end of the house to the other. We had two men helping us with our furniture, putting it in place. It was exciting to unpack everything. It felt as if we had just come back from our travels to all of the exotic places visited over the years.

Now we were by ourselves, it was marvelous. The mornings were busy; Basil working with the heavy equipment and generators, and me in the garden, looking after
my plants and watering them. Then I cleaned the yard and took the debris with the
tractor to the dump. Every day we went out on our boat for fishing, swimming or
just playing around Owen Island. In between, Basil chose the time for modeling
sessions, taking pictures of his adored subject. So we both had our fun.

One day, the police came over from the Brac. They saw me driving the tractor on the road and stopped me. "Mrs. Kassa, you have to have a driver's license when you travel on the road. We will send an examiner in a couple of days."

"That is fine with me," I responded. But soon I forgot the conversation. That is, until one afternoon when we were swimming in the nude around Owen Island. Someone hollered through a megaphone from Southern Cross Club.

"Mrs. Kassa, the license bureau examiner is here! You must take the driving test *now.*"

"Oh My Gosh! Basil! Please grab my bikini from the boat!"

Basil walked through the shallow water until he reached the boat while I swam behind him; then he handed me my bikini. Basil drove the boat back to our house where the inspector was waiting. I jumped onto the tractor and the inspector gave the directions. I also had to drive backwards. But his eyes were mostly somewhere else. I passed my driver's test with flying colors wearing a skimpy bikini.

Basil had a new hobby. When he heard a plane circle the island, he went with my car to the airport to greet the visitors to our island. Miss Sissy too walked towards the airport. Basil would pick her up sometimes on the way, which she liked very much. But most of the islanders were already waiting for the plane to land. I was not interested in who came or what was happening in the world. I was content to take care of our home and my garden. But mostly, I enjoyed being barefoot almost all day. In the evening, Basil had the pleasure of seeing me in stockings and high heels, cooking dinner. Sometimes we walked to the Southern Cross Club for dinner, or just drinks. There, Basil was the announcer of the news which he had heard from the visitors arriving that day. And soon people called Basil *Walter Cronkite* or the Governor of Little Cayman.

1982

It was spring, and my garden was producing vegetables and fruits in abundance. I enriched the soil by making compost. But something was missing. I thought it should be a little more lively around our house. I was thinking of the kinds of animals that would be good for the island and also would provide food for us. I asked Basil about it. "What do you think, Basil, of getting chickens, so we might have fresh eggs daily?"

Basil agreed, "That is a very good idea, Brigitte." There were a lot of chickens on the island already, but no one fenced them in. Uncle Joe was feeding them with coconuts. After his chickens had had enough to eat, they disappeared into the bush and laid their eggs. Then Uncle Joe followed the clucking sound to find a fresh egg. He had to cut the underbrush with his machete to get to the nest.

One day, Miss Sissy arrived to say, in an agitated voice, "Mrs. Kassa, Joe did not come back from his egg hunting." We followed the trail made by fresh cut branches and found Uncle Joe lying on the ground on top of the sharp cut sticks. He was bleeding from different parts of his body. We pulled him up and brought him to the house to clean his wounds. I cut a juicy piece of aloe vera into smaller pieces for salve while Basil bandaged the injuries tightly. We scolded him, but Uncle Joe just smiled and mumbled something under his mustache.

One night we awoke to the shrill cry of a rooster. Then it became unbearable. The crowing did not stop. We went outside and saw five roosters perching in our trees. They were crowing full force. In frustration, Basil made a fast decision. He grabbed his shotgun and we climbed in the jeep. I drove us around the trees. He took aim at his target. After ten minutes, we had our tranquility back. Basil had been a sharp shooter in the army and enjoyed making good use of his skills. There was a full moon and one might have thought it was daylight. We took a dip in the sea and then went back to our bed. The following day, I tried to cook one of the roosters, but he was too tough to eat.

We traveled to a hatchery in Miami and purchased a dozen three-day-old chicks, Leghorns. Then we looked around in the hatchery and I saw two little ducklings, also three days old. I fell hopelessly in love with them, and picked them up to show Basil. "Look how adorable the ducklings are!"

"Okay, Brigitte, we will take them too."

Then we bought all of the necessary supplies for the babies and ourselves, and flew back to Little Cayman. We put the chickens in a big wooden case that some of our furniture had come in. We covered the top with heavy screen. That way, they were protected from wild cats and rodents. The two little ducklings were named Stefan and Stefanie. I put them in a wheel barrow overnight. A couple of days later, Basil went to Cayman Brac to purchase some fencing for the chickens and for materials to make a chicken coop. I enjoyed my little family and became very attached to the birds, and they loved me too.

Three months later, the owner of the land next to our home offered up the lot for sale. I was very excited. "Oh Basil! We can leave it untouched. It will protect our privacy in years to come."

"Yes, Brigitte. If the price is right, I will buy it." And so he did. It was the same size as our first property.

By now, Basil was ready to travel again. I was worried for I didn't want to leave my ducks and chicks at home alone. But I had made a promise to Basil, that whenever he wanted to travel, I would be ready to go with him. Basil had kept his part of our agreement.

"Oh Basil, first I have to look for somebody who will feed the chickens and take care of my ducks." I went into the village and asked around, but everybody was busy with their own daily chores. I had just left Miss Rilly's house when she called me back in and said, "My Cousin Carsen is coming from England. He has nothing to do here. It would be a blessing if you can give him some work."

I was relieved and told Basil about it. Basil hired Carsen as our caretaker. Four days later, he arrived. We told him that he could work full days. First he would feed the chickens and ducks. Then he would take care of my vegetable garden and the rest of the property as needed. He seemed to be content with our arrangement. For one week, I worked with him. I instructed Carsen, "The chickens are easy to take care of. They are fenced in, you just have to give them water and food. My ducks need a little fence around them only for the night. First thing is to give them water and food in the morning and then let them out. They can graze by themselves. When you have finished your work, put the ducks back in their protected yard."

The day of our departure came; I wanted to stay with my pets. I instructed myself to show Basil a happy face and not to reveal my worries. This time we chartered a plane from the Brac. Basil had called the pilot and asked him to pick us up very early in the morning, by daybreak. The next morning, we went to the airport and waited and waited, no plane. Basil went to Miss Eleanor's and called Cayman Brac. Nobody knew where the pilot was. After a while, Basil called again and someone told him that the pilot was in no condition to fly, because he was still too drunk from the night before. We went back home, Basil was upset and very disappointed.

I had a plan to make good use of our unexpected time at home. I said to Basil, "Soon Carsen will come. Don't let him know that we are here. We can watch him from inside the house and see if he remembers everything I told him. Somehow, I don't have a good feeling about him."

Carsen came and began to weed. Then he took care of the chickens and went back to weeding. He ignored my ducks completely! He did not let them out or give them food or water. My heart sank and I was close to crying, but then I said to Basil, "Maybe it was meant to be that we could not fly out today. This is the reason."

We observed Carsen for one more hour. He did not go near my ducks. We both finally ran out calling to him. We frightened him so; he thought we were ghosts! He was confused and began to stutter. Basil told him he would have to hire some-one else, though we had no one else. Carsen didn't know that. He apologized for forgetting the ducks and promised to do right. Two days later, we left for the states. There we visited different cities and enjoyed dining and dancing. On the way back to Little Cayman we stopped at the hatchery and purchased more duck-lings, so that Stefan and Stefanie would not be lonely when we were away.

SEPTEMBER 12, 1982

Every morning we would wake up at sunrise and marvel at the colorful reflections on the sea.

"We are fortunate to live here in serenity and beauty," I remarked to Basil.

He agreed and then left for the generator to get it started. He returned to select a record. Soon, beautiful music filled our home. So our day began.

That same evening, after a full day of work, I fell asleep early. I had a strange dream. My duck, Stefanie, climbed up a tree. A swan was chasing her and fol-lowed her up. But he was too heavy and fell down. Stefanie was safe. The dream was so clear, that when I woke up, I could still see all of the details. I became wor-ried about Stefanie. It was still dark, so I quickly located the flashlight and went out to the ducks' yard. They all greeted me. But I took only Stefanie into my arms, checked her out, and decided everything was all right.

When I returned to bed, Basil was awake and asked me what was going on. I told him of my dream and he said, "You worry too much." Then he rolled over and began to snore. I couldn't sleep anymore and the whole following day, I did not have much energy.

Around 5 o'clock the morning of September 14, I had another terrible dream. I saw a newspaper which was all black. In the middle there was a diamond crown and under the crown it was written *Monaco*. But I could not read it all. Worse yet, I hardly could move my body; I felt paralyzed. I waited until Basil woke up, then I whispered to him my dream; also that I was very weak and could not even get up.

"I think the Duchess of Arenberg died, because I saw a crown and could read Monaco. She was very close to me and visited the Gipsy Club many times." I told him.

Basil made our breakfast and he helped me out of the bed. I could barely make it to the table. I sat down and prayed to never have another experience like this again. I said to Basil, "Do you remember in New Jersey when Jeno appeared in our bedroom, and I could not move for a while. This time it is even worse, I am exhausted." Then I asked, "Basil, please call Leslie in Monte Carlo." Leslie had been our bartender at the Gipsy Club. "Please Basil, go to Miss Eleanor's house and call Leslie; maybe you can get connected."

Instead, Basil took his radio outside, mounted a long antenna on it and tinkered around with it. The reception was rarely good, but Basil was lucky. He caught the news from the states; and what a shock it was. They were broadcasting that Princess Grace of Monaco had been in a fatal car accident. It happened on the same road up in the mountains where I almost had my accident when I was driving her former car and had brake failure. Her daughter Stefanie was safe. As in my previous dream, my duck Stefanie was safe.

"Basil, please help me back to bed. My energy is drained."

Two days later, I felt much better and was my own self again. Basil said, "I would like to go to Grand Cayman for three days. We haven't visited the big island for a long time. We've been too busy building the house."

"That's a wonderful idea, Basil. You're right. We have just been passing through on travel to the states and other countries.

The next day, we traveled to Grand Cayman. Basil rented a car and we headed for Seven Mile Beach. We saw the Hotel Galleon Beach and decided to check in. Then we drove around for sightseeing. It was a very different Grand Cayman from the one we knew ten years before in 1972 on our first visit. Now Grand Cayman had more hotels, restaurants, supermarkets, cars and people. We enjoyed the convenience of shopping.

"Now Basil, we don't have to fly all of the way to the states. You can even buy our liquor here!"

"That is very good, Brigitte. But what is even better is that tonight we are going out to dine, wine and dance!"

"Perfect, Basil!" I replied smiling.

In the evening, we met a charming couple. Sonny was the owner of the hotel. His companion, Dorothy, said, "Please call me Dottie." We all enjoyed a long and animated conversation. Dottie was lovely. We admired her thick blonde hair, brown eyes and stunning figure with a tiny waistline and full bosom. She spoke with a Southern charm and we were pleasantly surprised when she told us that she was from Tifton Georgia. We laughed and told her that we had purchased the tractor in Tifton.

Sonny was tall and slim, very handsome. His hair was gray, mixed with some brown streaks. He had a round friendly face. Sonny seemed very interested in us and our lives on Little Cayman. I think the admiration was mutual. The next day, they invited us to their home. Dottie prepared a superb meal, and Sonny let the Dom Perignon flow. It was a delightful day. Basil invited Sonny and Dottie to Little Cayman and they seemed very pleased with the chance to visit with us in our home.

Sonny said, "I will bring the champagne." Sonny had his own plane to fly to Little Cayman for the visit. We made a date for the following week.

Basil told him, "Before landing, circle around to see our house. We'll see you and head to the airport to pick you up."

Basil phoned the Executive Airline to set a time for the next day to take us back to Little Cayman. The next morning we went shopping and loaded the plane with all kinds of goods, delicatessen food and cases of liquor.

The day for Sonny's and Dottie's visit arrived. We heard Sonny's plane circle around our house and ran outside to wave. With excitement, we drove to the airport to pick up our new friends. Everything was ready to entertain our guests. I had prepared the food early in the morning. Our table was set for a sumptuous meal. They arrived with baskets of fruit and champagne. When they saw our house, they were much impressed. Immediately, Sonny asked Basil a lot of questions about the construction. I took Dottie outside and showed her my vegetable garden. She was very enthusiastic and admired our little paradise. So did Sonny. After our feast, he mentioned that he wanted to invest in Grand Cayman to build an upscale shopping mall. Instantly we said, "We know a high class shopping mall with beautiful landscaping."

"What is the location?" Sonny asked.

"Miami," replied Basil.

"Okay, whenever you would like to show us the shopping mall, let us know. We will pick you up and we'll all travel together to Miami."

"That's fantastic!" we happily agreed.

In conversation, Dottie asked me if my parents were still in Germany. I told her that both had passed away; but that my aunt and uncle were in Germany still. I told Sonny and Dottie about them; how my uncle was my mother's brother and my aunt was from Hungary. I mentioned that they came to visit us sometimes. Suddenly, Sonny said some greetings in Hungarian to me. I was surprised, but I answered back in Hungarian. Sonny explained that his first wife was Hungarian, and that he has an eighteen year old son from the marriage.

CHAPTER 25

Variety Gives Spice to our Life

1983

The population of all three islands had increased to seventeen thousand. The population on Cayman Brac was one thousand eight hundred. In 1971, when we first arrived, the population of all three islands was eleven thousand. Cayman Brac had only one thousand people. Little Cayman was still the same, with maybe twelve homes. But we were seeing more visitors and were happy and hopeful that it would stay uncrowded and undeveloped.

Early in January, Sonny and Dottie picked us up for our trip to Miami. It was great flying in a private plane. We showed them our favorite shopping center in Miami, The Falls. This mall featured top quality stores and restaurants. The wooden walkways circled around the spectacular landscaping, with lush tropical plants, fountains and waterfalls. The water was collected in large pools where waterlilies with showy flowers in multicolored shades were floating. In other ponds, many different species of fish were enjoying the water cascades. Sonny and Dottie were thrilled. He exclaimed, "This is exactly what I would like to see on Grand Cayman, and now we will celebrate to a successful future."

Back on Little Cayman, my ducks were happy to see me and I was glad to be home. I picked each one up and gave them kisses. Proudly they waddled towards the sea, with my lipstick marks on their white feathers. Then I went back to my garden and enjoyed the simple life. Basil inspected his equipment and the generators. I was very glad for Basil that we had such charming new friends who were refined and had many intellectual interests.

On a hot afternoon in May, my ducks Stefan and Stefanie announced that someone was approaching the house. Basil said, "It cannot be our friends Sunny and

Dotty! We would have heard their airplane circle our house." We didn't recognize the lady who was accompanied by the two ducks. She introduced herself as Jennifer, a journalist from Grand Cayman. She was a photographer and writer for a well-known magazine, the <u>Nor'wester</u>. Jennifer told us that she had heard about my garden and would like to write a story about it. I was proud and happily showed her around. She was impressed with the garden and amazed that I was having good success with such a variety of plants. Jennifer praised me and took a lot of photographs, especially of the breadfruit tree that Uncle Joe claimed could not be grown on Little Cayman. Stefan and Stefanie proudly posed with me, their Mommy, in front of the camera. Jennifer was delighted.

Two weeks later, what a pleasant surprise. When we opened the pages of the <u>Nor'wester</u>, there was a wonderful article written about my garden, with many lovely photographs and the title: *Mrs. Kassa's Garden Simply "Ducky"*.

rigitte Kassa's web-footed friends, Stefan and Stefanie   And they said it couldn't be done

Mrs. Kassa's garden simply 'ducky'

Can breadfruit trees be grown on Little Cayman?

Uncle Joe says, "no."

Mrs. Brigitte Kassa says, "yes!"

The breadfruit tree which she planted and diligently cared for, against all advice from the residents of Little Cayman, is now into its second season, and loaded with luscious-looking fruit.

The story is not as simple as that, however, for in order to reap the fruit of her labour, Mrs. Kassa really has to labour. Her extensive garden takes a great deal of care and she tends it single-handedly.

Protected by a wide-brimmed straw hat, and encouraged by her two beautiful white ducks, Stefan and Stefanie, she works barefoot in the garden from about 6:30 a.m. until noon every day.

A visit to Mrs. Kassa's garden is a truly gratifying experience. It is amazing that she has achieved such success with so many different varieties of plants, and one is simply caught up in her enthusiasm, and unflagging energy.

She refuses to believe that something which she wants to grow will not grow. She was told, for example, that lettuce would not grow in Little Cayman; she managed to grow more than enough leaf lettuce for her needs. She is even trying her hand at growing macadamia nuts. When she wishes to prepare a bed for

seaweed taken from the beach behind her house. (The seaweed acts as a type of mulch). On top of the seaweed she puts mold (fertile soil) taken from what she calls the "jungle." Then comes homemade compost, and the bed is finally ready for planting.

What does she plant? Everything. She has beds of herbs: thyme, oregano, dill, beds of vegetables: corn, peppers, lettuce, pumpkin, leeks and tomatoes, Stefan and Stefanie's favourite treat. They snitch the ripe fruit from the plants whenever the garden gate is left open.

Mrs. Kassa also has beds of what Cayman Brackers call "bread-kind," cassava. She has had roots weighing up to 20 pounds. In addition, she grows sweet potatoes, lovely, fat bananas and beautiful plantains.

She also grows numerous fruit trees, ackees, kumquats, Persian limes, guavas, pineapples, oranges and papayas, as well as lots of flowers. Her pride and joy is her bougainvillea border, an absolute riot of colour.

She has also had success with a hibiscus hedge, and proudly displays the unusual white flowers, which she has managed to coax from the plant with lots of tender, loving care and carefully applied plant food.

In addition to these, she has recently

In addition to her flowering trees and shrubs, Mrs. Kassa has managed to grow geraniums, roses, dahlias, orchids, and lots of marigolds, which she has planted among the vegetables, for, she says, she has been told that they will help to drive the bugs away.

Most of the plants which Mrs. Kassa tends so faithfully were imported by her from Miami. Before taking up residence in Little Cayman, she knew very little about gardening, she says, and most of her present knowledge has come from the books which she studies faithfully, and the experience which she has gathered since coming to live in Little Cayman. She is willing to give almost anything a try, and refuses to be deterred by well-meaning, but less adventurous neighbours.

Her ducks were also imported, and she has become so attached to them that she has decided to buy some more. Indeed, everyone who visits the Kassas admires the two beautiful birds, who come running whenever their 'mother' calls, and Mrs. Kassa has already had many requests for young ones.

Her next project is to build a swimming pool for Stefan and Stefanie (the actual labour will be undertaken by her husband, Basil) because the ducks have taken to crossing the road and going for

---

We went again for a short trip to Grand Cayman and stayed with our friends, Sonny and Dottie. They showed us another article in the Nor'wester. Sonny's project, *Cayman Falls*, was underway. A contract for the development was signed during April, to open the new shopping center on the land opposite the Galleon Beach Hotel just before Christmas. Sonny said, "We will celebrate our success in style." He invited us to take a cruise on his yacht in Florida. We were delighted. Then Sonny said, "But first, we will come to visit you. Dottie and I have fallen in love with Little Cayman."

We were overjoyed. Sonny continued, "I want to purchase Dr. Logan Robertson's place on Little Cayman to give my son something to do on the island."

We returned home. Miss Sissy said, "I am glad that you are back. We heard the news. You are in the magazine. We'd like to see it!"

"Look, Miss Sissy. We brought you flour, sugar and coffee. And for you, Uncle Joe, some tools and chewing tobacco. And I give each of you a Nor'wester magazine, the May 1983 issue."

Miss Sissy said, "Look Miss Brigitte, I baked bread and cooked a conch stew with dumplings for you."

"I thank you, Miss Sissy. That is very thoughtful of you." Then I opened the magazine and showed them the page of my story. Miss Sissy was in her mid-seventies and wore eyeglasses. Uncle Joe read without glasses still, and he was well into his eighties. It became quiet as they read the article. When they were finished, they both responded with emotion. Uncle Joe said fondly to me, "You are a case." He had a twinkle in his eyes and I knew that this was a high compliment from him, which was rare. Most of the time, Uncle Joe liked to tease me. Then Miss Sissy began to talk, and no one else had a chance to speak.

In the middle of May, Sonny and Dottie picked us up with their plane to enjoy a cruise around Florida. They told us that they had bought Dr. Robertson's place. We were thrilled. I changed from being barefoot almost all day back into high heels. We all were dressed stylishly and savored fine delicacies with Sonny's favorite champagne, Dom Perignon.

In June, Miss Eleanor came to our house and told us that Dr. Fraser from Cayman Brac had called. He would like to speak with Basil. Basil went to Eleanor's cottage.

After a while, he returned and smiled. "Dr. Bill Fraser and his wife Karen, would like us to go to Jamaica with them.

We were already good friends with Bill and Karen. Bill admired Basil and his capacity to endure the two terrible accidents with such good spirit and fortitude.

"What did you answer, Basil?"

"I told them that, of course, we would like to go to Jamaica. We will charter a plane with our friends."

"Basil, I will find Miss Leonie and ask her if she would take care of my ducks, chickens and the kitty cat."

I found Miss Leonie in her yard, chopping away bush and weeds. She was from Cayman Brac; a robust woman with a quick temper. She had beautiful thick auburn hair that was braided and pinned around her head. She was strong and hard work-ing. "What brings you here, Miss Brigitte?"

I explained to her that we wanted travel to Jamaica with our friends from the Brac, "But I have nobody to baby sit my animals."

"Don't you worry, Miss Brigitte; I will take good care of them." I was relieved and thanked Miss Leonie.

A couple of days later, a small plane picked us up. Then it stopped at Cayman Brac to Pick Bill and Karen up. Then off we all went to Jamaica. Dr. Fraser was born in Jamaica and was educated in England. Tall and slim with an athletic physique, he was very handsome. Karen was an attractive woman with short reddish brown hair. She had warm brown eyes and people liked her for her kindness.

Bill had many old friends with whom we all became acquainted. One afternoon, we were all invited to a beautiful villa up in the hills. When we arrived, my eyes widened and my heart beat faster.

"Look, Basil. See how many magnificent peacocks are strolling around in the yard!"

Basil looked at me, "Oh no, Brigitte. Don't you even think of it! Your menagerie is already overwhelming us, and besides, peacocks make a lot of noise!" My heart sank.

The lady of the house invited us back again the next day. This time she showed the baby peacocks to Karen and me. "Oh, how sweet they are, look Karen!" I exclaimed.

"It would be easy to take them with us," remarked Karen.

I showed Basil the adorable little peacocks and he softened, unable to resist, he said, "Okay, Brigitte, but you may only take home four babies." I was delighted. That evening we stayed in an elegant hotel in Montego Bay, and I put those four little peacocks in the bathtub, and gave them food and water.

Next day, we bought a large Jamaican basket from the open market. The babies traveled safely in the basket. We also filled our suitcase with vegetables. Our charter flight back to Little Cayman stopped first on the Brac. A customs officer was checking our belongings. I quickly placed a head of cabbage on top of the peachicks' basket and hoped that they wouldn't make any noise. But no such luck! "Peep, Peep," came the little voices out from under the cabbage.

The customs officer asked, "Mrs. Kassa, are you bringing young chickens into the country?"

I quickly agreed. The peachicks rested quietly for the rest of the trip to their new home on Little Cayman. We told everyone that they were baby chickens. The islanders liked chickens because they produce food for them, but they were not too keen on other animals. So now the peachicks simply became chicks!

It was such a joy to take care of my animals, my heart filled with contentment. The days were brimming with activity; my garden, the animals, managing the household and, of course, being Basil's playmate.

One day, we heard Sonny's plane circle around our house. We were in the middle of our work and had not expected company. At the airport, we had a surprise. Sonny's son had come with them. It was his birthday and the three of them wanted to celebrate it with us. We were delighted to see Dottie and Sonny, and to make the acquaintance of Danny, his son. It was a fabulous party. As always, Sonny brought along baskets of food, fruits and plenty of Dom Perignon. But they neglected to bring the birthday cake. I had an idea. I cut the fruits into small pieces and let them soak in Rum, mixed with some other liquors. My liquid cake was a tremendous success and knocked the socks off of everybody. The ambiance was at its peak when suddenly, the lights went out. We were sitting in the dark. Basil felt his way around and grabbed a flashlight, a candle and matches and, finally, the kerosene lamp. He commented, "Probably the generator ran out of fuel. I don't want to go down now to the generator house and get dirty. We should all go to bed now anyway, it's after midnight."

It was with great hilarity and unsteady steps that we went to bed. Next day, Sonny showed his son the cottage which he had bought from Dr. Robertson. Sonny told Danny that he would be in charge of the place, to make a small business out of it. Sonny also invested in a long stretch of land near the airport and by the sea on our island.

1984

Sonny's son tried to establish a small restaurant with some lodgings. But he was too young to cope with all of the responsibility. And there were difficulties in being on isolated Little Cayman. Later on, Sonny hired some help from the Brac. The McCoy family arrived in a small rubber boat from the Brac. There was Sammy, his wife, Mary, and six children. The weather wasn't cooperating, the sea was agitated and the waves tossed the rubber boat onto the reef, where it was cut into pieces. Most of the family could swim, and they made it safely to shore, with many cuts and bruises. They were very lucky. Sonny gave them work. He still hoped to create a business on Little Cayman.

Our island was changing. We had one district officer who was in charge of everything. Every day, he drove over rough road to the north coast to check the coastline and ensure that there were no unauthorized vessels off shore. He was also required to be present at the airfield to meet every plane, private or commercial, to check cargo. In the evening, he drove the mosquito spraying truck to keep the pests under control. In the winter months, most of the home owners spent their time on Little Cayman. Some remained for a few weeks, and some for longer periods of time. Another change on Little Cayman was that people on island were busier.

The Southern Cross Club's manager, a good friend of ours, presented us to a very nice couple. Howard and Lulu planned to stay at the club for two months. Lulu explained, "We don't like the winter weather in Wisconsin, it gets bitter cold!" Every morning they would take a walk from SCC to the airfield. On their way back, they liked to stop by our house where we would enjoy refreshing cool drinks and good conversation together. After this, Howard would go fly fishing and Lulu swimming. Sometimes I joined Lulu. In the afternoons, Basil invited them over for drinks. Lulu announced that their two daughters, living in New York, were coming for a visit the next day.

The next evening, we went to SCC and saw two gorgeous young ladies sitting with Lulu and Howard. Lulu proudly introduced them, "This is Sarah and her sister Ann.

Sarah and Ann had very lovely thick hair which cascaded in curls down to their shoulders. Both were tall and slim, like models in a fashion magazine. It was a fine evening. Basil invited the attractive family to a champagne party for the following day. After another enchanting evening together, we all became very good friends.

Ann soon left, but Sarah stayed because she could enjoy her hobby of fly fishing on Little Cayman. She came every morning to fetch coconut milk. Every day I opened six coconuts with my machete. The hard brown husks had white solid meat, but not much milk. Those were for my chickens and peacocks and peahens. They had all day to pick the meat out. The green coconuts were easier to open and were full of sweet water, or coconut milk. The "meat" was soft and I loosened it a little away from the husk with my knife. My ducks waited impatiently for their treat, and eagerly gobbled the soft meat down. Sometimes I put the open coconuts on top of the ducks' coop or on top of my car. The peacocks and hens liked this game. Sarah and I had fun playing with my pets; over the years she and I became very close friends.

The days passed smoothly. In the mornings, my ducks went swimming in the sea. In the afternoon, they sat under my car, the "Green Hornet". It was a Dodge Dart built in 1969. Basil had given me the car for Valentine's Day. I usually parked it in front of our living room entrance; considering it was outside all of the time, it remained in very good condition. I couldn't park the car in the garage, because it was full of Basil's tools and cases of liquor.

When I heard my ducks quacking, I knew a visitor was approaching. Then I heard the squeaky sound of wheels turning into our driveway. It was Sammy Mc Coy, who was working for our friend, Sonny. Sammy was a soft-spoken man who always had a pleasant smile. He was of medium height, his brown smooth skin was ageless.

"Miss Brigitte," he said, "I brought you something." He took a little box from his truck and gave it to me.

I called Basil, "Come to look, Sammy has given me something."

We heard a tiny voice peeping out from the box and Sammy said, "This is a baby whistling duck. He doesn't have a mommy and is crying all of the time! Miss Brigitte, you are so good with animals; my family and I decided to bring the little fellow to you."

I thanked Sammy. "I will do my best," I promised him. "Oh, what an adorable little duck this is! I have never seen one like this."

Sammy answered, "The whistling ducks breed on Little Cayman. Their plumage is quite different when they are older. You probably have seen the adult ducks."

"Yes, Sammy, you are right." I asked Basil to find a box into which I could put the little duckling. Basil returned with one that had originally contained tomatoes.

"This is perfect, Basil." I put newspaper on the bottom of the box, with soft tissue paper on top. Then I added water and dry duck food in tiny bowls. But the moment I set the duckling down, he began to cry pitifully again. So I picked him up and spoke tenderly, "Don't cry, sweet baby. I will be your mommy and will call you Teedee."

The moment Teedee did not feel the warmth of my body, he began again to cry. I put him into my skirt pocket and continued with my work.

The first night Teedee kept us awake. In our bedroom, we could hear him from the kitchen. Finally I brought him into our bed. I put paper towels under him, and immediately, he was quiet. Next day, we tried to figure out how to calm him down, but nothing worked well. I thought to myself, Teedee needs a mother. I cut a soft, old rag into strips and hung them on top of the open box. The strips almost touched the bottom. I put Teedee right under the soft rag strips and, to my surprise, he grew quiet. What a relief it was! Teedee thought that he was sitting under his mother's feathers. I put food and water on the uncovered side of the box. After a while, Teedee ventured out to drink some water; then he picked up the dry food and dropped it into his drinking water. When the food was softened, he gobbled it down, splashing all over and making a mess.

I called Basil, "You should see this, what messy eating habits Teedee has!" We were both amused.

"It is okay," Basil assured me, "as long as he does not cry anymore and we can sleep peacefully."

One day, I took the box outside so that Teedee could enjoy the sunshine. After a while, we heard the ducks making a lot of noise. "Look, Basil! They are all agitated and pushing something dark around with their bills! Oh no! It's Teedee!" The new little duckling was all curled up while the big ducks pecked on him!

I screamed at the ducks, "Stefan! Stefanie! Josephine! All of you, stop it!" I picked Teedee up and caressed him tenderly, then put him back into his box. Every day, it was the same scene. Teedee wanted to belong with my ducks.

I said to Basil, "The ducks will not accept Teedee. He looks different and his eating habits are not the same. He doesn't quack, he whistles."

Basil thought for a while and came up with an idea. "You remember, Brigitte, on our last trip to Miami, we bought a children's swimming pool from Sears Roebuck? It was meant for the new young ducks. I will bet you that if I set that pool up and we fill it with fresh water, the ducks will become so excited, they will forget about harassing Teedee."

"Basil, now that is a fantastic idea!" I said.

The next day, Basil worked quickly to install the pool. Soon the metal base was standing up. Next came the blue plastic liner which we shaped to the base and fastened with a metal ring to the top edge of the pool. "Now comes the fun part; filling the pool with water," Basil said.

"Please let me do it, Basil," I pleaded.

Basil said, "I will get the ramp so the ducks can walk right up to it and reach the water easily."

I heard the ducks coming. When they came close to their yard, I guided them towards the pool. First I took Stefan and Stefanie to walk up the ramp. Then one by one, each duck walked up. Teedee was the last. They looked like a little troop of soldiers. They began to dive and splash around, and could not care less about Teedee, who was busily enjoying himself in the middle of all of the ducks.

CHAPTER 26

Eventful Years

Come April, it was travel time again. We first flew to Mexico City, and visited the pyramids and the famous Floating Gardens of Xochimilco. We cruised in a blossom covered gondola through canals. We visited the spectacular Ballet Folklorico, presenting Mexican music and dance. In the evening, we dined in fine Mexican restaurants. One in particular we enjoyed was the Hacienda de los Morales. It was a 17th Century restored hacienda; a breathtaking location with beautiful gardens, courtyards and Mexican décor. The cocktail lounge, where we listened to the piano and string quintet performing, was charming and relaxing. The genuine Mexican cuisine with outstanding service made for a truly elegant, authentic restaurant. Our days were filled with sightseeing and sipping Margaritas.

After visiting Mexico City, Basil rented a car. We visited the Independence Route, through Central Mexico. Since Basil enjoyed driving in different countries, he was at ease driving in Mexico. We passed through old Spanish colonial towns and villages. We found lodging in restored haciendas, in small charming inns and elegant hotels. We loved San Miguel de Allende, a town in a colonial setting, so strikingly lovely in its architecture that it has been designated a national monument. We both agreed that we would return to explore different towns in Mexico.

In July, a big event happened on Little Cayman. The blasting at Salt Rocks. The government prepared the way for the future by building a concrete driveway and platform for unloading and loading ships. Accessibility for vehicles would be improved so as to be less dangerous. Basil was happy to help with his tractor.

Sometimes a religious minister came from Cayman Brac by boat and held service in the small wooden church. I enjoyed listening to the Reverend, he would bring us news from people who had left Little Cayman. Some were too old and could not take care of themselves; like Captain Edward Bodden and his wife, Miss Lila.

Their son took them to the rest home on Cayman Brac. The Reverend told us that the couple was not doing well; that they missed Little Cayman very much. Captain Bodden was going blind and his wife was very fragile. Miss Nada had left Little Cayman too, and was now living in the states with her sisters. Some guests from Southern Cross Club came to join us in the church. After the announcements, the little group rejoiced in singing favorite hymns with wonderful strong voices. Basil, who liked to sing, was happy to have the opportunity to participate.

In August, we received news from Sonny and Dottie, that the following week would be the inauguration of "The Falls" on Grand Cayman. We were invited to the grand event. The governor of the Cayman Islands opened the ceremony with a warm welcoming speech, wishing The Falls great success. We celebrated in style with Dom Perignon.

1985

One morning early in January, we heard Sonny's plane circling around our house. We didn't expect him for a visit, because he didn't notify us as he usually did. We drove to the airport and, to our surprise, there were two other men with Sonny, and Dottie was not with them. Curiously, we greeted Sonny who just smiled and asked the two men to unload the cargo from his plane. We couldn't believe our eyes. Sonny had brought a television for us! He said to Basil, "This is a gift from Dottie and me. Now you can listen to the news in your home. You don't have to go anymore to the airport to meet each plane and gather news from tourists."

The two men unloaded a dish and cables, everything that was needed to install the television and get good reception. Basil and I were flabbergasted; unable to speak. Basil had tears in his eyes. Sonny and Dottie were so kind.

Sonny then said, "Come on, you two. I don't have much time. We have to get this television working so you can see what is going on in the world. After many trips to the airport, we finally had all of the materials on our property. The men only needed two shovels, and the work began. We had to decide where we wanted to place the television. With the expertise of the two men, the installation progressed quickly. Instead of reading in the evening, our eyes were often glued to the television.

In March, we received a package from France. It was from our friends, Guy and Yolande in Paris. Featured in <u>The Figaro</u>, a well-known magazine, there was a long article paying tribute to the Cayman Islands. Next, there was an article written about Little Cayman and about us! The article covered many topics. Little Cayman is the smallest and most tranquil island of the three Caymans. Basil and Brigitte are a happy couple, owning one of the three houses right by the sea. Basil is an American who speaks remarkable French. He told the journalist that he courted Brigitte in Monte Carlo and continued the courtship even now; because his wife and he are living a perpetual honeymoon. My ducks and the garden were written about. And the article ended with how we had to be fanatic worshippers of nature and the sun in order to live on Little Cayman.

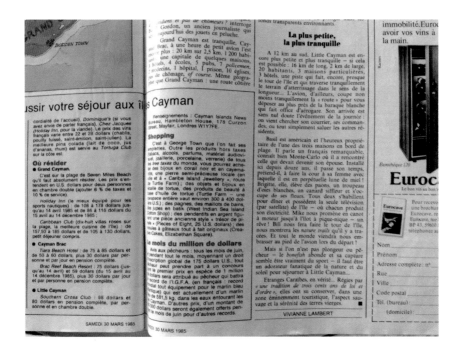

On May 26, we received news from our friend, Teddy in Hong Kong that he would be arriving in Indianapolis to participate in the *Indie 500*. He was bringing his own racing team with him. We traveled to Miami where Basil purchased a used car, a Chrysler.

Basil explained, "It is much more practical to have a car in Miami, because we have to find parts for the generators and other things that we cannot buy on Grand Cayman. We also have our winter clothes in air conditioned storage in Miami, it will be easier to get around in Miami. I spoke with the manager of this hotel. He will permit us to leave our car here in the parking lot, no charge. Basil had planned well.

We drove to Indianapolis where it was a great pleasure to see Teddy. We were invited to stay with our long-time friends, Kent, the owner of Southern Cross Club, and his wife, Elizabeth, while in Indianapolis, Kent's home town. Kent had purchased tickets to see the race. We presented Teddy to them. Unfortunately, Teddy's team did not win. Teddy made us promise to visit him and his family in Hong Kong soon.

We stayed on a couple of days longer with Kent and Elizabeth, enjoying our time together. Kent said that the next month they planned to travel to Little Cayman to look after the business. Then we drove back to Miami. We stayed one more week in Miami during which time we went shopping and enjoyed exuberant evenings of fine dining and dancing. However, it was very difficult for us to find the right supplier for our generators.

Back to Little Cayman! I was so happy to be home again, all of my animals came to greet me, and I spoke to them with joy. Miss Sissy gave Basil the island news; who had visited, who was here and for how long; everything was related in detail. Basil was pleased. As always, we brought tobacco for Uncle Joe and a selection of fishhooks for all of the islanders. For Miss Sissy and all of the women, we brought beans, salt, sugar and yeast. Uncle Joe went fishing right away, but not inside the reef. He rowed outside into the deep water.

I asked him, "Why are you going so far out with your boat, Uncle Joe?"

"Because the old wives, the triggerfish, out there taste better," he replied with certainty.

One evening, we were invited over by an American couple who owned a vacation cottage. They had also invited Uncle Joe and Miss Sissy, who we picked up in our car. When we all arrived, we saw more people standing outside and chatting. Some of them knew Miss Sissy and Uncle Joe, and they welcomed them. Uncle Joe set his feet on the ground and walked with fast steps towards a tall woman with a full bosom. It looked as if he jumped on her! He wrapped his arms around her breasts whereupon she screamed hysterically for help. She ran around the house to hide from him. Uncle Joe hobbled after the frightened woman until someone stopped him.

I hollered at him, hiding my amusement with a stern face, "You must not do such things! Now you should be ashamed of yourself," I scolded. Then I added, "I thought that *I* was your friend!"

Uncle Joe answered, "You are always here. And you are as skinny as a birch tree."

We were all trying to hide our laughter. I bit my lips and just said, "You remind me of your wild rooster. When he sees a hen in the distance, he runs after her and jumps on top of her."

Everyone released howls of laughter. The woman who visited, however, was not amused. She kept her distance from Uncle Joe.

More and more people came to visit Little Cayman, but we were still the only settlers; and we liked it like that!

In the fall and winter of 1985, China had opened the door to tourism. Basil was planning for a long trip. I prepared myself mentally to enjoy the new adventures; exploring the unknown China. First we traveled to Miami to pick up our winter clothes from storage. Then we began our trip. We stopped in Japan and stayed in the lovely Hotel Okura. Then we visited our friend Teddy and family in Hong Kong. Here we stayed in the luxurious Hotel Mandarin, as we had before. Then we flew to Canton China where we stayed in a simple guesthouse, they called it friendship lodging. The beds had wooden frames around them and were not long enough for Basil's legs. The food was mediocre, reminding me of Berlin after the war, when we didn't have enough and there was no variety. The people were not friendly. We were not allowed to travel around by ourselves, only with a guide or on guided tours. Next came Shanghai where we visited some factories. Workers in the most interesting one were making silk.

Next, we flew in a Russian plane to Xian. The flight itself was a memorable experience. The plane rattled, it was cold and noisy. But worse yet was when Basil returned from the toilet. He informed me, "There is no toilet; only a hole which opens up and the air sucks everything out."

After landing, a guide took us to the site which was discovered in 1974 by a farmer in his field. Statues of mounted soldiers of the Qin Dynasty were excavated. Then an army of soldiers made of ceramic were discovered. In addition, in 1980, two copper coaches were discovered along with the statues of two coachmen and four horses. They are considered to be among the most priceless treasures in the world. It surpassed all of our expectations and made up for the uncomfortable lodging. It was absolutely amazing.

Next came Guilin. Here we enjoyed completely different scenery. We floated downstream along the Lijiang River. Magnificent high rising hills in different shapes were appearing in front of us; all surrounded by water. Most of the hills in Guilin have caves, and some of the caves are spacious enough to hold ten thousand people. Some hills have winding tunnels which extend for several miles. We traveled in the boat to the caves and then walked for hours through the colorful stalactites, glittering palaces of nature. It was an extraordinary sight.

The next stop in China was Beijing. The accommodations here were also disappointing. The food was not appetizing. The streets and squares were enormous. The people traveled on bicycles, by foot and busses. We were guided to the Forbidden City, to the former Imperial Palace of the Ming Dynasties. It was very impressive and a magnificent priceless work of art. The last stop was the Great Wall; one of the wonders of the world. We were speechless as we walked to the wall. We started walking on the wall, but it was too steep. So we did not get far, since we were used to our flat little Cayman. We sat on top of the wall and admired the scenic country side.

We returned to Hong Kong, to our beautiful Hotel Mandarin, with all of its luxury and comfort. We were hungry for a good steak and champagne. When we took the first bite of our steaks and hastily chewed, our jaws began to hurt! We were both surprised, and wondered why. But then it dawned on us. We had not eaten a solid piece of meat in China for over a month. We ate using chopsticks. The food was always cut into small pieces. We even ate the noodle soups with chopsticks. Other dishes were soft and slippery. Our jaws had grown unaccustomed to chewing! So we began to chew again, but very slowly. After three months touring, we returned to our paradise on Little Cayman.

1986

It was a blessing to be home again. I think Basil was happy too. My garden was in full bloom. The thick hedge of bougainvillea was flowering in a striking variety of color. I harvested sweet pineapple. It was a joy to see my sunflower so tall and strong. My kitty cat was a mother now. She had two black kittens and two blondies, they were adorable. The peacocks were fully grown; the males spread their feathers like a fan and displayed the most brilliant colors of blue, green and gold. Teedee, my whistling duck, was also an adult now. He was very close to me, sometimes walking right between my feet. I knew he wanted to tell me that soon he would leave. Many nights he did leave; but came back early in the morning, circling around the house with his particular call, he announced his return. One morning though, he flew five times around the house and said goodbye. I was very sad, but also happy for Teedee that he had his own companion now.

In March, the children's pool for the ducks began to leak. The plastic lining had some holes in it. We decided to have a cement pool built. After the pool was finished, we went to the hatchery in Miami and purchased more baby ducks. It was such a pleasure seeing the ducklings splashing around in the new pool. My older ducks were busy in the daytime going into the sea, or crossing the road and checking out the pond. But in the evening, they joined the new ducks. One night I heard the ducks making a lot of noise in their yard. I grabbed the flashlight and went outside. To my horror, I saw my young ducks tumbling down and falling on their backs. I saw a cluster of soldier crabs eating the rest of the duck food. I picked the little ducks up and looked at their feet, because I thought that maybe the crabs had pinched them. But nothing seemed wrong. So I sat there and held them, caressing them. It seemed to help. I put them down again and went back to bed. I told Basil about it. Not long after, I heard the same helpless sound. I ran back outside and saw the same thing; the ducks were lying on their backs and were not able to get up. I held them and cried.

At dawn we looked first at the ducks' yard. Some of them were dead. Then we went all around our property and were shocked. The leaves on our shrubs and trees were black. Little birds were lying dead on the ground.

"Oh, Basil. It is the mosquito spray! Last night the truck came all around the house to keep the mosquitos away from us. But the poison must have been too strong!" We later learned that the poison had not been diluted at all.

We had to put most of our ducks to sleep. Some of the chickens too. Right away, I drained the pool and took the ducks into the sea. Then we went with the tractor to the fresh water well and filled the containers with good drinking water.

In May Little Cayman had a new addition. Our friend Sonny exchanged his establishment on Little Cayman for an oil well in Texas, owned by a woman named Gladys Howard. She converted the round houses into a small resort, which she called Pirates' Point. She had studied cooking under Julia child and turned the restaurant into a gourmet destination. Many of the islanders had little confidence in her. They said things like, "A woman alone cannot manage," and "this environment will be too tough for her." But they did not know Gladys. She was a strong character; and with her powerful voice, she achieved her goal. The business turned into a great success. She hired an engineer from the Brac who took care of the generator; giving more people from the Brac work. Soon people flew in on our local planes and in private planes from Grand Cayman, all to stay and dine with Miss Gladys. The weekends were always the busiest. We were very pleased to have another fine place to enjoy on island.

The population of Little Cayman grew slowly. One brave couple, John and Betty Jean Mulak, built a house on the northeast coast of the island. Betty Jean had a slim figure and was medium height. Her blond hair was cut and styled in a short pageboy. She had a lively personality, and her brown eyes sparkled when she laughed. John had an impressive stature, as he was tall and strongly built. He was also a very talented wood carver, specializing in carving duck decoys. To get to their place from Blossom Village, they had to drive on a long, narrow dirt road overgrown with high grasses. It took them almost one hour. They were the first settlers on that part of the island.

1987

It was Uncle Joe's birthday! Several of us gathered at the Southern Cross Club. I made a pumpkin cake in a coffee can. Basil put a candle on top and this actually nudged a smile out of dear Uncle Joe. We were a small celebratory group; Uncle Joe, Miss Sissy, Jack and Miss Rilly, Miss Eleanor and Mike, the club manager, and Basil and I.

Cayman Airways had a new plane, The Shorts. They were showcasing, and brought it to Little Cayman. A woman journalist interviewed us and took our photograph. Once more, we were in the newspaper.

In November, once again, Basil's lust for travel arose. This time we explored the southern states of Mexico. We drove through lush forests, green mountains and enjoyed the wide variety of flora and fauna. My favorite location was Oaxaca. It was high in the mountains and absolutely gorgeous. It has a superb climate year round. The church of Santo Domingo was built in 1670 and is considered one of the finest baroque churches; covered with gold and located in a charming location where a band played music. We traveled for two months, having fun and new adventures. We especially enjoyed the singing and playing of the Mariachis.

CHAPTER 27

Christmas 1987

Surprise! Santa landed on the grass airstrip on Little Cayman for the first time. It was a big event. Santa greeted everyone and had gifts for the children, who had come from Cayman Brac to visit. Santa must have been very hot in his suit; it was 80 degrees.

Now came the holiday modeling session. This time, I asked Basil to stand by the Christmas tree, and I made a very good picture of him. When Basil took a picture of me, my mama cat went in front of my legs and Basil was furious, he did not like it, but I did. Basil was becoming jealous of my ducks, especially Stefanie. I admit that Basil had reason to be resentful. When I was working in the garden, Stefanie would sneak up behind me and pinch my heels. Before I could turn around to holler at her, she would waddle contentedly off. I called the pinches "love bites" and I was the victim of them regularly. Basil was very annoyed, and wanted to get rid of her. He felt I paid more attention to Stefanie than to him. I had to figure out how to not get any more love bites. Whenever Stefanie would get close, I would throw a flip flop at her, and that would satisfy her. Stefanie would not play with the other ducks, she only liked her Mommy. Later on, we found out that I had misnamed her. Stefanie was a male!

CHAPTER 28

Hurricane Gilbert

1988

Until May, we stayed home working and playing. Then Basil grew restless and we headed out again. Our destination this time was England. We visited Basil's friends from his business years. They showed us the countryside and shared with us their English traditions. We dined in historic places. I loved the thatched roof pubs where we had to bend down to walk into a room.

After a cozy evening, I said to Basil, "This year, in October, it will be our twentieth wedding anniversary. I'm very happy! The only adjustment I would like to make is to wear my skirts and dresses a bit longer. It doesn't look right anymore, Basil, for them to be so short. I am forty-nine years old!"

Basil's face was flushed, his voice agitated, "I want you always to be my playmate; and I want to see your legs. Don't even think of covering them up."

"Basil, be reasonable. When will you allow me to wear my clothes at the length I want? When I am fifty?"

"Okay, Brigitte, when you are fifty, you can wear your clothes a little longer."

I was relieved. I don't think that Basil realized that I would be fifty years old the following year.

We visited my aunt and uncle in Germany. Now they had two houses near Lake Constance. One of the houses they rented out. In the other, they lived with a view of a picturesque landscape and a peek of Lake Constance. As always, it was a pleasure to be with them. This time Basil was embarrassed to ask for a loan from

Aunt Didi and Uncle Max. But with no formalities, they readily wrote Basil a check. Over the twenty years we had been together, Basil had taken money out of the bank as needed. He never invested much of his money, and now he was running out of it. I did not blame him, he had worked hard for it and deserved to live life as he wanted. I was thankful that I had been along "for the ride" with Basil. I learned a lot and enjoyed every minute of the journey with him.

I said to Basil, "But now, Basil, you have to be more careful. We should not travel so far and so often. How will you pay back Uncle Max and Aunt Didi?"

He thought for a moment and said, "We bought the large lot next to us. The prices will rise as more people become interested in buying on Little Cayman. I will sell the three acres, and that should keep us going for a while."

I was very sad; I loved the land and wanted to leave it undisturbed. I enjoyed our privacy.

"If I had the money, I would buy more land, and let nature take care of it. But if you have to sell it Basil, then go ahead."

The last stop on this trip was Rothenburg. The historical town was very charming, but I felt downcast and wanted to be home. It bothered me that we had borrowed money. But I put a smile on my face for Basil, who was not concerned about the loan.

SEPTEMBER 13, 1988 HURRICANE GILBERT

Early in September, we were having breakfast when it was announced on the radio news program that a tropical storm was forming off of the coast of Africa. We hoped it would not become a hurricane.

"Basil, you remember how in 1980, when Hurricane Alan hit, we had no communication."

"Yes, I remember," Basil replied.

We paid close attention every day to what was announced. It didn't look good for Little Cayman. On the 10th of September, the tropical depression was upgraded to a storm. It was predicted to become a hurricane which was on a path to hit Jamaica and then the Cayman Islands. I drove my car around the island, speaking with each resident and telling them to be prepared for the worst. The Southern Cross Club and Pirates Point sent their guests out on flights. We asked Uncle Joe and Miss Sissy to stay with us, but Uncle Joe emphatically stated, "I am not staying in your glass house!"

Basil and I covered the windows and doors with plywood. We placed empty gasoline drums in front of the plywood to fill them with water. We stored all outdoor furniture in the garage. Now we turned our attention to the duck coop. We put heavy cement blocks under the coop, a thick rope over the coop, and then threaded the rope through the holes of the cement blocks. We tied the whole thing down so it would not fly away. For the peacocks, we did the same. We took an old camper and used it as a roof. It took us a whole day. The next day, early morning, the clouds were an ominous gray, and a strange looking pale yellow cast was all around us. It was very eerie; the birds had left, everything was too, too quiet. We could only hear the waves pounding the shore. The water was brown and full of debris.

Basil hollered, "I almost forgot our boat!"

Since he couldn't swim, he put a rope around me with the other end around a coconut tree. Then he gave me another rope which I was supposed to fasten to the boat. It was scary, but it had to be done. Basil also brought the tractor down. The other end of the rope which was to be fastened to the boat would be fastened to the tractor. As I swam closer and closer to the boat, waves crashed over me. Planks torn loose from the docks were all around me with rusty nails exposed. I finally made it to the boat and signaled to Basil. He began to pull the boat in with the tractor. I held onto the boat tightly. When we landed on the beach, I had to lie down; all my energy was gone. It was a miracle that I was not hurt.

Now I worried about my pets. They were all tense and nervous. I brought the cat into the house. I opened the chicken coop and let the chickens out. The peacocks were given lodging under the camper roof; but they were free to leave to find a better place, if they could. Every one of my animals was free to fend for them-selves; they had better instincts and could respond to changing conditions. My beloved ducks were released from their pen. I put my car, the Green Hornet, close to the pen. By now, a strong gusty wind came and tore branches and leaves from the trees above us.

Basil yelled, "We still must disconnect the downspouts from the gutters!" The first rainstorm would carry salt spray, and we didn't want that to contaminate our drinking water in the cisterns.

Soon after, a heavy rain descended from the heavens. The sky became dark and the sea was stirred up by huge waves. The storm strengthened and the wind increased in violence. We could feel it hammering against the doors and windows. I was afraid it would break the glass.

Basil yelled, "Open the little bathroom window on the north side!"

This was to relieve the pressure. The windows and doors were all rattling. It sounded as if a train were passing by. The barometric pressure went lower and lower. My body felt heavier and heavier; all energy was sucked out of me. Then I saw water coming in under the bottom of the sliding glass door.

"Basil, quickly get pails and rags!"

We both rushed from room to room to try to soak up the water as it came in. As I entered our bedroom, I called for Basil to bring a couple of flashlights with him. I saw leaves wildly dancing up and down in front of the sliding door. It was totally dark. I couldn't figure out what was going on. We both shined our lights on the glass door and were shocked to see a sea grape tree floating and bobbing against the plywood in front of the door.

"Oh, Basil!" I cried out, "The sea has reached our house!" I had thought we would be better protected by the reef, and you built the house one hundred feet away from the ocean!"

"Calm down, Brigitte. Have faith that we will make it through this.

Basil and I were both exhausted. The storm raged on all night. Finally, at dawn, the winds eased up. We hurried outside. I called for the ducks and could hear them, but couldn't see them. We took our machetes and cut through piles of debris and big tree branches. We reached the car and found the ducks all sitting in a row, pressed against the car. They could not move because the debris was piled up against them. We cleared a path to them and they all gathered gratefully around me. Not one was hurt! I took them in my arms and they quacked happily. Then we went to the peacocks' yard. I called to them; the chickens and peacocks came flying in from all directions. We cleared an area for them near the Green Hornet and gave them food and fresh water. After this, we checked out the beach. There were hundreds of conchs and dead fish there. We also lost many singles from the roof.

Next, we took the tractor and headed out to see if everybody else was okay. As we made our way through our property to the road, we were both shocked by the amount of destruction. Almost all of my fruit trees were down, the entire road was washed out. We could barely get to the Southern Cross Club. There the hurricane had swept furniture from the cottages to the other side of the road, which was blocked with large rocks. We couldn't get beyond the SCC on the road because of the boulders in the way. Everyone at SCC was unhurt and in good spirits. However, sand was piled up into the toilets, along with all of the other destruction.

Next we made our way to Uncle Joe and Miss Sissy. They both came running out with big smiles. We opened our arms and hugged them tightly with relief. "Thank God you are alive!" I said to them. "Even your wooden houses are OK."

Uncle Joe grinned and said, "I told you so!"

Satisfied that they were safe, we climbed back onto the tractor and left to visit the rest of the locals. Miss Rilly's and Jack's home was half under water, but they were safe. Our last stop was Pirates Point. We had to see how Miss Gladys had fared. But we could not even get the tractor up their drive. All of the trees had been knocked down across the road. We pushed aside the broken branches and climbed over the trees. The roofs from every cottage were gone! Gladys greeted us with a loud and joyful "Hello!" She took us in her arms and held tightly. She had a marine radio and told us that Gilbert was a category four hurricane. We on Little Cayman were the lucky ones. We had generators. On Grand Cayman and the Brac, everyone depended on the electricity, which was totally destroyed. So all of their food was spoiling, and they had no way to save it. The work of cleaning up after the storm was made easier because of Basil's heavy equipment. The government asked him to rebuild the washed out roads, both on our side and on the north side of the island. Basil was happy to help. Other people needed his assistance and skills, so we kept very busy with work.

In October, we received a letter from Howie and Lulu asking if they could rent our little house for the winter, November through springtime. Repair work on the Southern Cross Club was not going to be finished in time for their stay. Normally, we would have said, "No," since we enjoyed our privacy, freedom, peace and quiet. But since we were living on money borrowed from my aunt and uncle, we gladly welcomed them.

The following week, we received a letter from their daughter, Sarah, who lived now in Montecito, California with her husband and two boys. We had met them at SCC and always enjoyed their company. Because we were having her mother and father stay in our little house, Sarah wanted to put together a first class party for us to celebrate our 20th wedding anniversary, in Sarah's home. Basil was delighted and I was honored.

We stopped our work and flew to Montecito, for one week. On the 17th of October, 1988, we celebrated our 20th wedding anniversary with close friends in their beautiful home. It was exquisite. We met many fascinating people, movie stars and the local high society. The food was superb. Their household consisted of a butler, a chauffeur, two maids and a cook.

CHAPTER 29

The Wardrobe Battle

We returned to Little Cayman and worked. In the middle of November, Lulu and Howie arrived. They were a very nice couple and we liked them right away. When Basil was resting after lunch, I would visit Lulu in the little house. It was so good to have another woman to talk to. I hadn't had a girlfriend on the island, except occasionally when friends visited. Lulu loved to bake; which I didn't enjoy. I preferred to be outdoors working in the garden and interacting with my animals.

Basil was not used to being alone; and became more and more possessive. Lulu baked more cookies and breads, which she shared with us, so Basil could not complain. One day, I told Lulu that the following year, in one month, I would be fifty! And that Basil had promised that once I turned fifty, I could wear my dresses a little longer.

"But I am afraid that he will not honor our agreement." I acknowledged.

Lulu and I put our heads together and hatched a plan. First I would bring two skirts over, while Basil was resting after lunch. We would open up the seams; lengthen the skirts by one or two inches, and then re-hem them. Lulu would iron them. Many of my dresses, especially the ones tailored to order, could not be altered.

1989

It seemed as if Basil had an intuition of what we were doing. He wanted me to wear one of the shortest skirts I owned for the celebration. On January 7th, 1989, we celebrated in harmony and good spirits. I let three days pass and then put on one of the longer length skirts, and wore my usual high heeled shoes. I did not say anything to Basil about it, and began nonchalantly to cook.

Basil entered the kitchen and sat down to watch me prepare the food. I thought, "So far all is Okay, maybe he will not even notice."

At that moment, Basil sprang from his chair and hollered at me, "What have you done? You have ruined your skirt!"

I said calmly, "Sit down, Basil. Don't you remember our agreement? You promised."

He shouted. "What promise? What agreement?"

"I am fifty now; and you promised that I can do what I like with my wardrobe. I may now decide how long I want my skirts."

"No! No! No!" he shouted.

"Yes! Yes! Yes!" I shouted right back at him.

"But you don't have to do it right away," he pleaded.

Needless to say; neither one of us ate anything, Basil complained all night. Finally, I said, "This is ridiculous to have such a big argument over the length of my skirts, Basil. I don't want to be only your *Barbie Doll* and playmate. I want to be your wife. It does not look good when we travel and I wear such short skirts and high heels. Especially when *you* look like a distinguished older gentleman who has *picked me up*. Do you think it makes *you* any younger looking?"

Well, he was furious. He stalked out of the house and behaved like a spoiled boy whose toy had been taken away unfairly.

Later, we went to bed, each pretending to sleep. Unexpectedly, Basil sprang out of our bed. He took his heart pills, the Phenobarbital, and threatened, "You will regret this. I am going to drive your car to the Salt Rocks and right into the sea."

"Don't be ridiculous," I scolded. "Come back to bed."

By now, it was close to midnight. Basil walked out to the car and left. I couldn't believe that he was really going to kill himself because of two inches off my skirt length. I almost laughed out loud. To me, there was a hilarious side to this disagreement and his childish actions. But in the next moment, I wondered, "What if he really does it if I stay in bed and let him go?"

So I ran out to the tractor and started the engine with the intention of following him. With the loud noise, Lulu and Howie came running out of the little house. "What's going on?" they wanted to know. I related to them quickly what had happened. Their first reaction, like mine, was to laugh. I joined in again with the amusing side of our situation. Then we all stopped laughing, and I took off.

I drove as quickly as possible with the tractor in the dark. When I reached Pirates Point and still had not reached him, I began to worry in earnest. As I came close to Salt Rocks, I could see a light! I drew closer, and there was Basil, driving towards me on the road. I stopped the tractor and he stopped the car.

"I just wanted to see if you would come after me." He insisted, protecting his pride after not carrying through with his threat.

I was upset, but I didn't say anything. We made our way home in the two vehicles. By the next morning, we had calmed down and were having breakfast. I said, "Look Basil, if the length of my skirts and viewing my legs mean more to you than letting me dress as I please, you should just travel to Thailand or somewhere else, where there are beautiful young girls who would be glad to do as you say. Take the rest of the money with you. I don't want anything. I just want to stay on Little Cayman."

He looked up at me and asked, "You really mean it?"

"Yes. I will not be angry if this is what would make you happy," I replied.

I could see that he was thinking and I was prepared for him to take the money and decide for the joyful life. His face then lit up, and he asked me again, "All the money?"

"Yes, Basil," I answered with resolve.

After a quiet moment, he asked me, "Tell me Brigitte. How will you live here without any money?"

"I will go fishing, plant vegetables and sell eggs and produce to Pirates Point. Miss Gladys is happy to have fresh eggs. If I need more money than that, I will rent out our castle to rich people from Grand Cayman for weekends; or even longer periods of time. I can stay in the little house."

"Ah, so you have figured everything out." I saw that this bothered him, that I could survive so well without him. "Well, no way will I leave you," he claimed. "Now, I will stay!"

It sounded to me as if he was jealous of my plan. Later we did come to a compromise. When we traveled, I could have the length that I wanted, with my skirts just above my knees. But in the privacy of our home, Basil wanted to have his playmate, and I would wear the miniskirts just for him.

In the middle of January, 1989, we flew to Miami to purchase some new dresses made for me, a little longer and more to my liking. One in particular I preferred. It was a cream colored chamois, with beautiful beads at the hem of the dress. I called it my "Pocahontas Dress". So ended our most serious argument ever; and all over two inches!

In May 1989, we traveled back to Mexico, visiting a variety of different places and enjoying the people, food and mojitos.

Months passed. People from the government on Grand Cayman came to visit. One wealthy Caymanian businessman made friends with Basil. He owned a lot of land on Little Cayman. Basil approached him and asked if he might be interested in buying the empty lot adjoining our home. He was very interested. After an official visit, he came back to shake hands; he purchased the prime three-acre lot. I was very sad, knowing that we should keep the land as it was for the natural setting it protected and for our privacy.

The buyer gave the land to his children. Most Caymanians do not like *Little* Cayman. They find it too quiet, with little to do and no night life. That attitude was lucky for us! When Basil received the money, he began to plan for another trip. I put my foot down. We first needed to pay back my aunt and uncle. Since Basil sold the land for a good price, he agreed right away.

BUDAPEST HUNGARY

In October, we arrived for my Aunt's eightieth birthday. She was overjoyed to see us. But it was a sad time too, as Uncle Max had passed away. The political doors had opened to Hungary, so we invited Aunt Didi to come with us to visit her homeland, for which she still held fond memories. She told us, however, that she did not want to see it now. She treasured her memories and preferred to keep them intact. She advised us though on where to stay and told us what she remembered.

The Saint Geller hotel was famous; a beautiful building that was decorated exquisitely. It still had the red plush sofas in the small sitting room, as in the old days. Before the war, the hotel was known for its man-made waves in the swimming pool. We checked out the pool first, and it was the same. All of the women wore bathing caps, as in the old days, and the waves gently lifted them up and down. It was fascinating to watch as we were gently taken back in time.

The architecture of most historical buildings was extraordinary; gothic, baroque, Turkish and classic styles, all managed to harmonize well. Budapest has over a hundred hot springs, which made it a premier health spa destination for over two thousand years. But the people had changed under the Russian regime. Once gallant, courteous and sociable, they had lost their joyfulness. Stores had little to offer. It was dreary. We asked our doorman if he would be able to find Beluga Caviar for us. At first, he was unfriendly. But two days later, he told us that he could obtain it from the black market. The transaction was made in secret as people did not trust each other and were afraid of being reported.

We shared the caviar with my aunt. I was glad that she had declined to accompany us. She would have been disappointed to see a cheerless Hungary. We spent two wonderful weeks with her. Near the end of our stay, she gave me her handwritten will and said, "There is the same will kept safe with my attorney in Munich."

Aunt Didi and I also visited her bank where she was well-known. She signed all holdings over to me. Then she showed me her safety deposit box. It was large and heavy, containing her beautiful jewelry and other valuables. There were several velvet pouches in different colors. Aunt Didi opened one of the little bags and showed me a roll of gold coins. I was astonished.

She said, "You see Brigitte, this is my inheritance from my mother." Here I saw gold coins from the late eighteen hundreds and early nineteen hundreds from Hungary and Germany. They were individually and neatly wrapped in soft paper.

My eyes were filled with tears as I said, "Aunt Didi. I hope that you will have a long life and we will have many wonderful times together."

"I intend to, but now is the time for you and me to be prepared." Then she told me that her father was a count, but there was a scandal in the family, and he had shot himself. After that, her mother had left Hungary. Aunt Didi grew up with her grandmother on Lake Balaton where they owned vineyards. She left for Germany when she was fifteen years old. She didn't like Germany, but her mother had insisted. I was thinking how my Uncle Max and I would always laugh over Aunt Didi when she wanted to teach us some manners. Now I realized that she truly had come from a much higher social class, she was a genuine aristocrat.

After a while, Aunt Didi drove us back to her house where Basil was waiting. On the way, she drove into a one-way street, the wrong way! "Oh, Aunt Didi, this is a one-way street!" I warned.

"Well the sign was not there yesterday," was her response. In spite of the danger, I had to laugh. I knew Uncle Max never allowed my aunt to drive, but now she enjoyed it; driving just as she pleased, even recklessly! Basil took over the driving.

It was difficult to say good bye to my aunt now. We were much closer than when I was living with them in my childhood. We invited her to live with us, but she declined. It's not what she wanted. We promised her we would visit every year and stay with her for a month. That made her happy.

1990

After a full year of enjoying time at home, Basil spread his wings again; we flew to Hawaii in October. This time we visited several of the islands, including Molokai, an island almost completely unspoiled by civilization. We saw the leper colony from high above. Visitors could arrange for a donkey to carry them down the steep mountain, or they would use an elevator. Since I was fearful of heights, we did neither. There were still people living in the colony and maintaining their gardens.

Then we traveled to Hong Kong to visit our friend, Teddy Yip. We boarded a boat together to sight see and enjoyed each other's company. After Hong Kong, we traveled to Thailand, Bangkok. This time we traveled by boat to see the amazing Chiang Mai water falls. We stayed in the best hotels and Basil spent money liberally. I did not feel so enthusiastic, uncomfortable with the knowledge that when our money ran out, there was no more.

December found us back on our island, larger ships were able to come in bringing building supplies and heavy equipment for the government, because now there was a well-built concrete dock at Salt Rocks. Ships also brought in food for the islanders. There was talk of building a power plant in the following year. They also planned a telephone communications center. By now there were about thirty-five people living on Little Cayman. None of the islanders were too keen on the encroaching civilization. We all loved our little paradise just as it was. On the other hand, I had to think about Basil on the 8th of December 1990 turning seventy-five. He was still going strong, but it would make everything much easier for me if he ever needed medical attention.

At the end of December, Basil was asked to help unload freight at Salt Rocks. He was glad to be of service and drove there with his crane. An hour later, someone drove rapidly into our driveway and blew the car horn. "Come fast, Miss Brigitte. Basil has had an accident with the crane."

I jumped into my car and followed them back to the Salt Rocks. When I arrived, I saw Basil's crane turned over with the wheels in the air and the boom in the sea! Anxiously, I called out, "Where is Basil?" By now, several people had gathered around and were trying to help Basil out from under. Thank God he was alive. Moments later, he managed to crawl out. He didn't have even a scratch on him. I held him tightly in my arms. Basil just smiled and made light of it.

"Brigitte, go home and bring me a bottle of cognac. I need it now!"

I replied, "No Basil, I will not!"

Just then the district officer arrived; he had notified the police.

"You cannot have alcohol on your breath when the officer arrives. He will think you were drunk while operating the machinery."

"Okay, Brigitte. I will wait," Basil relented.

"What did you do, Basil? Did you lift freight that was too heavy off of the ship?"

"Yes. I underestimated the load on my equipment." He admitted.

It was lucky that Scott Development had some heavy equipment on island and men were able to move Basil's crane out of the water and turn it upright.

CHAPTER 30

Struggles of Changing Times

1991

One morning, Miss Sissy came by to visit. She asked Basil if he could take her to the airport by car the following day. She was planning to fly to Grand Cayman.

"Of course, Miss Sissy," Basil answered.

After she lift, I remarked, "This is an unusual request. I hope she's feeling alright."

Miss Sissy was all dressed up, complete with a pretty little handbag. I accompanied Basil to see her off. When we came to Uncle Joe's house, I climbed out of the car and Miss Sissy proudly climbed into the front seat by Basil. I talked to Uncle Joe while he was feeding the chickens. He asked me if we would come by later on and bring him more coconuts.

"Sure, Uncle Joe. How long will Miss Sissy be away?" I asked him.

Joe replied that he didn't know. He thought she was going to visit relatives.

Well, Miss Sissy never came back. She checked herself into the hospital where she died. She had never been to a doctor before; had never complained of feeling ill or uncomfortable, and we never saw her sick. Now Uncle Joe was alone. We all loved Miss Sissy and would miss her knowledge of people, her cooking and her amazing ability to talk without ever taking a breath of air.

After that day, I visited Uncle Joe often. One day I told him to give me his sheets and dirty clothing. "I will put them in the washing machine and return them to you all clean."

"Oh no, you don't get my things," he said.

"Then I will just have to come by and take them!" I replied.

The next day, I returned to pick up his laundry. But Uncle Joe, that old fox, had everything soaking in a big tub of water. He wore a huge grin on his face when I scolded him. The following day, I saw every piece of clothing and linen spread out over the weeds to dry.

"Okay, Uncle Joe, as long as you can do it yourself, I will leave you to do your own laundry. Sometimes I will bring you food, and you can catch me some fish."

That was a good deal for the both of us. It was high season in my vegetable garden. From September through October I would sow vegetable and flower seeds. The winter time was for harvesting, from December to May. This year, my plants were producing plenty. Miss Gladys from Pirates Point was my best and most satisfied client. I also sold her chicken, peacock and duck eggs. My animals were all living in harmony. When the ducks were enjoying the pool, the peacocks kept them company. I felt blessed to have such a peaceful time of life.

In May, we traveled again to Germany and Mexico. On the return trip, we stopped in Miami, where Basil had his car parked at the hotel. After two days of rest, Basil told me that we were going to the Carolinas. He wanted to stop at Park Seeds Company in Greenwood, "So you can purchase your seeds for the winter time, Brigitte."

"I would like that very much, Basil."

But on our way back to Miami, Basil's legs were swelling up and he didn't feel well. We stopped at a hotel in the evening where he was able to put his legs up and rest. The next day, we did the same thing, but the swelling was increasing, going higher and higher up his legs. When we arrived in Florida, he went to a doctor who said that the water was almost up to Basil's lungs. "One more day and you would not have made it through this. You must check into the hospital." He advised.

Basil maintained that first we would have to go home to our island. We bought food for our animals and took it all home with us. The doctor had given Basil enough pills to keep the water down. Two days later, we returned to Miami. Basil checked into the Baptist Hospital, where he survived a quadruple bypass surgery. He had a room by himself, and soon he was joking with the nurses. I stayed at the holiday Inn by the airport, where our car was parked, and drove every morning to the hospital. Then I stayed all day with him until late, after traffic eased up. I didn't like to drive in the big city, especially now that I was used to the quiet road at home. After ten days, we arrived again on Little Cayman.

Not long after we came home, our friend, Sonny, came with his plane and circled around the house. I told Basil, "I will go to the airport this time; you are not yet allowed to drive."

"Okay," he relented.

I brought our friend home and we celebrated Basil's courage and strength. Sonny told Basil that he had come to ask him for a favor. "We have building material arriving tomorrow on a ship and I want to ask you if you can unload it for us. I didn't know about your operation, though."

We explained to Sonny what had happened and that there had been no time to contact anyone before Basil's operation. Basil then told Sonny, "Of course I will unload your building materials."

"No, Basil!" I protested. "The doctor said, 'No driving!' Your wound could open."

But Basil was stubborn. I couldn't reason with him. The next day, we agreed that Basil would drive the crane very slowly and would hold a pillow against his chest. I drove the tractor, which was the rougher ride. Basil lifted the material from the ship and put it on the tractor. I drove it up the hill to unload. Sonny and a helper were standing by. Everything went well, and we celebrated together again, relieved that Basil was okay.

1992

Electricity came to Little Cayman. We had the first two miles of electricity from the airport to the Southern Cross Club. A photograph of our sign, "Caution Duck Crossing" and the first electrical poles, appeared in the magazine and newspaper.

Basil invited to the island two of his nephews and their families. One couple was from New Jersey, with a young boy; and the other couple was from California. We accommodated the family with the young boy in the little house. Everything went well and we had fun together. They decided that they wanted to eat fish *every* day. I was cooking all of the meals, and had to procure enough fish for seven people, along with preparation of other dishes. I spread the word among the locals that I would buy fish.

The next day, a ten pound barracuda was delivered. The islander told me that he had caught it at the Pickle Banks, which is a popular fishing spot for larger fish, located between Little Cayman and Cuba. I thanked him and was relieved. For at least tonight, I had enough fish for everyone. But I remembered that barracuda meat could be poisonous, so I cut a piece and placed it near an ant nest in the garden. The piece was immediately covered with ants, they devoured it. I was satisfied that the test had a positive outcome for us, the fish was not poisonous. In the evening, I fried the barracuda and everyone exclaimed how delicious it was. I personally preferred the meat that was closest to the bone; it was tastier than the rest. Mama Cat came by as I was walking into the kitchen, nibbling on the bones that were nearest to the fish liver. I gave a piece to the cat, which she was eager to take, but immediately she spat it out.

"Kitty! Don't do this to me. No! It's a good fish. Here, please try another piece." She just sniffed at the piece, turned away and left. I was very concerned, now. I prayed in the kitchen, "Please, dear God, don't let the fish be poisoned." I was hoping that the cat just had no appetite.

I told Basil what had happened when we went to bed. "Don't worry, they all loved the fish, nothing is wrong."

Well, Basil was wrong. At around 2:00 am, the nightmare began. I ran to the bathroom, violently ill, and my distress continued all night. I became worse by the hour. At dawn, Basil's nephew from New Jersey came to tell Basil that he, his wife and their son suffered the same reaction. Interestingly, the nephew from California and Basil both took nitroglycerin for their hearts. Neither suffered a severe reaction. But the wife of the nephew from California was as sick as the rest of us. Our lips, eyes and hands began to swell. Basil called the hospital on Cayman Brac and chartered a plane from the Brac to pick us up. Five of us ended up in the hospital for much needed intravenous medication.

After three days, we returned to Little Cayman. The young boy felt better, but the four of us; the nephew from New Jersey, the two wives and I, were still ill. One of the wives continued to have heart palpitations. Our visitors went back to the states for more medical help. I felt awful that this had happened, that I had poisoned Basil's relatives. But they were good sports and all said that they would like to return to Little Cayman another time. I vowed never to serve them fish again.

My condition was not improving. Muscle pain was increasing. I still had diarrhea, nausea and vomiting. Worse yet, my senses were working in reverse; that is, hot water felt cold, cold water felt burning hot. The fish poisoning, ciguatera, attacked my nervous system. We flew to Miami and visited several doctors. A few of them had to look it up in a book, but no one could help me. There was no remedy.

We returned to Little Cayman, where some locals brewed tea out of local bushes. The islanders were aware of this kind of poisoning, and several had experienced it over the years. I was more acutely ill because I had nibbled on the bones next to the liver. I should have cut the liver out and given that to the ants. It took a full year for me to recover normal functions. In all of the twenty years that I lived on Little Cayman, my health was excellent. This incident was the one exception. What

I regretted most was that I could not enjoy a glass of champagne or wine for that year. Whenever I would have a sip of either of them, my skin would immediately begin to itch.

CHAPTER 31

Basil's Last Battle

1993

We received a call from Germany that my Aunt Didi died on the 17th of May. Basil and I flew to Germany. I brought my Aunt's handwritten testament with me. We sat in her house and began to sort through her things. I called her lawyer with the copy of her will. He had passed away, but a colleague answered for him. I requested his copy of the will; and he promised he would look for it. An hour later, he called back. The lawyer informed me that he would only give me the will if we split the profits. I could not believe his audacity. Heat rushed through my body and my skin began to itch. I felt my nerves tingling. The ciguatera can remain in a person's body for up to twenty years. Apparently stress immediately exacerbated the symptoms.

I called Basil, but he could not help me. He was sitting there, but could do nothing for me. He was beginning to show his age, slowing down noticeably. My aunt's house was on a hill; Basil could hardly make it up all of the steps. On the 8th of December, he would be 78.

I too was not feeling my best. I had little appetite. When I brushed my hair, it fell out in clumps. But instead of giving in to weakness and despondency, I became angry. I woke up one morning between four and six, suddenly knowing what to do. My wits were back! I went to the local mayor of the town, whom I had met at my Aunt's birthday a few years back. I showed him the handwritten will and related to him what had happened. He immediately took action. The mayor contacted the license department, which contacted the lawyer, warning him that he must send the testament right away or he would be disbarred.

The next day, I received the will from the lawyer, as requested. My Aunt had written down instructions about which realtor to work with to sell the houses. I placed an announcement in the newspaper to sell her car. I gave away most of her clothes. A few of her blouses fit me, I decided to keep them, as they were elegant and timeless. I also kept her beautiful royal blue dishes and crystal glasses; carrying them home with us in suitcases, packed very carefully.

It was necessary to make several trips between Germany and Little Cayman before the estate was fully settled. When both houses had been sold, within two months, I returned to my aunt's bank and deposited three quarters of the proceeds. The rest I transferred to a bank on Grand Cayman. I emptied her safe and took all of the treasures home with me. Aunt Didi's capital came to us at just the right time. Basil wanted me to transfer all of the money to our account in the Cayman Islands. But this was my money; and I was firm about how we were going to handle it. I wanted to invest some of it wisely, so as to increase our principle. We knew the president of the Cayman National Bank, and he gave me some good advice. I invested in bonds.

In October, Basil wanted to visit Mexico again and to return to all of the towns we enjoyed so much. I told him that was okay, but I would not let him drive anymore. "I want you to relax and enjoy. We will take a first class bus."

Surprisingly, he agreed. Truly, the bus was first class. We traveled to San Miguel de Allende, which took three and a half hours and only cost $15.00. We even had a stewardess, and could purchase drinks and snacks. We loved the town and people; they seemed to be happy to see us again too. Unfortunately, Basil tired easily and could not walk very far. There were many days I walked to the plaza alone. I purchased some soft flat leather shoes that were locally made. It was difficult to walk on the cobblestones in anything else. I saw a man with a donkey pass me; he took the donkey to the well and left him there. He didn't even tie him up. Then the man walked down the street and entered a bistro. I was curious about the donkey; would he stay there and wait? After about thirty minutes, the donkey ambled down to the bistro and waited right in front of the door. About five minutes later, the owner of the donkey came out, and they left. I laughed out loud at that; who was leading whom home?

We visited other little towns, all by bus. Then we traveled to our favorite place, Cuernavaca; close to Mexico City, but far enough away that the big city noise was not heard. The attraction of this town is the climate, always just like spring. It is also a weekend retreat for Mexico City businessmen and their families. We stayed in Las Mananitas, one of Cuernavaca's loveliest colonial hotels. It was our twenty-fifth wedding anniversary and an exquisite place to enjoy every single moment of it. Las Mananitas was an amazing hotel, with lush gardens and exotic cranes and peacocks wandering around the grounds. We admired the gardens and took many photographs. Little did we know that these would be the last pictures we would take together.

Back on Little Cayman, Basil grew weaker and tired easily. I did most of the work outdoors, cleaning up the weeds with a hand mower, raking leaves, knocking down coconut branches and picking up the debris; after which I would load up the tractor and take everything to the dump. I didn't mind the work, because it was for us. Most enjoyable were my animals. Soon came the time when I asked Basil to show me how to take care of the tractor; how to pump diesel fuel into it, make sure that there was enough transmission fluid, check the water level. Then I wrote down his instructions on how to maintain the generator.

Basil was a good teacher, and in time, I was glad I learned these lessons. I also had fun when Sonny and Dottie came to visit, which was quite often now. They were building a resort with a restaurant and dive shop, which was beginning to take shape. Dottie had a white sports car, a Mercedes, shipped over from Grand Cayman, and we would drive to Point of Sand where we snorkeled and swam together. I had to promise Basil that I would be back by 4:00.

One day, since I never carry a watch and didn't care about the time, Dottie and I left for Point of Sand, probably after 4:00. When we were half way home, we saw Basil coming toward us in my Green Hornet. He was very upset because we were so late. He was worried that something had happened to us. After the brief encounter, we drove on home, giggling together. I said, "Tomorrow we do the same thing, but I will bring *my* car." We thought that was a good idea, then Basil could not come after us. I reasoned that since I worked hard all day, I deserved to have some fun.

The next day, we did the same thing, except we drove both of our cars; and once again paid no attention to the time. We left Point of Sand and headed for home when, near Southern Cross Club, there was Basil, on the tractor! He was furious. It reminded me of his angry passion when I encountered him returning from Salt Rocks the night he threatened to kill himself, upset over the length of my skirts. I guess it was not very nice of me. But I resented Basil treating me like a little child who needed to be looked after.

Sometimes he was too possessive of me, expecting me to behave in whatever way he dictated. If he had an argument with someone, he would not talk to that person, and I was also not supposed to talk to that person. I had no reason to act that way. So, when someone Basil would not speak to, greeted *me*, and Basil was not around, I would greet him back. In small ways, I grew more independent of doing Basil's bidding. However, I always gave him his pleasure in the evenings. I would wear the stockings and high heels and short skirts while I cooked our dinner. Amazingly enough, after all of these years, Basil still became excited when I was dressed up as his playmate in the kitchen.

In December of 1994, Basil wanted to travel to South America. I had no desire to go; but to please Basil, I transferred funds to Cayman Islands from Germany. We had enough to travel in style. We visited Brazil, Argentina, Chile, Uruguay and

Ecuador. Basil took a helicopter ride over the Iguacu Falls on the border between Argentina and Brazil. I walked over the bridge. It pleased me that Basil could still enjoy himself. We then traveled to Santiago, Chile. Basil was getting weaker by the day. He could not walk for very long. We hired a private chauffeur to show us the city, and together enjoyed the panorama of the Andes Mountains. But often, I had to explore alone. It was difficult to watch Basil suffer; and to his credit, he never once complained. Even when he had his various accidents over the years, he did not complain.

We flew to Montevideo, Uruguay. I remembered how the Duchess of Arenberg spent her seasons in this location, and how she had wanted me to accompany her. I did not enjoy this trip, mostly because I was very worried about Basil. Our last stop was Quito, Ecuador. We hired a private guide with a car and drove to Cordova along the Galarza Highway; arriving in the middle of the world on the equator. Ecuador was my favorite destination of all of the places we visited on this trip. From our hotel, the Oro Verde, we could watch the indigenous people descending from the mountains at 5:00 am, hiking into the city to sell their goods. The first hours in the morning were quite cool, so they wore colorful layered shawls. As I watched, from hour to hour, they would peel off one shawl after another. I witnessed up to three or four shawls on each person. When the market opened, I would be the first to buy the fresh fruits and vegetables. Alas, Basil could not enjoy the food. Every day, it became more difficult for him. He had no appetite; it was hard for him to swallow. I was relieved when it came time for us to go home.

1995

After two days at home, we flew to Miami to check Basil into the Baptist Hospital. The first couple of days, the doctors were puzzled; they could not figure out what was wrong. They wanted to operate to learn more. They made marks on Basil's body where they planned to do the incisions, when at the last minute, they changed their plans and decided to give him ten chemotherapy treatments. The first one was given the following day. I entered the hospital that morning and was shocked to find Basil strapped onto his bed. I asked the doctor why; and was told that Basil had left his bed with all of the IV tubes and catheter attached. He had walked to the elevator and demanded to be released for home. I told the doctor, no more chemo. The doctor responded that they could peer into his body with a scope, and see just what was going on. I approved that procedure, but no more chemo.

Basil recognized me when I came every morning to sit at his bedside all day. I moved from the hotel near the airport to an apartment that adjoined the hospital. I took every one of my meals by his side. There was a beautiful fountain at the entrance to the hospital. On both sides of it there were lovely gardens and lakes. I was able to walk outside when I needed a break. The doctors finally determined that Basil had lymphoma. The swelling of the glands had turned his intestines around; his stomach was now in the back! After two months, I pleaded with the doctor to find a way to feed Basil and build up his strength enough for us to go home. It took another month before we could fly home. I was able to feed him through a tube on the side of his stomach. When I pushed his wheelchair towards the taxi for the airport, he asked me, "Where are we? Are we in Jamaica?"

"No, Basil. You have been three months in the Baptist Hospital in Miami. Now we are going home."

His face lit up then. When we landed on Grand Cayman, our dear friend Sonny was there waiting for us with his plane for the last part of the journey. It was a great relief to return to the peacefulness and security of our island home and neighbors; and my inner strength came back long enough for me to get Basil settled. He was very content to sit in front of the television that Sonny had installed, and watch programs beamed in with the satellite dish. He enjoyed listening to the news, over and over again. The difficult part was that he insisted I sit next to him the whole time. I explained to him that I had so much to do in the garden; and I still had a little troop of ducks, chickens and peacocks to tend to. Basil said, "Okay, Brigitte. Go do your work." But ten minutes later, he would call for me again. His condition steadily worsened.

Sometimes he wanted to walk around the house using his walker. The worst time was in the night when he could not fall asleep; he would get up to walk, stumble into things and hurt himself. In desperation, I tied a string on my arm and tied the other end onto his arm. This way, I would know when he arose, so I could walk with him. Sometimes I slept on the sofa while Basil sat next to me in the chair. Every time he stood up, I would tell him to sit down. It occurred to me that the first chemo treatment must have destroyed his ability to settle into sleep. It seemed that he never was able to stay asleep for longer than ten minutes.

After a month of this, I was completely exhausted. I became Basil's private nurse. He needed help with everything, from eating to going to the bathroom. The last night of his life, I called Dr. Mohanti on Cayman Brac and described Basil's condition and behavior, which had changed for the worse from the night before. I asked the doctor how I could help my husband. He was sympathetic, but had no advice for me; there was nothing more I could do, Basil's organs were beginning to shut down.

I walked with Basil back and forth throughout the house. Finally, he was exhausted. I pulled him onto our bed and lay down with him. I wrapped my legs, which he adored so much, around him. I cradled him as best I could. Basil's last request was expressed in a motion; he moved his finger to ask me for a kiss, and I kissed him. Then it seemed he "left me", although his eyes remained open. I wasn't sure if he was dead; so I stayed in the same position for over an hour. I finally arose and called the district officer, who promptly came to the house with one of the firemen who was an EMT. They verified that Basil had passed away.

A plastic sheet and ice were brought. They laid Basil on the sheet in the kitchen by the door. It was 11:00 pm, the 9th of May, 1995. Basil was 79 years old.

I sat in the living room and started calling friends to tell them the sad news. Around 2:00 am, Mama Cat came to the living room door, which was unusual for her so early. She must have sensed something wrong. Like her, I feared entering the kitchen and would not go in there. She remained close to me, on the sofa.

Suddenly, with a great bang, the kitchen door slammed closed. I felt the house shake. Both the cat and I sprang up; the cat wanted out and I opened the door for her. I was shaking as I made my way back to the sofa; I would not go near the kitchen. Maybe Basil was not dead after all. Maybe he had walked out of the house; he didn't want to be inside.

Sometime after daybreak, the officer and fireman returned. Since the kitchen door was not locked, they opened it and called to me. Now I had to enter the kitchen. Very slowly I walked in, wondering if Basil was still there. And so he was, with the ice melting in big pools surrounding him. Bruce, the district officer, had already called Island Air. I picked up the phone book and began to make the necessary arrangements. I phoned the funeral parlor in Grand Cayman. Preparations were made for them to send Basil's body to Miami, where he would be cremated. I selected an urn for his ashes. In time, I planned to scatter them around our property.

When that day came, I decorated Basil's tractor. On top was the urn. Next to it I placed his water jug. Then I brought sand to the tractor bucket with some pretty flowers, and a rope from a ship tied around it. Many people came from Grand Cayman and Little Cayman to celebrate Basil's life. After the little ceremony, I sprinkled his ashes around our property. I invited our friends to Pirates Point where Miss Gladys had prepared a feast. We toasted Basil with champagne, just as he would have liked. We celebrated his lifetime of achievements. I felt very grateful that he had built for us a home on Little Cayman.

Defence Attorney John   Sam Bulgin said he was   organisation, "The Eco-   auspices of the Public

Little Cayman 'pioneer' passed away

Little Cayman lost one of its oldest and most respected residents earlier this month when Basil Kassa died of cancer. He was 79.

He and his wife, Brigitte, had lived on the smaller of the sister islands since his retirement in 1976. They were among the first non-Caymanian settlers in the days when Little Cayman had no public utilities and irregular communication with the outside world.

Having bought a piece of land in South Hole Sound in 1972, the Kassas began to build a house, and brought in heavy equipment from the US. Their crane and tractor were the only ones on the island for many years, and Mr. Kassa, always a pioneering spirit, became the heavy equipment operator for many islanders, unloading ships at Salt Rocks and helping to

rocks would wash away, and he would have to repeat the process in order to unload the next ship.

Mr. Kassa, an engineer by profession, was well known for helping his fellow islanders. After a hurricane demolished the road on the island's north side in the early 1980s, he rebuilt it. Many people called on him for help with his equipment, and to consult him about building and engineering matters. He was generous with his time and his assistance.

His contribution to the development of tourism in Little Cayman in the 1970s is well documented. He used to meet incoming aeroplanes to greet the arriving passengers. Everybody knew him and looked forward to his greeting. He was kind, charming, friendly, and had a joie de vivre that was contagious. He travelled a good deal, and became a good-will am-

one occasion while building their house, Mr. Kassa fell 20 feet and badly hurt his back. He waited for six days until the boat arrived to take him to the medical clinic on the Brac. Another time while working on the island, he suffered a severe head injury and Brigitte had to nurse him until help arrived. But in spite of adversities, the Kassas were never daunted; they used herbs and home remedies to nurse their ailments.

Based on these experiences in the early days, the couple have appreciated the recent establishment of the medical clinic on Little Cayman and the services it offers, said Mr. Kassa's nephew, John Dettoni. Due to this interest, a memorial fund has been established in Mr. Kassa's memory to provide additional medical resources, Mr. Dettoni added.

including components for major electrical companies throughout the world, and parts for pacemakers, the US space programme, aeroplanes and televisions. He remained CEO and owner of his company until he retired in 1976.

One of eight children, Mr. Kassa is survived by his wife, who remains in Little Cayman, two daughters, four grandchildren, and many nephews and nieces.

Donations to Mr. Kassa's Little Cayman Medical Clinic memorial fund may be made to CNB, account no. 191845.

house, and brought in heavy equipment from the US. Their crane and tractor were the only ones on the island for many years, and Mr. Kassa, always a pioneering spirit, became the heavy equipment operator for many islanders, unloading ships at Salt Rocks and helping to build a dock. Before the dock was constructed, Mr. Kassa would move rocks to fill the rough terrain of the salt rocks, enabling him to drive his crane and unload ships anchored offshore. When a nor'wester blew in, the

1970s is well documented. He used to meet incoming aeroplanes to greet the arriving passengers. Everybody knew him and looked forward to his greeting. He was kind, charming, friendly, and had a joie de vivre that was contagious. He travelled a good deal and became a good-will ambassador for Little Cayman, talking about the island's charms wherever he went.

Many times the Kassas had needed medical help and, for several reasons, were not able to get immediate assistance. On

ated the recent establishment of the medical clinic on Little Cayman and the services it offers, said Mr. Kassa's nephew, John Dettoni. Due to this interest, a memorial fund has been established in Mr. Kassa's memory to provide additional medical resources, Mr. Dettoni added.

Born in 1915 in New Jersey, Mr. Kassa served in the US army during the second world war, and then went on to found his own engineering company in New Jersey. He invented and engineered many products,

CHAPTER 32

My Life after Basil:
A New Beginning, New Challenges,
Me One

After Basil's funeral, many people, including Basil's relatives, could not understand why I would want to stay on Little Cayman alone. I explained to them that Little Cayman was my only home. I loved the land and did not wish to go anywhere else. They were not convinced.

Basil had never been close to family members, who seemed more interested in his wealth and possessions than they were in him. One of Basil's relatives turned to me after everyone else had gone, and told me that I needed to write a will. He said that he had stayed to help me, because I would not know what to write or how to write it. I answered very calmly, "My testament was written a long time ago, and was handled by a lawyer."

He just looked at me, having nothing to say. Then I said to him, "You and your family are not in it."

Perplexed, he continued to look at me. I smiled. Then he managed to choke out a fake sounding laugh. "Me One" is a Caymanian phrase which translates as, "I am alone". It is also used as a salutation when someone is answering the telephone "Me one", "I am alone", or "I am here".

I was now alone, but definitely not lonely. I had difficult challenges before me. First, I looked at Basil's check book. Our assets were in both names. I had no idea how to write a check or balance a check book. It was partly my fault; once I had left the Gipsy Club in Monte Carlo, I told Basil that I no longer wanted anything to do with money. Now I was fifty-six and had a new beginning, which involved coping with finances.

I asked Betty, whom I had befriended when she settled on the island in 1994. Betty was a model figure, tall and slim. Her short blonde hair was cut stylishly. She had lovely blue eyes and always a friendly smile. She now worked in real estate. When Betty looked at the check book, she had a difficult time determining what the balance in the account was; it took her two days. In the end, $7,000 was unaccounted for. Betty showed me how to write a check and balance the book. I transferred all of the money in Germany to my account in Grand Cayman. Then I asked the bank manager for advice on investments.

The next challenge was my Green Hornet Chrysler Dodge Dart. Now twenty-five years old, the car had always been outdoors. One month after Basil died, the Green Hornet gave up. Now I could not ask anyone for advice, except Basil. One day, while I was dusting the knick knacks on the furniture, I asked Basil, "What should I buy, a Ford or a Chevy?" When I mentioned the word Chevy, one little Eskimo souvenir from Alaska toppled over.

Well, that must have been Basil communicating to me. "No Chevy." I decided I would buy a Ford. I should mention here that I was always talking to Basil, even though he was gone in person, he was very much still in my thoughts and life. I went to Grand Cayman to the Ford dealer and purchased a brand new white 1995 Taurus.

The third challenge was to operate the tractor completely by myself. I wanted to use it to help other people. For example, I wanted to help build the Little Cayman National Trust building. I had to remove the front bucket of the tractor and put on forks. It was difficult to do; it was very hard to see what I was doing. Once the forks were on the tractor, I was able to help lift the trusses for the Trust building. I gained more confidence in myself and loved my independence.

CHAPTER 33

1996

THE PERFECT NIGHT

It was September, 1996, over a year since Basil had passed away. Sonny's resort, Paradise Villas, had a restaurant named *The Hungry Iguana*. Sonny had hired a manager who was from Germany, Willy. He came to visit me with Sonny and his wife, Dottie. Later, Sonny said that Willy was a playboy and always pursued rich women. He was between forty-five and fifty years old. Dottie and I laughed, because he seemed too old to be a playboy. One thing he was good at was cooking. He made wonderful meals for us, often at my home. But I didn't like how Willy picked on me constantly.

"Why are you always at home? You should be out living life to the fullest. Why don't you have a boyfriend? Life is too short to close all of the doors." And so on and so forth, he would go on and on. I grew tired of hearing it all over and over again. I told him that if I wanted things to be different, then they would be different. I was perfectly capable of making my own decisions.

One evening, two of my girlfriends, Dottie and Mary, invited me to go to the Hungry Iguana with them for a snack and a drink. Willy took our orders and would occasionally join in our conversation. Afterwards, we went to the pool area and I put my legs into the water. A couple of people were having a good time playing in the pool and spraying water at each other. A handsome young man swam over to me and asked me to join him.

"No thank you, can't you see that I am not dressed for swimming?"

"I see, but that doesn't matter," he told me. He took hold of my legs and splashed water on them. My girlfriends stepped back to watch the show. I was pleasantly trapped, and could not move because he was holding onto my legs. He was charming when he spoke, and had such charisma that I could not bring myself to tell him off. Then he said, not quietly enough, "I want to make love to a blonde woman, and that is you." I laughed out loud at that. My girlfriends had heard it and moved closer to us, giggling, to see where this conversation was going.

"Finally, Brigitte, you again have love in your life," I thought.

The young man's name was James. He wanted to treat everyone to a margarita. Willy came out to take the order. When he took in the scene, and gave me a look! I looked right back at him, telling him with my eyes, "See? I am NOT such a home body."

As James sprang out of the pool, my girlfriends exclaimed in unison, "Wow!" More margaritas arrived. After we all were quite tipsy, I pretended that I needed to use the restroom. Instead, I jumped into my car and took off.

I arrived home alone, I thought. But as I opened my door, a voice behind me said, "Oh no, you cannot escape."

I had no idea that James had followed me in a jeep. I turned on all of the lights, opened the sliding door to the outdoor dance floor, and just stood there. I was intrigued. I felt excitement, but it was not sexual. I was content just to stand there and admire him.

Once again, he said, "I would like to make love to a blonde woman, and that is you."

I told him that I was not ready. He showed me that **he** was ready. As he stripped, his exquisite treasure appeared. He looked like a Greek statue. James was tall, with dark hair, brown eyes, and a well-trimmed mustache with a small beard around his chin. His torso was slightly covered with hair that tapered in a thin line down to below his navel. I stood there and marveled at his physical beauty. Then with a featherlike touch, I moved my fingertips gently tapping along his pulsing manhood. I could see that for him this move was very titillating.

"Now," I told him, "you have to go." I said good night! I am sure he was not used to this kind of response. Surely any other woman would be melting into his arms.

With a curious look, he obediently put his shorts on, gave me a lingering kiss and promised, "I will see you tomorrow."

The next morning, my girlfriends asked me anxiously, "What happened?" They had seen James follow me. I related my story and they gasped, "Really! You really turned him away?"

"I simply cannot jump into bed with a man. I need to have some connection with him first. And anyway, I did not have any condos."

"What? Why would you need condos?" They asked me, perplexed.

"For protection against diseases, of course." I replied.

They looked at each other and then burst into gales of laughter. My lovely, feminine girlfriends both snorted as they held their stomachs in laughter. I looked at them dumbfounded. "Do you have condos?" I asked.

"Brigitte, it is not 'condo'. A condo is an apartment. You mean condoms!" Now I joined them in the riotous laughter until tears were rolling down my cheeks.

Later, James picked me up and we drove around the island. He invited me to lunch back at the Hungry Iguana, where we had a fun conversation. He told me that he lived in New York, overlooking Central Park.

I said, "I thought so. You are a rich young man who is trying out his hunting skills."

He didn't deny it and said, "I liked how you touched me." We continued our conversation more intimately now, and I invited him to dinner the following evening.

After dinner, we went swimming in the sea by moonlight, it was very romantic. Then we took a shower together and thoroughly enjoyed our perfect night. I didn't expect to hear from him again; but three weeks later, a letter arrived in which he thanked me for the unforgettable night.

CHAPTER 34

More Fun to Come

1997

I experienced another funny episode. By now, there were three lodgings on Little Cayman. One of them was a new hotel, the Little Cayman Beach Resort. The owner of the resort had just finished building the first two story condos on the island, the Conch Club. They were now ready to be sold. He presented me to the sales manager for the Conch Club whose name was Andrew. He was a very nice man, but I was not attracted to him. We were friendly, sometimes he invited me out and sometimes I cooked for him.

One day, Andrew was sick, so I made chicken soup for him. He was supposed to pick it up later. I was just pouring the soup into a covered container when Playboy Willy appeared. He said he wanted to swim from my beach to Southern Cross Club. I told him to go ahead. As I watched him from the terrace, I saw Willy strip all of his clothes off as he headed towards the beach. I yelled out to him, "Willy, Willy! You cannot do that here by me. What are you thinking?"

"In Germany they all do it," he hollered back.

"Not so," I replied. "Only in the nudist colonies."

But he didn't care and continued on into the water and swam away. I was upset and hoped that no one would visit me. Half an hour later, Andrew dropped by. I was a nervous wreck. He wanted to stay and chat; I only wanted him to leave, in case Willy came back. Within moments, Willy appeared, stark naked! Andrew looked at me, then he looked again at Willy, then back to me in disbelief. I began to babble, "Willy is from Germany and he thinks he can skinny dip here."

Willy came closer to Andrew to shake his hand, but Andrew ran out of the house as if he had been stung by a bee. I was angry with Willy, "See what you have done!"

I took the chicken soup over to Andrew's house and tried to explain, and to calm him down. But he didn't want the soup. I told him, "You could at least have shaken his hand."

"What do you want me to shake?" Andrew spit out.

I had to laugh. It was too comical. In the end, Andrew finally accepted the soup.\

CHAPTER 35

Stormy Weather

Many months passed. At the end of 1997, we had a bad storm and I lost shingles from the roof. I hired a young man and his crew; they fixed the roof in no time. Several birds were hurt in the storm and I went around the island, rescuing them. There were red footed booby birds, whistling ducks and several smaller birds. At one point, after the storm, I had four baby mourning doves, two baby mocking birds and two baby ching chings, black birds. I also grew flowers, created arrangements and sold them to the hotels on the island. I became known as either "The Bird Lady" or "The Flower Lady". I also volunteered at the Little Cayman National Trust House every day. I kept myself busy.

Later on, the handsome young man who had repaired my roof began to court me, with great persistence. After a couple of weeks of resistance; he finally persuaded me to go out for dinner. We went out several times. Then one night, as he was getting ready to leave, he held me tightly against his body. I felt his erection. Then he said, quite bluntly, "I am sexually interested in you."

I felt the heat in my body rising and thought about it. "Well, I will see about that," I told him. Then I closed the door.

I was very flattered. But on the other hand, the difference in our ages bothered me. He was quite a few years younger than I. He was a very nice man, but I was astonished that this man, from the younger generation, spoke out in such a forward manner. To my old-fashioned way of thinking, it sounded too much like a business deal. I must confess, I was hungry for a sexual relationship. It had now been over two years since I had been with Basil. I had only enjoyed the one perfect evening in all of that time. I was ready for some rain to come to my desert.

The following day, we met and I spoke his language. "Okay, we do it – but without clothes!"

His eyebrows shot up. "What other way is there?" he asked.

We stayed together for eight years; had our ups and downs, but physically, I always felt fulfilled.

CHAPTER 36

Hurricane Ivan

2004

Hurricane Ivan was the worst Hurricane ever to hit Grand Cayman Island. It was a Category 5 when it hit the islands on the 11th and 12th of September 2004. Many houses were destroyed. Large boats were swept onto city streets. And water was up to the rooftops of many homes. At one time, Grand Cayman was all under water.

I stayed inland during this hurricane. It was mandated that everyone on the waterfront had to leave their houses. The police went from door to door to make sure that people were obeying the order. I stayed with a couple of friends at a private home. Some homes on Little Cayman were totally destroyed. A Southern Cross Club boat was hurled into the mangroves. My house had roof damage, the trees and vegetation also sustained a great deal of damage. We still counted ourselves as the lucky ones. It had been much worse on Grand Cayman Island. We still had our generators to get us through the aftermath of the storm when electricity is off. I will always keep a generator for storms to come.

CHAPTER 37

Brigitte in the Spotlight

2005

In the spring of 2005, I published a children's book, <u>Brenetta and Her Menagerie</u>, a story for children and the young at heart. The events in this story actually happened. I wrote about my beloved animals; ducks, chickens, peacocks, cats and wild birds. It was how the animals demonstrate their personalities as they interact with each other and me. A lady journalist from Cayman Net News wrote an article about my life. She included that I was born in Germany, managed a night club in Monte Carlo and lived a glamorous life for years on another side of the world, where my customers included many famous people including Aristotle Onassis with opera star Maria Callas, Zsa Zsa Gabor, James Garner, Brigitte Bardot with Gunter Sachs, as well as European and Indian royalty. Monte Carlo was very pristine in the early sixties.

Articles appeared in the Cayman Net News and I signed and sold my books at the Little Cayman Trust House. I went book signing to all of the resorts on Little Cayman. Then I went to Grand Cayman book stores and hotels, and signed and sold more books. In October of 2005, Governor Dinwiddy and his wife, Emma, came to visit Little Cayman. They stopped by the Little Cayman Museum, the Central Caribbean Marine Institute and the Little Cayman District for the National

Trust. I presented a copy of my book to the governor and his wife. A couple of days later, I was honored to receive a thank you letter. I also visited the school on Cayman Brac and the small school on Little Cayman which had four students. I read for the children from my stories. Many of my books were given away to underprivileged school children in the states. I received hundreds of thank you letters, art sketches and photographs from children throughout the years.

Brigitte Kassa hands her book to the Governor and Mrs Dinwiddy at the National Trust Little Cayma

CAYMAN NET NEWS • Issue 1273 • Friday, 22 December 2006

"Brenetta" comes to the Brac Library

CHILDREN'S author Brigitte Kassa (second from left) with the children she read to from her book, "Brenetta and her Menagerie" at the Cayman Brac Library on Saturday, 16 December.

While she read, her friend Dulce Connolly (far left) showed them the book's illustrations by Mary McTaggart Christoffers

The book tells stories of Ms Kassa's life on Little Cayman over the past thirty-five years from the point of view of the many animal friends she has had.

In July 2005, Cayman Net News featured me on the front page. The article, "*Up Close With Nature*", is about my rescue of a fledgling bird on Little Cayman. My friend, Betty, and I tried to determine what kind of bird it was. She put the picture on her computer and sent it out to some friends and experts in that field. But no one could identify the bird. It was quite an ugly young bird, but later it grew into a beautiful mourning dove. I called her Bee Bee. She has produced many offspring, as have my other birds; mocking birds and ching chings. I had rescued and raised their parents, given them names, and always they responded to my call. Some fly onto my head, some I feed by hand, sometimes they are arguing among them-selves. But all are free and happy, like me!

CHAPTER 38

Hurricane Gustav

2008

Hurricane Gustav came through on the 29th and 30th of August, 2008. It was the storm that hit the island of Little Cayman harder than Grand Cayman or Cayman Brac. It was not supposed to happen! It had been announced that Gustav would pass by us without damaging the islands, but then it turned and came straight towards our island without warning. On the evening of the 29th of August, rain and heavy winds began. The soffits from the overhang of my house were soon damaged or destroyed. At first I thought they were blankets floating in the wind. I actually thought people must have left their blankets on the beach before the storm. Then there were more and more flying around. I looked up at my overhang, and there were no more soffits. The screws which were old and corroded had broken.

Everything went quickly then. The ceiling in the kitchen was soaked and the rain came in! The ceiling actually crumbled; I caught the lamp that had been hanging over the glass table in the kitchen before it crashed. Then I ran into the living room, and with a bang, the glass from the cupola broke and rain poured in. I panicked and called my friend, Betty, asking her to come with her husband to help me. Then I called two other friends, George the fireman and my friend, Robin. By the time I pulled the furniture away from the windows and took my paintings and treasures off of the walls, my friends had arrived.

Betty and her husband were happy to be in my house, because theirs was shaking from the wind. Robin arrived last. He told us that it was the most difficult and dangerous terrain he had ever driven over. At that time, he was living on the north coast. He said trees and light poles were breaking down and almost hit his truck. Now the three men went to the garage to get the large tarp out. They hardly could stand up against the storm winds. We moved the heavy furniture to the dryer side of the living room, away from the sea.

Then we looked into the guest bedroom. The ceiling was ready to fall in. We took the bed and other furniture to the next room; then put plastic sheeting over the floor. We completed the preparations for disaster just in time. The ceiling crumbled and fell down.

Every half hour, I swept the water off of the kitchen floor and from the tarp in the living room. After midnight, we were all exhausted; there was no dry place to sit, so we all just plopped down on the kitchen floor together, next to the refrigerator. I brought out a couple of bottles of wine and we drank together, which helped us to calm down, as we waited for the morning to arrive. Most of the people on Little Cayman still had generators, which saved our food.

By 8:00 am, the storm had calmed down a bit. We went outside and looked around. It was a disaster, only the little house had survived undamaged. For my friends, it was a very difficult drive home. The electric poles were on the ground, live wires made travel very dangerous. Some roads were completely blocked. Most houses had some damage, whether it was to the roof or water damage, or mountains of sand piled up inside. I was fortunate; I had extra shingles to cover the roof temporarily, until I could have a new roof made. It took six weeks for the house damage to be repaired. I needed a new ceiling and new shingles to cover my roof.

We had just finished painting the new ceiling when it was announced on the radio that another storm was approaching the Cayman Islands. This was to be another direct hit. Hurricane Paloma hit the north side of Little Cayman, but the most destruction was on Cayman Brac. It brought a lot of rain to us; I walked that night from room to room. To my horror, I watched my new ceiling begin to bubble. There was water underneath the new paint. The roof had not been fully repaired. I quickly brought out the stepladder and put pans and pails under the bubbles.

Then I took a knife and poked holes to allow the water to run out. Now it even dripped in my cedar closet, where I kept all of my clothing. This was just too much for me! I sat down on the bathroom floor and prayed, "Dear God, if you don't want me to live in this house, it is fine with me. I give up. I will stay in the little house." My nerves could not take it anymore.

Well, maybe He heard me! The rain began to slow down and eventually stopped. Six months later, I finally had a new roof. It was February 2009 and Little Cayman became a sunny paradise again.

CHAPTER 39

Support the Boobies: December 2007 through January 2009 Calendar

It all began with "Ladies' Day" years ago when there were only three or four ladies on the island. My friend, Betty Jean, from the north side of the island, and I would meet once a week at various places on the island. We brought food with us and would have a picnic; we exchanged news and gossip. Then we would go swimming and snorkeling; enjoying our afternoon together.

As time went on, Betty found a job selling real estate and we all were busy doing other things. No more "Ladies' Day" for a while. Ms. Gladys at Pirates Point Resort, the founder of The Little Cayman District for the National Trust, asked me to help at the Trust House. It was time for me to give back to the community. I donated two hours a day minimum for sixteen years, volunteering at the trust house. I would do tours, informing visitors about the red footed booby birds, frigates and other wildlife, flora and fauna of the island. We sold local art, souvenirs, wood carvings, books and general merchandise from which all proceeds would go to the trust. More people joined the Little Cayman District Committee for the National Trust and we all contributed in one way or another to preserve our island environment and the wildlife in our paradise.

Ladies' Day became Ladies' Night, and we would meet once a week in one of the local resort restaurants at 6:30 for dinner, enjoying together a few drinks and discussion of how to raise money for the trust. One night in particular we were quite a large and lively group. The ambiance was very invigorating as we had a few extra glasses of wine. We decided that we needed a new project to raise funds to purchase more land at the Booby Pond Sanctuary and the land adjacent to the nesting sites visible from the deck at the trust house, where there were telescopes for viewing. As the evening progressed, everyone grew excited about the new project. It was now time to come up with ideas of how to get needed funding. With everyone's enthusiasm, ladies began expressing their ideas and someone yelled, "Let's do a calendar!"

Amidst all of the laughter and ideas being shouted out, another lady said, "Protect the Boobies!" That was it! This was the beginning of "Support the Boobies" calendar for December 2007 through January 2009. That night, our friend Melissa, from Grand Cayman, a professional photographer, offered to come back and take the photographs of us for the calendar. Once the word was out on the island, many lady members were willing to pose for the various months on the calendar. It was a tremendous success. Through this and other trust functions such as the Mardi Gras Parade, The annual Easter Auction and many generous donations, we raised the funds needed for land purchases to protect our Booby Birds.

Support The Boobies

Ladies of Little Cayman "Ladies Night" Presents – December 2007 through January 2009 Calendar

CHAPTER 40

My Little Miracle

2011

It was the 26ᵗʰ of February when I returned to Little Cayman from Grand Cayman on a Cayman Airways Express, a nineteen-seat plane. People all around me were coughing and sneezing. I was hoping I would not catch anything. Two days later, on the 28ᵗʰ of February, at close to noon, I finished working in my garden and entered my kitchen. I became suddenly dizzy, spun around and realized I was about to faint. I was afraid I would hit my head on the hard floor. Then I passed out. When I regained consciousness, I couldn't get up. A terrible pain shot through my body. Luckily, I had my cell phone in my hand. I called a friend. My voice was so hoarse, that at first my friend could not understand me and asked who I was. I told him, "It is your friend, Brigitte."

He said, "Oh no, I just spoke to her an hour ago."

With great effort, I was able to whisper, "Charlie, I fell. It's me!" I had called the right person. Charlie was a retired orthopedic surgeon. He came to the house, lifted me up and carried me over to the living room sofa, where he laid me down. He could not believe how sick I had become, so quickly. I suffered a high fever, and a hoarse voice. The island nurse came to see me. We have a clinic on the island, but no doctor. Everyone thought I should go by air ambulance and check into the hospital on Cayman Brac. I was adamant. "I will not go to the hospital!"

I was certain that I had caught a virus which had weakened me; and then strained a muscle when I fell. I was hoarse, feverish and unable to walk. If I went to the hospital, they would never let me out. I asked my German friends who were vacationing on Little Cayman to locate Basil's walker and cane in my attic. They found both items after digging around; and helped me that evening into bed, putting a container beside the bed for when I had to go to the bathroom during the night. For this I rolled out of bed, gritted my teeth from pain and relieved myself. Then I had to endure the agony of getting back into bed; it felt as if it took hours. My whole body trembled with pain, especially my right side from the waist down, which was excruciatingly painful. Although it was almost unbearable, I didn't cry.

The next day, my friends descended upon me to convince me that I must go to the hospital. I remained stubborn. I asked them please to make me chicken soup. I promised them that if I couldn't walk with the walker within three days, then maybe I would consider going to the hospital.

I channeled all of my inner strength to walk to the kitchen, using the walker. Now I would not have to fight the hospital battle any more. I did ask for an injection, which didn't help at all. After that, I refused to take any medicine; no pain killers, nothing! One week later, the fever was gone. My voice was back, but the pain remained. Every day and night, it changed. Sometimes my leg swelled up. My hip always hurt, the exact point of pain changed. I could not sleep on my right side.

During the day, I would joke about the pain; but at night, it was no laughing matter. I would put a pillow between my legs. When my leg became very swollen, I put an ice pack on it. Then I changed from ice to heat. After ten days, I was able to walk with the cane. There was still constant pain, no matter what I did. But now I could go outside and water my plants. The moment I could no longer bear my pain, I would break out into a sweat and grow weak. I listened to my body and would immediately go inside to rest.

After six weeks, I could climb the steps onto the airplane, with help. I couldn't understand why it was still hurting after so long. Maybe now I should go to the doctor. He could give me something for my muscle pain. My girlfriend, Karin, greeted me at the Cayman Brac airport and took me to see Dr. Reed. He checked me out and couldn't diagnose anything; but sent me to the hospital for an x-ray. As we came back to the office, he lovingly put his arm around me and said, "You have no muscle sprain or tear. What happened is you fractured your right hip! The neck of the femur is broken and the bone has reattached itself. It is a miracle! How did you do it?"

I told him that I endured the pain without medications, because, if I took painkillers, I would not feel the pain and would possibly turn the wrong way and further injure myself.

He agreed with me, saying that if I had gone to the hospital, they would have operated on me and put a pin in my hip. "You were very wise; not many people can stand that kind of pain," he told me.

"But it still hurts, and I cannot squat down. I want to heal more quickly. Should I take anything now for it?"

Dr. Reed scolded me. "Get out of here. You know best what to do and what not to do."

I arrived on Little Cayman and was greeted by a little parade of people waiting for me. They all applauded, and the nurse said that Dr. Reed had phoned her to give her the good news. They all wished me well. It was lovely to get the attention, but I was a little embarrassed at the same time. I was not used to any fuss being made over me.

CHAPTER 41

To Spain on a Cane

On the 18th of May, 2011, my friend Ali and I met in Spain. Long before my accident, we had planned our vacation, and the time was finally here. Ali had suggested we cancel the trip, that it would be too hard on me.

"No, Ali, I am fine. I will bring the cane with me and make arrangements for a wheelchair at the airports in Miami and Madrid." I flew to Miami and then traveled business class on Iberian Airlines to Madrid the following morning. I could not have made it without the aid of the wheelchair. Madrid is one of the largest airports I have ever traveled into. Ali came from Canada. We stayed in a small hostel in the old section of Madrid and went out sightseeing every day.

The weather was a little cool for me; I brought a sweater and panty hose to keep me warm. I couldn't get the panty hose on or off by myself; it hurt too much to get into the right position. I was embarrassed, but had to ask Ali for help. It ended up being very funny. She would kneel at my feet and get the pantyhose onto my feet. Then she would work them up my legs to my knees. The rest I could do.

Almost every day, while we were in Madrid, we went to Plaza de Mayor. It became our resting place. We had everything we wanted there; good restaurants, entertainment and people-watching time. After three days, we took the train to Cordoba. At the train station, we grabbed a taxi to the historic part of the city. As we entered the street where our hotel was, the taxi driver pulled over. We watched him pull each of his side mirrors in so that they were against the car. We wondered, "What is he doing?" Then as we traveled down the street, we realized that the roads were so narrow, the car barely fit, and the mirrors would have been knocked off of the taxi.

It was fascinating. Here we were in a medieval city with cobblestone streets, whitewashed houses with balconies overflowing with flowering plants, and patios placed under ancient trees. There were also lovely plazas where people gathered and visited happily together. We stayed in the Hotel Gonzalez, rich with Moorish décor. We enjoyed our breakfasts at the lovely outdoor café across the street. We couldn't wait to change out of our traveling clothes, so that we could begin exploring the historic city.

Ali kindly helped me with my pantyhose once again. I felt like a child; dependent upon Mother to get me dressed. Once again, we giggled. I am seventeen years older than Ali. She has beautiful long brown hair, exotic greenish eyes and is slim and taller than me. She is very active in sports; this is the one area in which we are very different. She would always wear tennis shoes; and I would wear shoes with heels. Not anymore! But otherwise, we have the same interests in traveling, gardening and a shared love for Little Cayman. Mostly we laughed over simple things and at ourselves. It was awkward and difficult for me to walk on the cobblestones, even with my cane. Ali helped me along, tucking her hand under my arm.

"Now I feel like your grandmother. In the morning I am a child that you must dress and during the day, I am your grandmother!" I exclaimed.

The Mezquita Mosque impressed us the most. It was an incredible creation of Islamic architecture with its shimmering gold and rows and rows of red and white striped arches. Centered inside the mosque was a Christian cathedral. It is the largest Mosque in the world, covering twenty-three thousand square meters. Back in time, Cordoba was the largest city in Western Europe. There were libraries, aqueducts, auditoriums, gardens, universities and artisans who were skilled in metal, paint, glass tiles and leather. Cordoba was the center of civilization. It was a multicultural city, home to Jews, Christians and Muslims alike. Then we found a 14th Century synagogue. It is one of the few remaining medieval synagogues in Spain. After the great historical attractions, we entered a lovely restaurant in the Jewish section. The meal was thoroughly enjoyable, and we were entertained with the friendly conversation with locals. Upon reflection, of all of the wonderful things we saw, it was a perfect day, ending with a fiery flamenco dancing. The next day, Ali snapped a photo of a caballero riding his horse down our narrow cobblestone street. He was coming back from a fiesta. She was delighted with the photograph, but the proud caballero showed his displeasure by his expression directed towards her as she pressed the camera's shutter button down, and pressed herself into the doorway in an effort to give him and his horse room to pass.

On another day, we took an excursion by bus to Toledo. The whole City is a museum! Walking the tangled medieval streets was a challenge. We visited a church, a mosque and a synagogue. It was an intriguing combination. It was also the first time that I could not follow Ali all of the way. I told her that this particular cobblestone street was too steep and difficult to walk. "I will sit down in a restaurant and wait for you." I watched the people go by. There were many tourist groups which dimmed the charm of the picturesque city.

Back to Cordoba after 5:00, we had all of the streets to ourselves and could explore in tranquility. On a small street, we discovered Hamman de Al Andalus, an Arab bath which recovered the traditionally splendor with its mosaics, archways and columns.

CHAPTER 42

A Short Visit to Germany

2014

In June, from the 10th the 25th, I visited Germany. Because my friends from Bavaria could not come to Little Cayman anymore due to health issues, I thought it would be a good time to visit them. I had not been to Germany for many years. I decided to combine this European trip with a visit to Bremen to see a friend, and my last stop to see a girlfriend in Berlin.

I traveled from Little Cayman to Grand, then took British Air to London on business class. It was comfortable, but I never can sleep on an airplane. From London, I had a good connection to Munich, Munchen. My friends were happy to see me. Ingrid and Emo were living in a beautiful area with a lovely garden only one half hour by train from the city. I liked how Munich had not changed too much; between the old buildings there were some new stores where the structures were glass. It was June and for my friends, it was warm. But for me, the weather in Germany felt too cool, as always, since my childhood. The temperature could change dramatically three times a day.

My friends took me to the lovely country side where we had lunch in a traditional Bavarian restaurant. The waitresses were dressed in a dirndl, a white blouse with a generous "decollete", deep cut and a colorful, full length skirt, gathered at the waist. We enjoyed a heavy, hearty meal with many tall glasses of beer. I was relaxed and content.

Next day, my friends said, "Today we will show you something new for you." Emo drove for a while and then stopped the car and we walked up onto a bridge. Emo said, "That is the River Isar, Brigitte. We have an old tradition here from May to September, we recreate the ancient ways of how the people traveled from one place to another, before the train was invented." The people were building rafts from tree logs and it took them all day to get from one village to another. Ingrid shouted, "Look, Brigitte, there! The floats are coming." What a great show that was. Each float had an orchestra, the people were singing, eating and drinking. They even had a small square area staked out for a toilet. We had fun observing everything from above the bridge which we stood upon. All of a sudden, six or seven men sprang from the float into the cold water and proceeded to swim to the land. They walked up onto the bridge, where we were. All were dressed only in "Lederhosen", leather shorts. They climbed on top of the bridge and jumped back into the water. They were each pulled upon the float again. I thoroughly enjoyed the four days with my friends.

Next stop was Bremen. Alas, my friend did not feel very well. So I visited the old part of Bremen alone. I admired the architecture and took a photograph of Grimm's Fairy Tale, Bremen Town Musicians, (die Bremer Stadt Musikanten). I had a very tasty lunch and was pleasantly surprised to see the train still passing through the middle of the town.

My last stop was Berlin. This was the city where I was born, but *never* did I feel at home here. I visited a longtime girlfriend, Regina. She had an elegant apartment in a nice quiet section of the city; not far from the center. She also had a terrace with lovely flowering pots hanging and standing adjoined to a small garden, where a raspberry hedge fenced off her place. I enjoyed the ripe berries. Regina took me around Berlin. I didn't recognize the city anymore. It was super modern, surrounded by high rise glass and steel buildings. I saw the clock of the half-destroyed tower from the Memorial Church. I recognized the names of the streets, also some names of department stores on the main street, Kurfurstendamm. Then we took the tram, the train and a boat, all kinds of public transportation. We arrived at checkpoint Charlie, where the US Army still were posing as a reminder of the war, and when Berlin was split into sections.

Next Regina showed me the completely new Berlin, which was once East Berlin, Russian occupied territory. We took a boat tour to see it from the waterfront. There were some beautiful monuments left, also some sturdy old houses with new face lifts, but the rest of the city was ultra-modern. On our boat ride, we enjoyed a Berliner lunch, sausage and Beer, (Bockwurst und Bier). After the boat ride, we walked through a nice old section where the houses were still intact and the façades were ornate. Regina said, "I have a surprise for you, Brigitte," and she pointed at an imposing grand ornamental house. "Read the name, Brigitte."

I did, it was "Sasswenoer". "Regina, that doesn't tell me anything."

"Well, that is the oldest chocolate factory. It survived the war and is well-known. I call it Chocolate Ecstasy, or Extravagant, and now we will savor it."

I could not believe my eyes. There were castles, monuments, toys and figurines all made from chocolate. We went upstairs and Regina ordered a delicious chocolate dessert for us. Later on, I bought Chocolate filled with ginger to take home with me. I didn't have to be afraid of the chocolate melting; it was June, but it was cold, especially for me, being around 69 degrees F.

Then Regina had another surprise for me. We walked back close to the waterfront and now I could not believe my ears and my eyes. Tango music filled the air. "Come on, Brigitte. Look down there." We were close to a wall. I looked down, people of all ages were seriously dancing the Tango, my favorite dance in Monte Carlo. Some of the women brought their high heel shoes with them to change for dancing. Unbelievable. In the Middle of the city, on a lower place close to the water, decorated with potted palm trees, the Tango came alive again.

I had two interesting weeks of travel, enjoyed the company of my friends and satisfied my lingering curiosity about Germany. Now I am back home on my beloved, sunny Little Cayman, and take a deep breath of clean air.

Appreciation of Life

Today I finish telling my story. I feel Little Cayman is a fundamental part of me, filling me with contentment and peace in my heart. The challenges have always proved inspirational, encouraging me to become self-sufficient. Faith in myself grew strong on this island which I call my true home.

Because of all of my experiences, good and bad, throughout my younger years; I was led to this island, which became my beloved place in the sun. I have reached my goal. My desire now is to give back to nature, to help the environment and the animals that are indigenous to the island. I don't have any regrets. If I were given the chance to change my past decisions, I would choose the very same path I have taken. I only have one little regret; that I was spoiled and snobbish and refused to dance with James Garner. I was sure that he would ask me again. Alas, he did not.

Everyone carries a backpack of his own. It is up to you how much to take out and turn into goods you can use. If you leave all of the weight in the backpack, it will burden you, instead of providing you with what you need to move forward with your life.

Brigitte Kassa
7th of June, 2015

ADDENDUM

12TH OF MAY 2017

WERNER ISRAEL BAB

The answer to my lifelong question finally came to me from beyond the grave.

In March of 2017, my attractive and vivacious friend, Susan Ploplys, gladly accepted the position as editor of my handwritten memoirs. When more than half of my text was typed, we planned a working lunch at my home. I greeted her at the door, and together we entered my kitchen. Susan placed our day's work on the table. We both sat down.

I said to Susan, "Before we begin, I would like to thank you." I paused for a moment before continuing.

"You have been persistent and resourceful in transcribing my manuscript. You are searching into the depths of my story with your mind. But it is your heart speaking as you write my words; my life. I am very grateful to you, Susan."

Susan smiled. With tears in her eyes, she reached to hug me. We were both silent for a moment.

Then Susan sat back in her chair, looked intently at me and said, "I have come to you with two important questions, Brigitte."

"Okay, Susan."

Her first question was very easy to answer, but Susan began a little nervously, "My mother is 97 years old. She is not very active anymore, so she enjoys reading books, and is very interested in reading your memoirs. She told me that she would like to know more about you. May my mother read your work as I continue to edit and type?"

"Of course, Susan. I will write a little note to your mother. What is her name?"

"Marjorie Williams Muench." She wrote it down. "Thank you so much, Brigitte. It means a lot to both of us, something we can share and discuss."

Then Susan hesitated. The expression on her face grew serious.

"What is the second question, Susan?" I gently urged her.

"When was the last time you saw Werner Bab?"

When I heard his name, my heart began to beat very fast. I was confused. Why would Susan ask me such a question?

"I don't know, Susan. It was so long ago. I think when I returned to Germany in 1973, when my father was sick. But why do you ask me about Werner? Is he still alive?"

"No, Brigitte," Susan answered sadly. "But I researched on the internet and found information about him right away. He died in 2010. He was eighty-five years old. I will show you the information I found. Here is a picture of him shortly before he died. Do you recognize him?"

I looked at the picture, saw an older man with white hair and a gentle face. But, not Werner.

Then Susan showed me a photograph which she had saved on her iPad. It was taken much earlier, when Werner was a young man.

"That is Werner!" I exclaimed. It was a picture from a passport, exactly as I remembered Werner. Thoughts were flashing through my mind. I remembered the intense, passionate love I had for him. Werner has never been forgotten.

Susan opened a link on the web and pointed to the title, "Look here, Brigitte. Werner was a prominent person in Berlin. Here are articles written about Werner. Many Jews, like Werner, were sent to concentration camps. But he was in the small minority of those who survived.

We found out much more through further research. Werner was in the camps in Auschwitz, as well as Mauthausen, Melk and Ebensee. He was liberated by the Americans. Werner spoke little of his past when we were together. I did not pressure him to do so, as I could see it was painful for him.

When Steven Spielberg produced the film, Schindler's List, he searched for the truth, and interviewed more than 50,000 Jews who witnessed and survived the Holocaust. Werner was one of these witnesses to history. The interview, in Werner's later years, gave him the opportunity he sought. With courage and strong sentiment, Werner told his compelling life story to those who would listen, those who desired to know the truth and to share it.

Sixty years after WWII, Werner returned to Auschwitz to create a documentary film which was translated into nineteen languages. Furthermore, Werner gave lectures to educate the youth of Germany about the history of WWII and the concentration camps; heartrending stories from his experiences. He related how he had miraculously survived the Holocaust; and how we must never forget the past. He spoke eloquently and with passion to more than 20,000 students in seminars held in universities. He was honored and received a medal for this service.

Now, finally, I have the answer to my life long question.

"Why did Werner leave America to return to Berlin, Germany in 1958?"

Werner lived to fulfill his purpose in life, to tell his story. He was grateful to be alive, for he had witnessed the deaths of countless others who were not so fortunate. Werner Bab paid his debt of gratitude by returning to Berlin and living his life in service to the truth; to share his personal narrative in the hope that through education, future generations will not repeat the past.